Derivatives Engineering

A Guide to Structuring, Pricing, and Marketing Derivatives

THE GLOBECON GROUP, LTD.

IRWIN
Professional Publishing®

Chicago • Bogotá • Boston • Buenos Aires • Caracas
London • Madrid • Mexico City • Sydney • Toronto

ISBN 1-55738-759-1

Printed in the United States of America

BB

1 2 3 4 5 6 7 8 9 0

PSG

Contents

READING THE MARKET

Part III
Foreign Exchange Derivatives   **133**

Part IV
Commodity Derivatives   **169**

Part V
Capital Markets Applications   **201**

INTEREST RATES

EQUITIES

Preface

This book is the product of the philosophical approach to wholesale banking that the Globecon Group brings to the market. The chapters in this book were originally created for Globecon's **Finance Update Service**, a monthly service for the clients of Globecon. The chapters were written with one overarching purpose: to enhance knowledge among bankers of financial techniques and market developments that can benefit their clients.

The chapters presented here all deal with an important financial tool: derivatives. Much has been written about this tool over the past year as companies, financial institutions and even government entities have gained notoriety through huge derivatives-related losses. In truth, however, the losses so vividly reported in the media had less to do with derivatives than with weak managerial control and reckless judgment on the part of users. Any tool used in the wrong way can cause damage. Any highly leveraged position used to bet on a market movement can yield such a result, regardless of whether a derivatives component is present.

On the other hand, when derivatives are used to reduce risk and arbitrage market inefficiencies, they bring tremendous benefits to the financial and business community. By facilitating risk management, derivatives have made business transactions and capital raising more efficient and less costly. That is why the volume of outstanding derivatives deals has grown to trillions of dollars. That is also why these financial tools are not likely to disappear. Indeed, their use will continue to grow. Finally, this is why Globecon has elected to make this material available to the general financial community.

The chapters in this book were written as the subjects became topical. But by no means are they outdated in content. Each chapter deals with a specific aspect of derivatives from the viewpoint of the bank and, more importantly, the bank's clients. A companion volume, *The Derivatives Engineering Workbook,* contains workshops keyed to most of the chapters in this book. Although each book stands on its own, it is recommended that the workbook be used in conjunction with this volume.

All the consultants at Globecon contributed to the **Finance Update Service**. As a result, these chapters were authored by a variety of people. Nevertheless, each chapter has two common elements. First, all are informed by Globecon's philosophy of building long-term relationships by basing service on client solutions. Second, all were written not by journalists or academicians, but by people with extensive practical banking experience, particularly in the derivatives area. Since all Globecon consultants have responsibility for teaching and advising wholesale banking clients throughout the world, the content is always relevant to the real issues faced by banks in the derivatives marketplace.

Over the years, our clients have found Globecon's **Finance Update Service** to be exceptionally useful. We hope that *The Derivatives Engineering Handbook* provokes the same reaction in you.

Gerald Kramer
President
The Globecon Group
New York

PART I

Marketing Derivatives to the Corporate Customer

Although the main users of derivatives have always been financial institutions themselves because of the nature of their business, the corporate community also represents a huge user base. Derivatives have a wide variety of applications to corporations that seek to manage risk. The problem for the bank marketer, however, is that the risk management choices of every company are influenced by different factors. Moreover, the negative publicity concerning the role of derivatives has tended to make corporate users very cautious. Nevertheless, corporations in general understand the usefulness of these financial tools and will continue to seek beneficial applications.

Successful marketers can draw on a comprehensive knowledge of their clients' business and specific problems, supported by an understanding of the range of derivative tools and the ways in which they can be applied. The combination of product, market and customer knowledge is the key to adding value when advising the corporate customer. The following four papers provide insights into the ways corporates view derivatives and make decisions on their use.

1

Value-Added Banking
Providing Product Advice to Clients

There are a variety of financial tools available to the corporate client that can solve financing and rate risk-management problems. The question is one of choice. Deciding which product or technique best fits a specific situation will depend upon many factors—one of which is always going to be cost, i.e., price. But other factors are qualitative in nature—and they have nothing to do with price and a lot to do with such things as visibility, liquidity, accounting, taxation, risk, market forecasts, financial sophistication, etc.

Complicating the decision is the fact that the financial marketplace has advanced quite dramatically in the past 10 years. Financial tools and techniques are now integrated. Indeed, every technique can be substituted in one form or another for every other technique. Raising fixed-rate financing, for example, can be done directly (public issue, private placement, bank borrowing, etc.) or synthetically (combining variable-rate financing with swaps or other products). Similarly, rate risk-management problems can be solved using a variety of different techniques that achieve the same results. For example, forward contracts may be a solution in one instance, but by combining two options the net result can be the same as the forward contract and might be more useful in another situation.

Exhibit 1   Consultative Matrix

Objectives/ Hedge Technique	Minimize Cost/ Visibility	Maximum Liquidity	Maximum Structural Flexibility	Best Hedge Fit	Minimum Credit Exposure	Lowest Explanation Risk*	Tax & Accounting Simplicity**
Cash Market	Yes	No	Yes	Yes	Yes	Yes	Yes
Swaps	Yes	No	Yes	Yes	No	No	Yes
Forwards	Yes	No	Yes	Yes	No	No	No
Futures	No	Yes	No	No	Yes	No	No

* The risk that the financial executive takes when trying something new.

**Much depends upon whether the transaction meets "hedge" test qualifications. If not, treatment is more complex.

The above categories are not definitive. The shorter the maturity and the more basic the transaction, the more distinctions will blur.

All too often, however, when the corporate client is called upon by his or her banker, the banker's objective is to sell a specific product or technique (the "flavor of the month") rather than look at the range of possible solutions and identify the best fit for the client. But this is precisely where the banker can offer added value to the corporate customer, enhancing the relationship and the bank's profitability.

Differentiating Your Bank

Value-added banking has become the new buzzword in banking in the 1980s —and rightly so. In an era where the competition is intense and the profit margins are shrinking, how can a banker differentiate himself or herself?

On the face of it, the answer is easy: by differentiating his or her product. But what exactly is the product that the banker is selling? The answer: The banker sells financial information and advice.

In other words, the banker who differentiates his or her advice from that of the competition can provide value. The banker who understands the policies, business, financial structure, investment plan, constraints, past experiences, strategies, risk tolerance, etc., of the customer will be able to differentiate and provide value.

The banker who has an understanding of all the financial products and techniques available (not just the ones the bank is pushing), including their advantages, disadvantages, risks, pricing, liquidity, taxation, accounting, documentation, etc., will be able to differentiate and provide value.

The banker who has current rates and prices readily available and understands and anticipates market trends in product usage will be able to differentiate and provide value.

And finally, the banker who is aware of the delivery capabilities of his or her own institution can offer and deliver efficient service, which will provide value.

What we look at next is an example of this process at work. Taking a simple hypothetical problem, we will analyze the many possible solutions. And in doing so, we will take a look at how the solutions are interchangeable and what factors will influence the decision choice.

The Problem

Fretting Company Inc. has an outstanding $10 million liability with 15 months remaining before maturity. The liability is based on the three-month London Inter-Bank Offer Rate (LIBOR) index, and the rate setting for the next three months has just been determined and communicated to the company.

Although Fretting Company understood that interest rates were rising, the current rate it is being charged together with market forecasts of more rapid increases is heightening company concern about interest expenses. The company has asked its banker for advice.

The Choices
Obviously, the initial decision involves only two choices.
Does the company attempt to protect itself against rising interest rates, i.e., hedge?
Or, does the company accept the risk, despite its concern, and do nothing?

The Value-Added Solution

We have a situation where value can be added through the proper advice. However, providing the proper advice will require a considerable amount of homework and understanding.

Homework
How well do you know the company? Is the interest rate risk acceptable in the context of the company's operations? How much of an impact will interest expense have on the reported earnings of the company? What is the company's tolerance for risk? And, any other questions you can think of that are relevant.

Understanding the Options

How sophisticated is the treasurer or finance director? Does this person truly believe in the company's interest rate forecast, and is this person willing to act upon it? How does the company evaluate treasurer's performance? How much risk does the financial executive take in trying something new?

The banker/advisor who can realistically answer these questions is well positioned to provide value. Let's make the assumption that the decision is made to hedge the interest rate risk. The question becomes, how? What are the techniques that are available and the factors attributable to each that will influence the choice?

Six Techniques for Adding Value

Even for this very simple hypothetical situation there are six basic techniques (and derivations of each are possible) that will provide interest rate protection: the cash market, swaps, futures, forwards, caps, and collars (which will be discussed later in this book). The banker/advisor cannot simply suggest the technique that the bank is good at providing or capable of delivering. Adding value requires giving advice that is objective. The appropriate question: What is best for the company?

The answer can be ascertained by analyzing the alternatives and considering all their elements.

The Cash Market Alternative

This is simply a matter of refinancing. If the company truly thinks that interest rates will rise and it doesn't want the risk of variable-rate debt, it can borrow at a fixed rate and pay off the LIBOR-indexed loan. Of course, if the yield curve is positively sloped, the interest rate the company will obtain for one year will be higher than that for three months. However, this will be true for all of the alternatives. But if interest rates do rise as expected, the cost to the company at the loan's maturity will be less than if it had done nothing.

Advantages

The advantage to using the cash market is its simplicity and the fact that the concept doesn't have to be explained to anyone. At times the cash market can be the cheapest of the alternatives.

Disadvantages

The disadvantages of the cash market are the renegotiation of the loan, covenants that may have to be changed, prepayment penalties, new commission fees, limited flexibility (what does the company do if interest rates don't rise or, perhaps, fall), etc. In this simple example it is unlikely that any of these factors will cause a problem, but for more complicated refinancings, they may.

Exhibit 2   Interest Hedging Alternatives

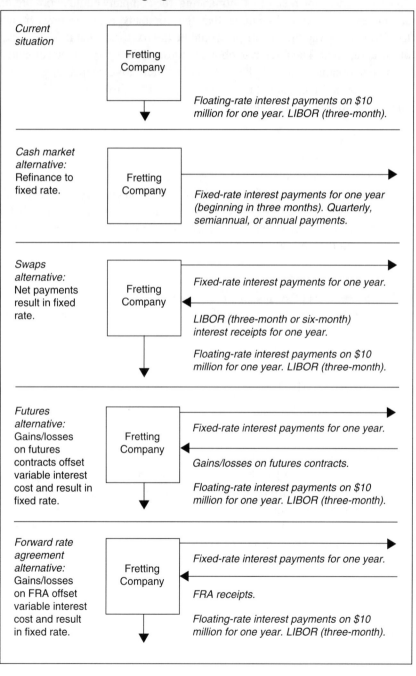

The Interest-Rate Swap Alternative

To achieve the same result as a refinancing, the company could choose to do an interest-rate swap. Assuming that the company receives three-month LIBOR in the swap, the net result would be the fixed rate that it pays as part of the agreement. The fixed rate obtained through the swap can be compared to the rate obtained through the cash market alternative. Depending on supply and demand factors, the rates probably will be different, thereby influencing the company's decision.

Advantages

The advantages of the swap are the ease of implementation, straightforward documentation, negation of all the disadvantages of refinancing (because a swap is, in effect, a synthetic refinancing), off-balance-sheet treatment (although the accounting procedure is undergoing changes that will call for more disclosure on these types of transactions), and simple accounting and tax treatment (assuming the swap remains on the books until maturity).

Disadvantages

The disadvantages of swaps are credit exposure to the bank (companies are concerned about this), lack of liquidity (especially for complex swaps), more complex tax treatment if the swap is reversed, and generally, management approval must be obtained.

The Futures Alternative

An effective fixed rate for the company can also be achieved through a series of futures contracts that lock in the rate of interest for each of the quarterly-rate-fixing dates that the company will face under its current liability structure. The quarterly rates are locked in, for any change in the market LIBOR rate will be directly offset by a gain or loss on the futures contract. By combining the four quarterly rates (adding the principal and multiplying the series), a fixed rate is obtained.

This fixed rate is also comparable to the rates achieved by the other alternatives. Indeed, in the absence of a counterparty to a swap, the futures markets are often used to synthetically construct one.

Advantages

The advantages of the futures contracts approach are liquidity (reversing the transaction and negating the position is easy for one-year maturities), reduced institutional credit risk (the Regulated Futures Exchange is assumed by some to have negligible credit risk), ease of implementation (once the procedures and margin deposit accounts have been set), and maximum flexibility for structuring.

Disadvantages

The disadvantages of the futures markets are that margin deposits are required up-front before contracts can be bought or sold; contracts are marked to market each day with settlement on gains and losses, which requires an administrative function; margin calls may affect the company's cash flow management; visibility of the transaction (margin calls are not easy to hide); and determination of the hedge structure may be complex owing to standard contract sizes and maturity dates.

The Forward-Rate Agreement Alternative

As with futures contracts, an effective fixed rate for one year can be achieved using forward rate agreements (FRAs), which are nothing more than futures contracts implemented with the financial institution as the counterparty rather than some exchange. The bank will contract with the company to guarantee in advance an interest rate for the period(s) in question. At maturity the bank will either make or take payment depending on market rates compared with the contracted rate.

As with futures, the interest for each rate-setting date is locked in, and combining them will result in a synthetic fixed rate for the year. Again, the fixed rate obtained is comparable to the rates in the other alternatives.

Advantages

The advantages of FRAs are flexibility (there are no standards for contracts either in amounts or dates), lack of margin requirements (credit approval is, however, always required), no cash flow until maturity, and low visibility (off-balance-sheet treatment).

Disadvantages

The disadvantages are reduced liquidity/transferability (because of the lack of standardization), institutional credit risk, general inability to net out transactions, and availability of maturities out to only one year (Eurodollar futures contracts are available for three years and swaps even longer).

Conclusion

Four different methods have thus far been described that can achieve interest-rate protection for the company. The resulting cost to the company using each of the methods is likely to be comparable, making the price a less important factor in the final decision. The other factors, therefore, will be very influential. The banker/advisor who wants to add value will be fully cognizant of these factors and their relative importance to the company.

The techniques discussed in this chapter are termed symmetrical hedges, because the ultimate result for each one is the same regardless of what happens in the market. Two other possibilities exist: caps and collars. These will be covered in other chapters.

2

Financial Risk

Marketing Derivatives to the Corporate Treasurer

Few transactions require more coaxing on the part of the banker than hedging with derivatives. For a variety of reasons, corporate treasurers face huge obstacles in using derivatives to hedge the risks arising from changes in interest rates, exchange rates, or commodity prices. Overcoming these obstacles requires more than a high degree of product and market knowledge; it requires sufficient intimacy with the customer's business to understand the company's exposures and risk tolerances.

On the most basic level, however, marketing derivatives successfully—especially to middle-market companies—requires the ability to convince a customer simply that hedging is useful. The widespread acceptance of efficient market theory, a growing awareness of transaction costs, and the fear of bad publicity over "speculative" trading have encouraged the perception that derivatives do little to reduce risk and, in fact, may expose a company (or, on a personal level, the treasurer himself or herself) to new risks.

This chapter highlights the fallacies inherent in four time-worn arguments against hedging. In doing so, it provides ammunition for bankers seeking to help customers answer the question "Why hedge?" Once a corporate customer arrives at the belief that hedging can be useful, the next step is creating corporate hedging policies and strategies and, finally, the execution of transactions.

Dealing with Financial Risk

Risk is a word that brings together two ideas: hope and fear. In dealing with financial risk, most companies want to retain the hope of a favorable outcome while eliminating the fear of an unfavorable outcome.

Every company starts the risk-management process by attempting to analyze and measure its interest rate, currency, and commodity exposures. Once the exposures are known, however, companies approach their management in a variety of ways, from simply absorbing volatility and passing higher costs on to customers to setting up full-scale derivatives hedging programs. Risk-management strategies differ among companies, depending on:

- competitive structures in the industry
- degree of tolerance for cash flow volatility
- access to financing sources
- sophistication/understanding of the financial alternatives available
- compensation strategies for the treasury group/finance function

The ways companies manage risk are summarized in Exhibit 1. However, not every method is available to every company. Competition may prevent a company from raising prices, or the lack of a high credit rating may prevent a company from issuing long-term debt. These companies must turn to other techniques.

Exhibit 1   Methods of Offsetting Financial Risk

Operational Alternatives	Cash Market Alternatives	Derivatives Alternatives
Changing pricing strategy	Aligning assets more closely with liabilities	Using symmetrical or "lock-in" hedge products
Changing purchasing strategy	Altering debt structure	Using asymmetrical or option products

The proliferation of derivative products in the past decade has expanded the hedging alternatives available to the corporate treasurer. But while every company has a pricing policy and a financing strategy, not every treasurer sees derivatives in the same benign light.

To Hedge or Not to Hedge?

Over the relatively short history of derivatives, several arguments have developed both for and against their use. These are summarized in Exhibit 2. It is possible to refute every one of the arguments in the second column against hedging.

ARGUMENT NO. 1

HOPE OF FAVORABLE PRICE OR RATE MOVEMENTS

Some companies don't hedge because hedging can make it impossible to benefit from favorable price or rate movements. These companies are making an implicit choice: to protect potential gains by exposing the company to real losses that could quickly put the company out of business.

For example, the Middle East crisis in January of 1991 pushed up the level and volatility of oil prices. Unprotected end-users suffered millions of dollars in losses. U.S. airlines were particularly exposed to fuel costs. Several

Exhibit 2   To Hedge or Not to Hedge?

To Hedge	Not to Hedge
Fear of adverse price or rate movement	Hope of favorable price or rate movement
Taking advantage of a view—trading for profit	"We're not in the business of speculating; we make widgets."
Locking in costs and revenues	Shareholder diversification argument: Shareholders buy a stock to benefit from positive movements in the underlying product, so hedging is undesirable.
Ability to forecast cash flows better	Efficient market argument: On average, over time, the cost of hedging should equal the cost of not hedging.

U.S. carriers had recently initiated routes to Europe. Competition prevented U.S. carriers from hiking fares on those routes to cover higher fuel costs; some of their competitors did not have to raise prices, because they had already hedged against a higher cost of fuel.

In some cases, financial price risk is so great it can bankrupt a company. A famous case is Laker Airlines, which brought British tourists to the United States in the late 1970s. Laker bought five new aircraft when the pound was strong, contracting to pay in U.S. dollars. Unfortunately, the dollar strengthened and Laker needed more pounds to buy the planes. But at the same time, British tourists stopped traveling to the United States. The appreciation of the dollar put Laker out of business.

These companies failed to hedge in order to take advantage of possible gains. In doing so, they exposed themselves to potentially catastrophic losses.

ARGUMENT NO. 2
"IT'S NOT OUR BUSINESS"
A common argument among treasurers is that "We're not in the business of speculating on interest rates; we make widgets." But by failing to hedge, widget makers are speculating. They are betting that interest rates (and therefore interest expense) will fall; that exchange rates (and therefore profits from exporting or importing) will improve; and that commodity prices (and therefore their cost of goods sold) will decline. Should these events fail to happen, the company will suffer. Only by controlling these factors can the company prosper by making the best widgets on the market.

The current reputation of risk management as a speculative activity has resulted in part from publicity about companies such as Allied Lyons, which recently lost an estimated £250 million by speculating in currency options. In 1991, the company sold U.S. dollar puts that were not expected to be exercised, earning premium income with little apparent risk—that is, until the dollar reversed course. The resulting losses shocked the financial community and led several British corporations to announce publicly that they neither sell nor buy currency options. However, currency options can provide valuable protection against unfavorable exchange-rate movements while allowing hedgers to gain from improvements in rates. The effect is that some British companies increased their risk in order to prove that they are not risk-takers like Allied Lyons.

Losing money by trading for profit is visible. Losing money by doing nothing often goes unnoticed. Allied Lyons may have lost £250 million by speculating, but many other companies have lost even more by failing to hedge.

ARGUMENT NO. 3

"LET THE SHAREHOLDERS HEDGE"

Other naysayers pull out the shareholder argument. The owners of a company's shares can choose to hold a diversified asset portfolio with offsetting risks. Because the shareholder can hedge, there is no reason for the company's management to hedge. In fact, management's decision to hedge could make the stock more unattractive. An often-cited example is a gold mining company. Because investors buy shares of such a company for the gold play, hedging the price of gold removes the investors' motive for buying.

The argument that shareholders can hedge for themselves is correct as long as they have a detailed knowledge of the timing and magnitude of risks faced by the corporation. Shareholders do not know the purchasing or excavating plans of the company. They are not aware of the levels of debt or repayment schedules. The timing of receivables and payables is not public knowledge. Nor should this information be divulged to shareholders, for the information could help competitors. The lack of access to this information puts the shareholder seeking to control risk on his or her own at a disadvantage.

This argument also assumes that investors have the same access to hedging instruments as does management. In fact, the instruments used to hedge financial risks often have minimum contract sizes that far exceed the needs of all but large investors. Transaction costs for small and medium-sized investors would also be greater than those of the corporation.

The strongest challenge to this argument is the fact that hedging can prevent the firm from going bankrupt. Although the order of magnitude of financial risks varies greatly among companies, financial risk has put many firms out of business.

ARGUMENT NO. 4

"ON AVERAGE, OVER TIME"

This argument, which is often used by efficient market adherents, is stated as follows: "On average, over time, the results of a firm that hedges will be the same as if it did not hedge. In fact, because there are costs associated with hedging, companies that hedge may actually be worse off."

This argument is correct—but the key qualification is "on average, over time." While two firms may end up in the same place, the one that does not hedge will encounter much more volatility along the way:

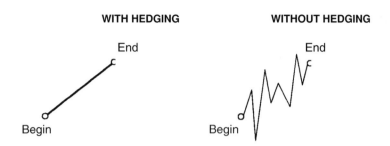

The "without hedging" company is scrutinized not only at the "end" mark, but at every stage between "begin" and "end." Information moves quickly. The performance of companies (and increasingly individuals) is measured today, not "on average, over time."

Derivatives enable companies to smooth their cash flows over time. Exhibit 3 compares the expected cash flows of two companies: one that hedges and one that does not. The firm that hedges has a smaller range of cash flow possibilities, as Exhibit 3 illustrates. This firm, with lower cash flow volatility, has three advantages over the nonhedger:

Exhibit 3   How Hedging Affects the Value of the Firm

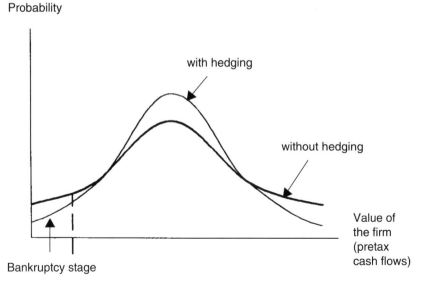

1) The hedger, with a more accurate forecast of the future relationship between costs and revenues, can better plan its business strategy and operate with a lower likelihood of entering bankruptcy.

2) The hedger will most likely have lower borrowing costs because lenders perceive lower risk in a company with less volatile cash flows.

3) Shareholders ascribe a higher value to companies with less volatile future cash flows.

Volatility and Share Prices

The case of Bankers Trust Corporation and Banc One—shown in Exhibit 4—makes a powerful argument for reducing cash flow and earnings volatility. Although both institutions are banks, the two are in entirely different businesses. Bankers Trust makes money by engaging in short-term trading. While profitable and professionally managed, the business is transaction-oriented and is perceived by investors to be volatile. Banc One has been successful in retail banking and credit card processing—areas perceived as more relationship-oriented and less risky.

These perceptions are manifested in the price/earnings multiples of the two banks. Bankers Trust trades at a P/E multiple of 8; Banc One's P/E is 16. Investors pay twice as much for Banc One because of its lower volatility.

Exhibit 4   Bankers Trust Versus Banc One

	Bankers Trust	Banc One
Business	Short-term trading in currencies, interest rates, and some equities; transaction-oriented	Consumer banking, credit card processing
Investor Expectations	Profitable but unpredictable; expectations of volatile cash flows	Profitable and stable; expectations of smooth cash flows
P/E Multiple	8	16

Conclusion

Derivatives are a tool for reducing volatility through hedging. The use of derivatives is not speculation; the objective is not to "beat the market," but to help a company meet its earnings and cash flow objectives. By using derivatives intelligently and in combination with operating and cash market alternatives, management can avoid financial danger while taking advantage of market opportunity.

Hedging is a process, not a transaction. Once a company has been convinced that hedging is useful, the banker should begin to work with the treasurer to develop policies and strategies that address the company's exposures, risk tolerances, and choice of hedging alternatives. A subsequent chapter will discuss the selection of appropriate hedging instruments given different exposures and expectations. This process begins with the identification of a company's exposures and ends with an execution plan.

3

Corporate Hedging Strategies

Linking Expectations to Hedging Choices

Many financial tools are available to the corporate treasurer seeking to hedge against financial risk. The decision on which hedging instrument to use depends on several factors, one of which will always be quantitative, i.e., cost. Other factors are qualitative: They have nothing to do with cost and a great deal to do with such things as credit risk, hedge effectiveness, flexibility, visibility, liquidity, and administrative, tax, and accounting issues.

The quantitative decision-making process is the most straightforward. It involves comparing the all-in cost of the various hedging alternatives to the customer's expectations about interest rates, exchange rates, or commodity prices. Once the marketer is able to discover these expectations, he or she will be able to target a hedging strategy that is consistent with these expectations and therefore is most cost-effective.

Cost is not the sole force driving decisions about how to hedge. Other customer considerations are less clear-cut; they can only be discovered and evaluated by a banker with a close relationship with the customer. Information such as how the treasury group is structured and compensated, who approves hedging transactions, and how willing the company is to try new things will affect the types of hedging methods that should be offered to a customer.

The previous chapter, "Financial Risk: Marketing Derivatives to the Corporate Treasurer," was intended to help bankers show customers how hedging can be useful, even necessary, despite arguments against hedging by academics and others. This chapter illustrates a way to use the strength and direction of the customer's expectations—i.e., the interest-rate forecast—to choose among hedging alternatives. In addition, the chapter reviews the qualitative factors that drive the choice of hedging methods.

The Quantitative Approach

Cost is not the only consideration in choosing a hedging method, but for many customers it is the most important. Cost is defined here as the all-in cost of a hedge combined with an underlying financing. For example, a customer should look not only at the rate on a swap or the premium on a cap, but also how using the products in conjunction with an underlying borrowing will change the expense of the combined structure.

Unfortunately, when the resulting financing has a floating interest rate, the all-in cost cannot be known until maturity. And when the result is a fixed-rate financing, the cost cannot be compared to floating-rate alternatives. To be able to analyze such costs, assumptions about future interest rates are required. Ideally, these assumptions, or interest-rate forecasts, should come from the customer.

For the insightful banker, a forecast is more than a number. Risk combines elements of hope and fear. A customer's decision to hedge interest-rate risk is driven by both fear of rates rising and hopes of rates falling. This mix

---

Exhibit 1   Hedging Strategies in a Rising Interest-Rate Environment

Underlying Exposure:		Risk:			
Floating-rate debt		Interest rates rise			

HEDGING ALTERNATIVES

Cash Market	FRA	Futures	Swaps	Cap	Floor
Repay loan; borrow at fixed rate	Buy FRA (pay fixed, receive floating)	Sell Euro-dollar futures contracts	Pay fixed; receive floating	Buy cap	Sell floor (to receive premium income)*

*Not a pure hedging strategy

Exhibit 2   Customer Expectations and Hedging Strategies

INTEREST-RATE EXPECTATIONS		HEDGING STRATEGY
Degree of Certainty	*Direction of Movement*	
Certain	▲	Pay fixed in an interest-rate swap
Probable	▲	Buy an in-the-money (expensive) cap
No view	▲▼	Use a collar
Probable	▼	Buy an out-of-the-money (cheap) cap
Certain	▼	Do nothing

---

gives insight into the kind of risk/reward profile—and, consequently, the type of hedging instruments—that the customer will seek.

None of the hedging alternatives listed in Exhibit 1 eliminates risk. Each simply redefines the risk. For example, a swap locks in a borrower's interest rate over a specific period. The borrower is hedged against the risk that rates will rise, but is still exposed to the possibility that floating interest rates may fall and the borrower would have been better off remaining unhedged. A swap may appear less risky because of the fixed cost associated with it. But in fact, entering into a swap requires a strong view about interest-rate movements—in this case, that interest rates are rising.

The choice of a swap (or any other symmetrical or "lock-in" product such as a futures contract, a forward-rate agreement, or a foreign-exchange forward) is at one extreme of the spectrum (see Exhibit 2) of hedging possibilities because of the strong view required. At the other extreme is the "do nothing" strategy, which also requires a strong view: By not hedging, the floating-rate borrower makes the statement that rates will fall. These borrowers are "speculating" on rates by betting that rates will drop.

The Floating-Rate Borrower

An example can illustrate how the customer's view drives the choice among hedging alternatives. A company has a three-year $25 million loan, indexed to six-month LIBOR. Because the borrowing is floating rate, the borrower is exposed to a rising LIBOR. The yield curve is upward sloping, indicating market expectations of rising rates. The company has five hedging alternatives:

Maturity	Instrument	Rate or Strike	Premium	Level
3 years	swap	5.50%	N.A.	N.A.
3 years	cap	5.50%	70 basis points	at the money (ATM)
3 years	cap	7.00%	30 basis points	out of the money (OTM)
3 years	cap	5.00%	90 basis points	in the money (ITM)
3 years	floor	5.00%	40 basis points	out of the money (OTM)

DO NOTHING
Here the borrower's cost will equal LIBOR over the three-year term of the loan. There is no maximum or minimum cost.

THREE-YEAR SWAP
The borrower receives LIBOR, which offsets the LIBOR payments on the loan and pays 5.50%. The interest cost is fixed at 5.50%, regardless of what happens to LIBOR.

THREE-YEAR AT-THE-MONEY CAP
A 5.50% cap protects the borrower from an increase in rates over 5.50%. The borrower pays LIBOR when it is below 5.50%. But if LIBOR rises above 5.50%, the borrower receives cash inflows to compensate the borrower for the interest expense over 5.50%. In return for this protection, the borrower pays a premium that, if amortized, boosts the borrower's cost by 70 basis points.

The highest cost to the borrower is 6.20% (the 5.50% cap level plus a 70 basis points per-annum premium). Because the cap level is the same as the swap rate, the cap is at the money.

OUT-OF-THE-MONEY CAP
This is the 7.00% cap; because the borrower accepts the risk of interest rates rising to 7.00%, the premium is lower than that of the 5.50% cap. The

maximum cost is 7.30% (the 7.00% cap level plus a 30 basis points per-annum premium). Because the strike rate is higher than the prevailing swap offer rate, the cap is out of the money.

IN-THE-MONEY CAP

A three-year 5.00% cap costs the most among the cap alternatives because it offers the borrower the lowest maximum cost. The most the borrower will pay during the term of the loan is 5.90% (the 5.00% cap level plus the 90 basis points premium). Because the strike rate is below the prevailing three-year swap offer rate, the cap is in the money.

COLLAR

A collar involves simultaneously buying a cap and selling a floor. The sale of the floor generates premium income to offset the cost of the cap. The lower the floor level, the less premium is earned. The collar here combines an at-the-money cap and an out-of-the-money floor. At 5.00%, the floor generates 40 basis points of premium income. Thus, the customer's maximum and minimum costs are:

Cap level	5.50%	Floor level	5.00%
Cost of cap	+ 0.70%	Cost of cap	+ 0.70%
Receipt from floor	– 0.40%	Receipt from floor	– 0.40%
Maximum cost	5.80%	Minimum cost	5.30%

Exhibit 3 compares each of the alternatives. Each has a different personality; each performs differently under different interest-rate scenarios. The question of which product is best depends on the customer's view of the direction of rates.

Strong Expectations

The "do nothing" and "swap" alternatives appeal to the borrowers with strong expectations. The do nothing alternative suggests a strong view that rates will fall; the swap alternative, a strong view that rates will rise.

These strategies require strong views on rates because they can result in very high costs if the customer's view is wrong. If rates remain below 5.50%, the do nothing strategy bears the lowest cost, but if rates rise, the do nothing strategy could have the highest cost.

At the other extreme, the swap also requires a strong view. It appeals to the borrower with strong expectations that rates will rise and remain above

---

Exhibit 3   Hedging Alternatives

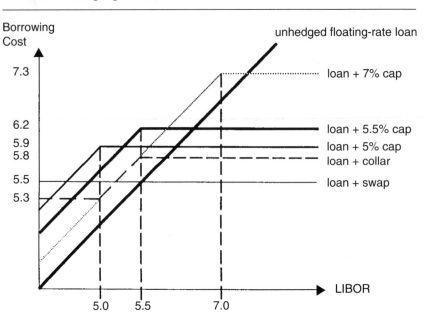

5.50%. A strong view is required because the borrower gives up potential gains from a lower rate in exchange for the protection against higher rates.

Moderate Expectations

Between the do nothing and swap extremes lie the option strategies. Options combine aspects of both the do nothing and swap alternatives, allowing the user to tailor the hedge to a specific view. Options are appropriate for customers with medium views or even no view because they are asymmetrical hedge products—that is, they allow the user some protection against rates or prices moving in either direction.

A strategy involving the purchase of options will never be the lowest-cost hedge. If interest rates fall, a do nothing strategy will be the best; if interest rates rise, a swap will be the best. The purchase of options always involves paying premiums, while the "do nothing" and swap strategies entail no explicit cost.

The examples that follow explore four option structures, but the number of approaches is limitless.

AT-THE-MONEY CAP

The cap struck at the swap offer rate—in this case, 5.5%—offers similar protection against rising rates as does the swap. Like the user of the swap alternative, this customer expects interest rates to rise. Unlike the user of the swap alternative, the customer is not entirely sure about his or her rate prediction. In the customer's mind, the possibility of rates remaining the same or falling still exists. The fixed nature of the swap—which precludes any possibility of benefiting from an interest-rate drop—makes it inappropriate.

OUT-OF-THE-MONEY CAP

A cap struck above the swap offer rate—in this case, 7%—is also appropriate for a medium view. In this case, however, the borrower must believe that rates are more likely to fall, but is also afraid of the possibility of rates rising. If the customer felt certain that rates would fall, there would be no reason to pay the cap premium.

The out-of-the-money cap could also be a good strategy for a borrower who, though he or she believes in falling rates, has a mandate to hedge a certain amount of debt. Another possibility might be a difference of opinion within the company. An option can satisfy both points of view.

Exhibit 4　All-in Cost of Hedging Strategies

VIEW		INTEREST RATE EXPECTATIONS			STRATEGY	ALL-IN COST
		Probability of rise to 7.5%	Probability of fall to 3.5%		Rates rise to 7.5%*	Rates fall to 3.5%*
Strong	▼	0%	100%	Do nothing	7.5%	3.5%
Strong	▲	100%	0%	Swap (5.5%)	5.5%	5.5%
Probable	▼	25%	75%	OTM Cap (7%)	7.3%	3.8%
Probable	▲	75%	25%	ITM Cap (5%)	5.9%	4.4%
Probable	▲	60%	40%	ATM Cap (5.5%)	6.2%	4.2%
No View	↕	50%	50%	Collar**	5.8%	5.3%

*Average over 3-year period
** Combines cap at 5.50% and floor at 5.00%

Exhibit 5   Hedging Strategies Ranked by Cost

INTEREST-RATE SCENARIO

Big Rise (7.50%*)			Big Fall (3.50%*)			Moderate Rise (6%*)		
Rank	Strategy	Cost	Rank	Strategy	Cost	Rank	Strategy	Cost
1	Swap	5.50%	1	Do nothing	3.50%	1	Swap	5.50%
2	ITM cap	5.90%	2	OTM cap	3.80%	2	ITM cap	5.90%
3	ATM cap	6.20%	3	ATM cap	4.20%	3	Do nothing	6.00%
4	OTM cap	7.30%	4	ITM cap	4.40%	4	ATM cap	6.20%
5	Do nothing	7.50%	5	Swap	5.50%	5	OTM cap	6.30%

Average over 3-year period

IN-THE-MONEY CAP

The 5% cap suggests a fairly strong belief that rates will rise, but not strong enough to give up the possibility that rates (and therefore the borrowing cost) will fall. This borrower believes more strongly than the buyer of the 5.5% cap that rates will rise, yet is still uncertain.

The view of the 7% (out-of-the-money) cap buyer is the opposite of that of the 5% (in-the-money) cap buyer. The 7% buyer thinks rates are falling, but is not sure; the 5% cap buyer says rates are rising, but is not sure.

COLLAR

Collars impose on the borrower a maximum and minimum cost. The borrower buys a cap because he or she thinks rates may rise but also may fall or fail to rise substantially. The borrower adds a floor because he or she thinks rates will fail to fall far enough to pay for the cap. The borrower therefore sells some of the cap's potential benefit in the form of a floor. The premium received for selling the floor reduces the cost of the cap and lowers the premium expense.

Some borrowers believe that if they are not sure about the direction of rates, they should "be conservative" and do nothing. Exhibit 3 shows that the do nothing strategy is far from conservative. Instead, it expresses a very strong view about rates. Collar-type products are a far better alternative for those with uncertain expectations. They are inexpensive and offer the possibility of gains, yet provide protection against an increase in borrowing costs.

The Qualitative Approach

View and all-in cost are one way to determine the most appropriate hedging strategy for a customer. But companies do not always base their decisions solely on cost. The qualitative factors that impact choice of hedging strategy include:

CREDIT RISK

Some companies restrict counterparties by credit quality. A typical require- ment is a rating at or above single-A or double-A. If credit is a top concern, futures are the alternative with the lowest credit risk.

HEDGE EFFECTIVENESS

Hedging involves offsetting the cash flows of an underlying exposure. Companies concerned about matching precisely the size and timing of the cash flows would avoid futures contracts or hedges entailing basis risk.

FLEXIBILITY

Flexibility is similar to hedge effectiveness: it refers to the ability to tailor a solution to specific client needs. Over-the-counter products are preferable if flexibility is important.

VISIBILITY/EXPLAINABILITY

The biggest risk facing a treasurer is often the risk that he or she is making the right decision. The best alternative may be the one that requires the least explaining or is most "invisible." Complex alternatives are appropriate only when the treasurer feels competent to discuss them and will not be penalized for a wrong decision.

LIQUIDITY

For some customers, it is as important to be able to get out of a contract as easily as it was to get into it. These customers view liquidity as very important. The more tailored the product, the less liquid. The most liquid of all interest rate hedging alternatives is the futures contract.

ADMINISTRATION/DOCUMENTATION

Some hedge alternatives require more administration than others. Clients may lack the ability to handle complex cash flows such as those resulting from a margin account. This implies a more straightforward alternative—for instance, a swap or forward-rate agreement.

TAX/ACCOUNTING

Often neglected by bankers, tax and accounting implications are always a concern to corporate customers. If the customer is concerned, the banker should also be concerned.

Conclusion

Both quantitative and qualitative factors are important to each client. A quantitative evaluation involves understanding the direction and strength of the customer's rate forecast, helping the customer to understand the true risks involved, and translating the customer's view into an appropriate hedge structure. Qualitative factors are more subtle but involve an understanding of the customer's organization, hedging style, corporate culture, and level of sophistication. Knowing the customer's expectations, and understanding the customer well enough to evaluate the importance of the qualitative factors, will help bankers target marketing efforts effectively by appealing to the client's specific needs.

4

The Future of Futures
Will Corporate Use Increase?

Who will profit most from the growth in risk-management products—banks or futures exchanges? In the past, banks have stood between corporate end-users and the futures exchanges. As exchanges gear up to capture more end-user business, corporations may increasingly bypass banks and deal directly with the exchanges. An understanding of how the exchanges are changing, and how these changes affect the ultimate corporate consumer of swaps, FRAs, caps, collars, and other products is essential for anyone marketing rate-risk management products.

The growth in risk-management transactions has both benefited and frustrated participants in the exchange market. These markets have enjoyed a surge in volume, but most of it has come from financial intermediaries. A large number of ultimate borrowers, investors, and even speculators continue to look to commercial and investment banks for risk-management products. Some portion of these bank transactions are inevitably offset on the exchanges, but the exchanges do not receive the full volume of these transactions.

By customizing risk-management strategies, banks create value and make the products more effective and less intimidating for corporate customers.

(See "The Bank as Intermediary" in Chapters 7, 8, and 9.) However, in many cases corporate treasury staffers can customize their own risk management products using exchange-traded contracts. Indeed, many sophisticated corporates are already doing just that. The exchanges are hoping to accelerate this process and disintermediate the banks further.

This global competition for the business of the end-user has compelled the exchanges to make a number of dramatic changes. New futures and options contracts are being introduced. New exchanges are opening in several countries. Technological innovations are changing the way trades are executed. These are all functions of global competition. The exchanges, both individually and as a group, are trying to:

- encourage customers to bypass the financial intermediaries, using the primary markets directly
- expand the potential market for risk-management products/transactions
- increase volume on the exchanges.

By becoming more attractive to end-users, the exchanges will open the door to an even greater explosion in trading volume—and potential profitability. The coming changes will benefit all current and potential users of futures, options, swaps, and derivative products—including corporate clients of all sizes—whether they use bank products or go directly to the exchanges.

The Role of the Exchange

To understand the reasons behind the coming changes, it is necessary to under-stand the role of a futures exchange. A futures exchange is comprised of the members who have purchased seats on the exchange. By buying seats, the members obtain the right to trade on the exchange (there are different

---

Exhibit 1   The End-User Perspective on Exchange Products

Advantages	Disadvantages
Liquid	Inflexible contract amounts
Efficient	Possible date mismatch
Good price	Potential basis risk
Low default risk	Irregular cash flows (margin)
	Access to market
	Administrative burden
	Cosmetic factors (public perception)

types of seats, allowing access to different trading opportunities). The members generate profits in two ways.

- Commission revenue comes from fees charged to clients for executing buy/sell orders.

- Trading profits are generated by taking positions in the market.

Exhibit 2   Bank Intermediation Versus Futures Exchange

Company A would like to convert $50 million in debt from three-month LIBOR to a two-year fixed rate. It can either pay fixed in an interest-rate swap or short Eurodollar futures for each quarterly reset date. Company B would like to do the opposite on $35 million in debt.

While several scenarios are possible, two common alternatives are described here.

Scenario 1
Company A pays a fixed rate to a bank on $50 million and receives floating in an interest-rate swap. The bank pays fixed to Company B and receives floating on $35 million. The bank has $15 million in exposure remaining, which it hedges by shorting futures contracts. The exchange benefits by an increase in volume (and commissions) on only the $15 million. In effect, the bank has disintermediated the futures exchange by standing between the two companies and matching $35 million of the $50 million total volume. The more the bank can do this, the more the bank will benefit at the expense of the exchange.

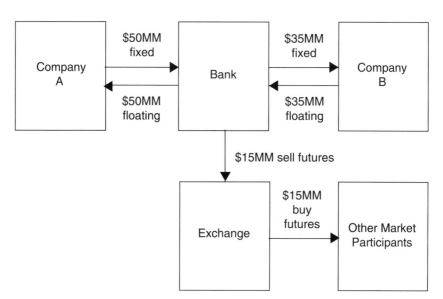

Scenario 2
Company A shorts $50 million in futures contracts for each quarterly reset date, creating the same effect as a two-year swap. Company B buys $35 million in futures for the same period. The exchange captures $85 million in end-user volume.

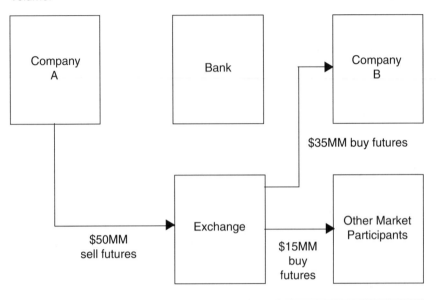

Volume Considerations

Because commission revenue is a major source of profits to members, transaction volume is a major consideration. More volume implies more commission revenue. It also implies more opportunities for both day traders and market makers to generate additional trading profits.

Although the exchanges can take actions that will generate additional volume in the short term, the ultimate objective is to increase the extent to which end-users transact business directly on the exchange, bypassing financial intermediaries.

When banks act as intermediaries in risk-management transactions, many of the derivative products they sell create offsetting risks. To the extent that two transactions partially or completely offset the risk, the level of residual risk that is hedged on an exchange is reduced. This results in less commission income for the member firms. Reducing the disadvantages to end-users of exchange transactions will lead to an increase in trading volume and a commensurate increase in commission revenue, liquidity, and potential trading profits for members.

How can the exchanges stimulate additional volume? Several actions have been taken in the past, and many will be implemented in the near future. Some solutions will provide benefits almost immediately, while others are longer term in nature.

Short-Term Improvements

Many actions will increase trading volume quickly. However, many of these steps have negative side effects and do not stimulate volume among the most desired constituency, the end-users. Rather than reducing or eliminating the major disadvantages to end-users, these actions frequently make trading easier and/or more efficient for financial intermediaries.

Margin Requirements

One such action is to cut the level of margin required. Because exchanges can alter margin requirements at any time, this change is easy to implement and can be done for all contracts or only specific ones. When market volatility is low, the margin requirement on many contracts might be reduced. Trading volume on a new contract could be increased quickly by instituting a very low margin requirement.

When margin requirements are low, less capital is required to trade. The cost of trading is reduced. This is a significant consideration for high-volume participants, generally financial intermediaries and speculators, but does not overcome any major disadvantage to end-users.

Reducing margin requirements also carries a big drawback. Margin serves to guarantee the performance of obligations by market participants and insulate the exchange from loss. Lowering margins increases the level of default risk borne by the exchange clearinghouse.

Expanded Trading Hours

Most of the exchanges engage in trading for approximately eight hours each day, ending in midafternoon. This makes the use of futures more cumbersome by placing time constraints on end-users.

Many exchanges circumvent this obstacle by establishing "mutual offset agreements" with other exchanges. Two exchanges list the same contract with exactly the same terms and agree that positions opened on one exchange can be closed on the other. The most prominent links are the Chicago Mercantile Exchange (CME)/Singapore International Monetary Exchange (SIMEX) and the London International Financial Futures Exchange (LIFFE)/ Sidney Futures Exchange (SFE).

Another alternative is expanding trading hours. The Chicago Board of Trade (CBOT) was the first major exchange to institute an evening trading session. Designed to coincide with the period of greatest trading activity in the Asian market for U.S. government securities, this session has successfully increased volume in the CBOT's Treasury futures and options contracts. The CBOT's move induced other exchanges to lengthen trading sessions, including the currency futures and options section of the Philadelphia Stock Exchange.

The use of mutual offset links and increased trading hours have removed one major obstacle to the use of exchange products by reducing the time constraint.

Increase in Contract Alternatives

The pace at which new contracts are added continues to increase. Not only have new contracts appeared—for instance, a greater maturity spectrum of U.S. Treasuries—but the contract cycles have been extended as well. As the markets become increasingly liquid, the pace will continue to accelerate.

This is one of the few actions that stimulates trading over both the short and long term. By allowing users greater flexibility in terms of the underlying instrument (i.e., Treasuries versus corporate bonds) and extending the maturity of contract cycles (i.e., Eurodollar contracts trading three years in the future), the exchanges reduce major disadvantages to end-users.

Long-Term Growth

To capture more of the growth in risk-management transactions, the exchanges must reduce the disadvantages to end-users. Some disadvantages, such as margin and inflexible contract amounts, can never be fully eliminated. However, other obstacles to end-users can be removed.

The most important factors inhibiting the use of exchange products are:

- basis risk, due to the difference between contract instruments and the underlying position

- market access (partially overcome by mutual offset links and expanded trading hours)

- cosmetic factors, including the perception by an uninformed public that the exchanges are a disorderly market

- the potential for a date mismatch between the underlying position and the exchange hedge.

The exchanges, generally acting independently of each other, are taking a number of actions to overcome these factors. These actions include introducing new contracts, opening new exchanges, and using modern communication technology to improve and expand trading.

Expanding the Contracts Available

While the most popular financial futures contracts (ignoring equity) have existed for several years, several relatively new contracts have captured impressive volume levels. This volume has often come from new business rather than cannibalization of existing contracts.

Given the diversity of contracts now available, short-term borrowers, investors, and intermediaries in almost every major currency have the ability to hedge themselves on an exchange. The short-term contracts are listed in the table that follows.

Exhibit 3   Selected Short-Term Futures Contracts

Underlying Asset	Option Exchange	Option Available?	Applications
Three-month Eurodollar	CME	yes	Borrowers: Hedge
	SIMEX	yes	future short-term
	LIFFE	yes	borrowings or resets
	SFE	no	against increase.
Three-month sterling (£)	LIFFE	yes	Depending on tenor,
Ninety-day Australian bank bills (A$)	SFE	yes	synthesize swap.
Three-month Euro DM	LIFFE	no	
	MATIF*	no	
Three-month Paris Interbank Offered Rate (FFr)	MATIF	no	Investors: Protect against lower rates
Three-month Dublin Interbank Offered Rate (I£)	Irish Futures & Options Exchange	no	(opposite of above).
Ninety-day New Zealand bank bills (NZ$)	New Zealand Futures Exchange	no	Intermediaries: Asset/liability management, swap book management.

*MATIF is the Marche à Terme International de France in Paris.

In many of the currencies noted in Exhibit 3, other short-term instruments exist as well. When multiple short-term contracts exist, as in the U.S. dollar with Treasury bill and Fed funds contracts, the user can select the one that minimizes or eliminates basis risk.

There has been a similar proliferation of contracts on long-term instruments. Most of the contracts are based on long-term government securities, but several other instruments have been introduced or are under consideration.

Exhibit 4   Selected Long-Term Government Futures Contracts

Underlying Asset	Option Exchange	Option Available?	Applications
U.S. dollar T-bonds	CBOT	yes	Borrowers: Hedge
	LIFFE	yes	future long-term
	SFE	no	debt issue or swap.
U.S. dollar T-notes (10-year)	CBOT	yes	
U.S. dollar T-notes (five-year)	CBOT	no	Investors: Protect
	NY Cotton	yes	asset value from
UK sterling long gilt	LIFFE	yes	rise in rates.
UK sterling short gilt	LIFFE	no	
	SFE	no	Intermediaries:
Yen 10-year bonds	Tokyo	no	Asset/liability
Yen 20-year bonds	Tokyo	no	management, swap book
Yen bonds	LIFFE	no	management,
French franc bonds	MATIF	yes	hedging of currency
DM government bonds	LIFFE	yes	swaps.
Australian dollar Commonwealth bonds	SFE		yes

Contracts have also been introduced in the United States that are based on corporate bonds and municipal bonds. Contracts on mortgage-backed securities are scheduled to start trading on the CBOT later this month.

As contracts gain liquidity, exchanges will add contracts to extend contract cycles into longer maturities. An increasing variety of contracts will help make basis risk more manageable by end-users. If contract cycles are expanded, the expansion will also help the end-users overcome the problem of date mismatches.

More Recently Established Exchanges

At the same time that existing exchanges are broadening the range of contracts available, other exchanges are opening. To capitalize on the potential for futures and options business, exchanges are being organized in several locations throughout the world. Other exchanges are banding together, and some that have been burdened by regulatory restrictions or failed to react to changes in the business have failed.

Exchanges in the start-up phase include the following:

- The Swiss Options & Futures Exchange (SOFFEX) opened for business in May of 1988. Activities include options on specific equities and futures and options on an equity index.

- The Deutsche TerminBoerse (DTB), sponsored by several German financial institutions, began operations in early 1990. The primary activity is a German government bond futures contract. The contract is similar to one that has been successful on the LIFFE since its introduction in September of 1988. It is also likely that there will be equity options and an equity index future.

- The Irish Futures and Options Exchange (IFOX) opened in March of 1989, with contracts based on long-term Irish Gilts, three-month time deposits, and the I£:US$ exchange rate.

The increasing number of exchanges will inevitably lead to more new contracts as each exchange searches for a niche to exploit. Greater competition and a wider choice of hedging alternatives will work in favor of end-users. Futures and options will become more flexible, applications will be better understood, and transaction costs will fall.

Any exchange that cannot sustain adequate volume will be unable to maintain the infrastructure required for an "open-outcry" transaction system. These exchanges will ultimately fail or seek some form of alliance with other exchanges.

Global Trading Systems

Many firms have touted "24-hour trading" capability for years. In most cases, this is a goal rather than reality. Very few markets are liquid for 24 hours. Inhibiting 24-hour trading is the lack of a central marketplace and/or communication system.

To capitalize on the demand for risk-management products, and also to maintain their position as the leading futures and options exchanges, both the CME and CBOT have introduced electronic trading systems. Globex, the CME system, became operational in October of 1989. The CBOT's version, Aurora, was completed in 1990.

Both systems provide the capability to trade "around the world/around the clock." Each of the two exchanges has formed alliances with different vendors in the fields of computers and communications and is seeking other exchanges to join the networks.

The two systems are similar in many respects. Both are seeking to enlist other exchanges. All contracts offered by member exchanges are eligible for listing on the systems. No contracts will trade on the electronic systems during the hours they trade on the sponsoring exchange. The systems will provide a more effective audit trail of transactions, simplifying administration and also reducing concerns of improper trading practices.

Aurora, the CBOT system, is a computer replication of the open-outcry system. Participants enter bids and offers. Other participants can counter those prices or accept them. A button is pushed to execute a trade. Globex, the CME system, automatically matches trades based on price, on a first-come first-served basis. The Globex system appears to be the most popular. So far, Globex has enlisted three other exchanges: MATIF, SFE, and the New York Mercantile Exchange (NYMEX).

Only members will have access to trading terminals, but a greater amount of market information will also be disseminated over financial information networks like Reuters. In the long run, both systems will provide many advantages: an increase in overall volume; broader participation by end-users as contracts become more easily available in different time zones; and streamlined administration and record keeping.

Another major advantage of the systems is an enhanced public perception of the futures markets. Using the computer networks, the markets will appear to be more orderly and "legitimate" to the unsophisticated users who have been reluctant to use the exchanges in the past. This is an important step in increasing the level of end-user participation in the markets.

One unanswered question is the level of liquidity. In the early stages, individual contracts will probably have greater liquidity on the exchange floors than on the electronic systems. Locals are unlikely to trade extensively on the systems. For the systems to be successful, financial intermediaries and end-users must generate sufficient volume to maintain liquidity. In the introductory phase of the systems, the sponsors may have to offer incentives to accomplish this.

Future of Risk-Management Products

The use of risk-management products will continue to spread. The introduction of new tools and techniques and the further dissemination of information will aid this process. Exchanges, intermediaries, and end-users will be forced to adapt to this evolutionary change. Some will flourish with the changes; others will be hurt.

The Exchanges

Exchanges currently rely on financial intermediaries for a large share of volume. At the same time, exchanges compete with intermediaries for the business of end-users. This situation is further complicated by the fact that most major banks and investment banks are members of the exchanges. Banks are indirectly competing with themselves for the business of end-users.

The introduction of new contracts, opening of new exchanges, and introduction of electronic trading will make the use of futures and options easier in many ways. New end-users will be attracted to the exchange markets. However, it is unlikely that there will be sufficient volume or other justification for trading the same type of instrument on multiple exchanges. In fact, systems like Globex make multiple listings of the same contract redundant.

In the long run, exchanges that successfully meet end-user needs will flourish. However, the industry will probably be much different than it is today. Much like the airlines and other deregulated businesses, the futures industry will reach a point where some rationalization of capacity will occur. Unsuccessful contracts will be eliminated, and some exchanges will probably close. Electronic trading may completely replace the open-outcry system, effectively acting as a single exchange for futures and options.

The End-User Perspective

The implications for end-users of risk-management products are nothing but favorable. New futures and options contracts provide more flexibility to those wishing to hedge directly on an exchange. For those who prefer the ease and simplicity of "custom-designed" bank products, the increased ease of hedging (due to the new contracts) will drive down the cost to banks of intermediating, thereby reducing the cost to end-users.

The electronic trading systems will also benefit end-users. By moving toward a liquid, 24-hour market, any hedger can centrally manage exposure. A U.S. middle market company receiving subsidized financing to establish a new manufacturing facility in Ireland might wish to hedge against higher rates. In the future, the treasurer might use the IFOX (via an electronic system) to hedge either short- or long-term I£ interest rates, rather than maintaining a local treasury staff or getting out of bed in the middle of the night to implement a hedge.

As the markets evolve, high-volume hedgers will find it increasingly easier to go directly to the exchanges. End-users who have only occasional needs, are ultraconservative, or have very special needs or small treasury staffs will continue to use the banks.

Conclusion

The banking industry's success in risk-management products has given exchanges the motivation and opportunity to capture a larger share of end-user business. The expansion of exchange capabilities will make exchange-traded products more attractive to end-users. This is not necessarily bad news for banks. It merely highlights the importance of adopting a realistic competitive strategy and implementing it well.

Few banks can successfully fill every market need in risk management, just as a single bank cannot dominate any other market/product segment. Each bank must identify its strengths and weaknesses—as applied to the bank's client base—and adopt a strategy that emphasizes the appropriate capabilities.

Multinationals (MNCs) typically generate a large volume of transactions to create a variety of hedges of domestic and foreign interest rates and exchange rates. MNCs also have the sophistication to accept minor basis risk and the infrastructure to handle the administrative requirements of exchange-traded products.

For this type of end-user, access to the exchanges will be important. Many banks have affiliates that are futures and options brokers, and members of the major exchanges, which can be used to service this type of client. Historically, however, banks have not aggressively marketed these services to corporate clients. In the future, this will become increasingly necessary.

Large domestic corporate clients may not have the same volume or diversity of transactions, but may still be candidates for standardized exchange products. The deciding factor will be the sophistication of the treasury staff and the relative importance of the treasury function. Some of these clients will provide tremendous opportunities for continued intermediation by banks. Others will look to the exchanges directly. The relationship officer must make this determination.

Many middle market clients are still learning about risk-management products and techniques. It is unlikely that middle market customers would bypass banks and move quickly to futures and options. However, to obtain and maintain this business, banks must be at the forefront of the education process. By demonstrating the need for a service, a bank will have an advantage in meeting the need.

The most successful risk-management banks must examine their client base and product capabilities. Continued success among large and sophisticated clients will require direct access to the exchanges or outstanding product innovation that clearly adds value. The middle market is currently an attractive opportunity, but expansion by the exchanges and competition from other banks means that success requires moving quickly to build a presence in this market. Maintaining success will require excellent delivery capability and some degree of value-added service.

PART II

Interest Rate Derivatives

Since virtually every entity in business or government faces interest rate risk, the variety of interest rate derivative products has proliferated. Interest rate derivatives take the form of simple forward rate agreements, futures, swaps, swaptions, caps, collars and combinations thereof. Their application to a multitude of different situations is limited only by the imaginations of product specialists.

Chapters 5 and 6 provide an introduction to interest rate derivatives. Chapter 5 covers forward rate agreements, the building block for all other interest rate derivatives. Chapter 6 applies a product life cycle framework to derivatives, showing how swaps quickly moved from a radical innovation to a commodity business, forcing banks to innovate anew in order to maintain high margins.

The five chapters in the options section focus first on the bank's role and then on specific over-the-counter products. Chapters 7, 8 and 9 examine the bank's function as an intermediary between exchange-traded futures and tailored derivatives. Chapters 10 and 11 cover the development of the cap and swaption markets.

The final two chapters in this section take the view that trends in the financial markets influence the marketing opportunities available to corporate relationship managers. Specifically, these papers examine interest rate swap spreads and how they affect the hedging, financing and arbitrage opportunities available to clients.

5

Forward-Rate Agreements

The Fundamental Hedging Product

Forward-rate agreements (FRAs) are simple and effective tools for managing interest-rate risk. Customers like FRAs because of their flexibility, simplicity, and lack of up-front fees; banks like them because they are liquid and involve little credit risk. Because an FRA is used to hedge interest-rate risk one period at a time, it is an easy commitment for customers unsure about the need to cover. And because FRAs are the simplest of all derivatives, they are an excellent way to introduce less sophisticated customers to interest-rate hedging.

Like any forward contract, an FRA is a legally binding agreement to buy or sell some commodity at a specific future time, place, and price. With FRAs, the "commodity" bought or sold is money and the future "price" is, therefore, an interest rate. FRAs involve the exchange of a fixed rate for a floating one over a single, specified period of time. An FRA is simply a one-period interest-rate swap. The sister product of the FRA is a standardized futures contract bought or sold on a regulated exchange. But an FRA—an over-the-counter futures contract—offers customers far more flexibility.

Characteristics of FRAs

FRAs are the first derivative of the cash market. They are the basic building block for all other interest-rate risk-management products. The Eurodollar futures contract, as well as contracts on sterling and Deutschemark LIBOR, are simply exchange-traded FRAs. An interest-rate swap rate is simply a blended rate on a series of FRAs out to the maturity of the swap. The FRA rate defines the at-the-money on options on FRAs, a series of which will make up a cap or floor, just as the futures contract denies the at-the-money for exchange-traded futures options. All interest-rate risk-management products are closely linked to the simplest product, the FRA.

FRAs are available on all major currencies. The largest FRA markets are in U.S. dollars, pounds sterling, and Deutschemarks. Short-term interest-rate futures contracts are also available on these three currencies, so hedgers in these markets can choose between FRAs and futures contracts. Other active FRA markets include yen, Canadian dollars, and Australian dollars. Portuguese escudo FRAs became available this year following the introduction of an FRA on Spanish pesetas. FRAs are also available on French and Swiss francs.

Summary Sheet   Forward-Rate Agreements (FRAs)

Buyer	Issuers of floating-rate debt and investors in fixed-rate assets (customers hurt by rising rates)
Seller	Investors in floating-rate assets seeking protection against falling rates
Intermediary	Commercial and investment banks, insurance firms
How Bank Profits	Bid-offer spread and position-taking
Deal Size	Interbank average is $25 million; for end-users, as low as $100,000
Credit Considerations	Minimal credit risk due to lack of principal exchange, short period, and net settlement at value date
Major Players	Bankers Trust, Chase, Chemical, Citibank, Continental, First Chicago, MHT

Bankers often complain that FRAs are not profitable. Because FRAs are so simple and liquid, spreads on U.S. dollar FRAs have been squeezed to an average of 4 to 7 basis points. But FRAs can still be profitable in currencies without an active futures market, for in these markets, an FRA is the customer's only hedging alternative. Where futures contracts offer competition, large or longer-dated FRA trades can still be lucrative. Bankers can also charge a wider spread to less sophisticated customers unlikely to shop the deal. As banks drop out of the FRA market, spreads may once again widen.

The Concept of Hedging

A corporation can protect itself against adverse price or rate changes by buying or selling a contract that establishes a price now for something to be paid at a later date. This is called hedging. Hedge instruments, of which FRAs are one, do not replace the underlying exposure that caused the price risk in the first place. On the contrary, a hedge is another product layered onto an existing risk position. It is designed to generate gains as the underlying position generates losses. Hedging products are simply additional sets of cash flows that offset the underlying position.

Suppose a corporation has floating-rate liabilities. As interest rates rise, its interest expense will rise. Graphically, the corporation's risk profile looks like:

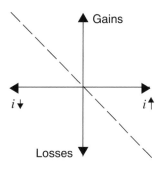

Rising interest expense means falling net income. The company takes losses every time it enters the bottom right quadrant. To hedge, the company seeks an equal gain to offset the loss. Achieving this requires layering on a product that will generate gains as interest rates rise. The profile of such a product would be:

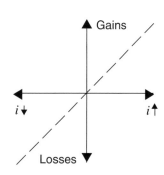

By layering the hedge product onto the underlying exposure, the profits from the hedge offset the losses on the exposure and the two net at the X axis, which represents the strike price—the locked-in price resulting from the hedge.

This concept of hedging applies not only to FRAs, but to any hedge that locks in a price or rate, including futures, swaps, and forward contracts on currencies.

How FRAs Work

FRAs involve the exchange of a fixed rate for a floating rate over a single period. The fixed rate is set when the contract is bought or sold, but the floating rate (and therefore the settlement value) is not known until the first day of the exposure period. The floating rate is usually LIBOR. If the contract is for a three-month period in the future, then the floating rate is the then-current three-month LIBOR rate; if the contract period is one month, the then-current one-month LIBOR is used. The exchange will look like:

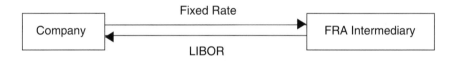

The LIBOR inflow (based on a notional principal amount) will offset the LIBOR payment on the loan (the principal of which is equal to the notional principal of the FRA). The net result is a payment of the fixed rate agreed to when the contract was purchased. The FRA has insulated the company from the risk of rising rates, but for one period only.

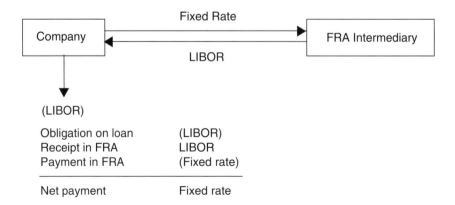

Depending on whether the user is the payer of the fixed rate or the receiver, the user buys or sells the FRA. The buyer pays the fixed rate and receives floating; the seller receives fixed and pays floating. The bank, as intermediary, profits from the bid/offer spread.

The Futures Alternative

The sister product of the FRA is the futures contract; the most common and liquid is the three-month Eurodollar futures contract traded in Chicago, London, and Singapore. Futures achieve the same goal of locking in future rates but differ from FRAs in several ways. These are shown in Exhibit 1.

For all their differences, the two products are inextricably linked. The forward interest rates determined on the futures exchange drive the interest rates in the cash market. And banks trading FRAs use futures to hedge their positions. Only the inflexibility of futures prevents most corporate customers from using the futures market directly and ensures that banks remain intermediaries between the futures exchanges and corporate hedgers.

The Settlement Process

With an FRA there is only one settlement, made on a net basis. If current LIBOR is below the agreed-upon fixed rate, the FRA buyer makes a net payment; if LIBOR is higher, the seller makes the net payment. The net settle-

Exhibit 1   Eurodollar Futures Contracts Versus FRAs

	Eurodollar Futures	FRAs
Trading Hours	Hours on CME, LIFFE, and SIMEX add up to 24 hours*	24 hours
Contract Amounts	$1 million	Flexible
Margin Requirements	Yes; depends on client	No; only credit approval
Delivery Risk	No; cash settlement	Yes
Daily Settlement	Yes	No
Fixed Maturity Date	Yes	No

* Contracts in other currencies are traded on only one exchange, generally LIFFE; trading hours are more limited.

ment feature reduces the credit risk of each party to the other. In fact, because the notional principal is never exchanged, and because there is only one settlement that is netted, the credit risk of FRAs is quite low.

On a LIBOR-based loan, the rate is set at the beginning of the borrowing and paid in arrears, upon maturity. The customer knows its interest expense at the start of the borrowing period but does not need to pay until the end of the period. With FRAs, because the floating rate is known at the onset, settlement usually occurs at that time. Early settlement reduces credit exposure for both parties. On a time line, the events associated with the purchase of an FRA locking in the three-months forward three-month LIBOR rate are as follows:

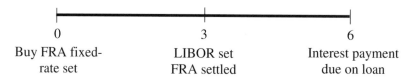

0	3	6
Buy FRA fixed- rate set	LIBOR set FRA settled	Interest payment due on loan

The LIBOR set at time 3 is good for the 3–6 period and is used to calculate the interest to be paid at time 6. The fixed rate set on the FRA is also a rate effective for the period 3–6, and it too is calculated to be paid at time 6. To settle the FRA at time 3—that is, to net the fixed rate and LIBOR—it is necessary to discount back from time 6 to time 3 the value of the difference in the interest payments. This process is covered in more detail in Exhibit 2.

Pricing FRAs: Forward Interest Rates

Critical to the FRA settlement process in particular, and hedging in general, is the rate on the FRA. This rate is derived from the cash market yield curve. For example, given three-month and six-month cash rates, it is easy to find the exact three-months forward three-month rate. It is literally the rate that allows the rate of the first period to "catch up with" or "slow down to" the full longer maturity rate. It is the rate that makes an investor indifferent between two alternatives: to invest for six months or to invest for three and then reinvest for a second three months. Only one forward rate will make an investor indifferent. This is the rate used for the 3×6 (three-month rate three-months forward) FRA. Chapter 2 of *The Derivation Engineering Workbook* covers the derivation of forward rates in depth.

Of course, because the three-month and six-month rates are constantly changing, so too is the forward rate. The beauty of FRAs is that they lock in that forward rate. Once the rate is locked in, the user need not worry about current cash market rates, nor what the three-month rate will turn out to be in three months.

Exhibit 2   Finding the Present Value of the Net Payment on an FRA

The present value of the net payment for a 3×6 FRA (three-months forward three-month rate) is found as follows:

$$\frac{NP \times [(\text{Fixed Rate} \times DM/360) - (\text{LIBOR} \times DM/360)]}{1 + (\text{LIBOR} \times DM/360)}$$

NP	=	notional principal
Fixed Rate	=	rate contracted at time of FRA purchase
DM	=	days to maturity
LIBOR	=	settlement rate (the then-current LIBOR)

Using the HP-12C:

FV	=	difference between interest expense based on fixed rate and LIBOR rate
PMT	=	0
n	=	1
i	=	3-month effective LIBOR rate
PV	=	settlement value

Using an FRA

Suppose a customer faces a rollover on a $10 million LIBOR-based loan in February for the next three months and is afraid of interest rates rising in the interim. One way of hedging this exposure is to buy a 3×6 FRA that would lock in that three-months forward three-month interest rate. Exhibit 3 shows how this hedge would work, assuming an FRA rate of 7.62%.

Because the risk is that interest rates may rise, the customer would buy the FRA so that it can receive the floating rate and pay the fixed rate set today. The FRA contract is bought today, but no cash changes hands. Not until February will the actual LIBOR rate be known, so settlement cannot occur before then. But regardless of what LIBOR turns out to be in February, the company will achieve the all-in rate fixed today.

The grid shows three scenarios for LIBOR in February: 7.50%, 8.00% and 8.50%. The next line calculates interest expense owed for the 89-day period. This obligation does not go away simply because the company has hedged; it is the actual interest expense the company will have to pay. As LIBOR rises, so does interest expense, pushing the firm with each basis-point rise in LIBOR further into the loss quadrant of the risk profile shown previously.

Exhibit 3   How a Customer Would Use an FRA

Today is November 20. On February 20, customer has three-month (89 days) rollover of $10MM loan.

Risk: Rates rise
Action: Buy 3 × 6 FRA (rate = 7.62%)

Actual LIBOR on 2/2/90	**7.50%**	**8.00%**	**8.50%**
Interest Expense	$185,417	$197,778	$210,139
Using the FRA:			
Rate Paid	7.62%	7.62%	7.62%
Rate Received	7.50%	8.00%	8.50%
Net Payment/(Receipt)			
in percent:	0.12%	0.38%	0.88%
in dollars:	$2,967	$9,394	$21,755
Total Expense	$188,384	$188,384	$188,384
All-in Rate	7.62%	7.62%	7.62%

The next line shows the FRA hedge. Because the company bought the FRA, the fixed rate it pays in the FRA is 7.62%. This is consistent throughout all three rate scenarios. The floating rate (LIBOR) is the variable in the FRA; it changes as LIBOR changes. In the first scenario, the fixed payment is 7.62% and the receipt is the current LIBOR of 7.50%. Because the LIBOR receipt was lower, the customer had to make the net payment. In the second and last cases, however, LIBOR rises to 8.00% and 8.50%, respectively, and the customer receives the net payment. Again, the hedge is just another cash flow layered on to the existing position.

In cases where the customer is a net payer, the payment is considered a loss to the company and must be added to its interest expense. That's why, in the first case, total expense is higher than interest expense. Total expense is the interest expense plus any losses or less any gains on the FRA. Total expense will be the same regardless of the actual LIBOR rate. It represents an all-in cost to the borrower of the FRA rate—the locked-in rate. By using this lock-in product, the gains from the FRA offset the losses on the underlying loan to bring interest expense to the all-in rate of 7.80%.

The Cash Yield Curve and FRAs

In an upward-sloping yield curve environment, the customer must feel that interest rates will rise in order to use an FRA. The customer has locked into a borrowing rate for the February through May period and by doing so, has given up the opportunity to benefit should rates fall. In addition, because the yield curve is downward sloping for that time period, the company was actually "bumped down" the yield curve to determine the forward rate of 7.62%. If rates fall, the company will have net payments under the FRA, thus increasing its total expense. However, if rates do rise as feared, the FRA realizes gains that serve to reduce interest expense down to the fixed level of 7.62%.

In an inverted yield curve environment, where short-term rates are higher than long-term rates, forward rates are lower than the cash yield curve. As corporate relationship officers discovered in a number of countries in 1989— the United States, Canada, the United Kingdom, and Australia—FRAs are relatively easy to sell in this type of environment because they allow customers to immediately lock in lower interest expense.

Conclusion

FRAs can be a relatively easy product to market. Because they are so flexible, they can be custom-tailored to suit the customer's needs exactly. They also represent a painless introduction to hedging for hesitant customers who feel that hedging is risky. FRAs are actively traded in many currencies and serve a particularly vital role in those currencies in which there is no short-term interest-rate futures contract.

6

What Drives Product Innovation?
Examining Interest-Rate Swaps

Since interest-rate swaps first gained notoriety in the early 1980s, much has been written and said about the "creativity" and degree of innovation employed in this product area. While it is true that the range of swap applications and potential users has expanded dramatically, this is not necessarily the result of technical improvements on the basic swap. Rather, it is the result of applying the same basic principles to a variety of situations, leading to combinations of multiple swaps and swaps with other products. What role have these factors played in the development of the swap market? Do these factors represent innovation?

The Early Swap Market
One of the earliest swaps to receive significant publicity was the IBM/World Bank currency swap in late 1981. The fact that two such well-respected institutions used the technique provided a certain degree of credibility to swaps. Since then, both interest-rate and currency swaps have grown dramatically in terms of popularity, though interest-rate swaps are in greater favor.

Exhibit 1   U.S. Dollar Interest-Rate Swap Transactions* *(in $ billions)*

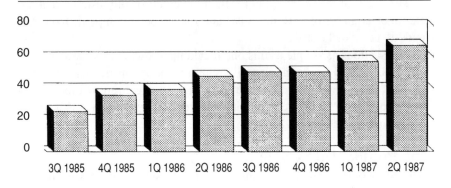

*Notional Principal Amount

Source: ISDA

Many of the early interest-rate swap transactions involved an institution with very high credit quality issuing fixed-rate debt and exchanging it for floating-rate debt with a medium credit quality corporation (see Exhibit 1). As a result, both parties obtained funds less expensively than if they issued directly into the desired market. This was possible because the fixed-rate market tends to distinguish among quality grades to a greater extent than the floating market. Another important factor was that many of the high-quality issuers were European banks, which historically had never before issued large amounts of fixed-rate debt. Consequently, fixed-rate investors were

Exhibit 2   Generic Interest-Rate Swap

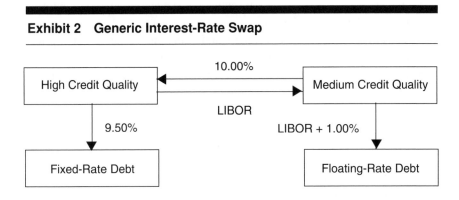

willing to accept yields somewhat below market rates to diversify their portfolios.

The result of this transaction for the high credit quality user is floating-rate funds at a cost of LIBOR–.50%, and for the other company, fixed-rate funds at a cost of 11.00%.

Transactions as simple as this one fueled the growth of the swap market from 1981 to 1984, providing attractive returns to the arrangers/inter-mediaries. At about that time, most major market participants realized that the market was becoming so highly "commodity-oriented" and competitive that profitability was on the decline.

The Product Life Cycle

In the sense of traditional marketing management, swaps have passed through the **introduction** and **growth** stages of a product's life cycle and into the **maturity** phase in a period of less than three years. Of the four phases in the life of a product (introduction, growth, maturity, and decline), the growth stage is the most attractive from the standpoint of a producer, for it does not contain the high level of risk inherent in the introduction phase, yet still affords attractive profit opportunities. This profit potential is due to several factors: a limited (but increasing) number of suppliers; expansion of the market; product differentiation; and more efficient product management.

The Four Phases of the Product Life Cycle

INTRODUCTION

During this stage, the producers of the product (commercial and investment banks) achieve minimal profitability, due to the high level of costs involved in producing and distributing the product. With swaps, this involved the need to train marketing officers, develop sophisticated accounting and monitoring systems, and develop documentation. Additionally, relatively large expenditures are needed to educate consumers and stimulate demand. While prices may be high for the product, the costs of production are also quite high. At this point, there are relatively few competitors providing a rather simple product.

GROWTH

As a result of efforts to stimulate demand, volume increases dramatically. This, combined with more efficient production methods, significantly decreases the cost of production. Because demand continues to increase, however, prices fall little, if at all. There is a continuing emphasis on promotion to expand the size of the market and to defend against new competitors. Nevertheless, profits increase due to the increase in volume. Product differentiation occurs.

MATURITY

The longest phase in the cycle is characterized by a slowdown in the rate of growth. This is caused primarily by market saturation. In reaction, producers intensify the effort to provide product innovation either to stimulate demand or to increase the profit margin. Eventually, volume may begin to fall, leading to an overcapacity in the industry.

DECLINE

This is the most difficult phase for producers. Should the product with only minimal profits be eliminated, or will the market improve? As product usage declines, either due to technological advances or a shift in attitudes, many competitors leave the field. Oftentimes, the remaining ones will scale back to cut costs and enhance profitability.

The Effect on Financial Products

In the swap business, the introduction and growth stages were very short-lived. In the current environment, the entry of a large number of competitors (commercial, investment, and merchant banks, as well as nonbank banks) providing a relatively uniform product has invariably forced profit margins to fall. In the future, this is likely to be even more dramatic when capital requirements on swaps are imposed by regulators. This effect is compounded by the slowing of the rate of growth in demand for the product. The graph on page 58 and the table demonstrate the slowing in growth rates that has occurred recently.

The compression of the product life cycle that is apparent in the swap market is becoming the norm for almost all financial products. As products pass through the various stages of the life cycle, the effects are felt in both London and New York. In London, the slowdown in the Eurobond business, especially coming so soon after the problems in the floating-rate note market, has led many firms including Lloyds, Schroeder, and Salomon Brothers to leave certain business areas. In the United States, the most dramatic situation is taking place in the municipal bond business, which several firms have also recently left. As the distinctions between commercial, investment, and merchant banks continue to be eliminated, other casualties are inevitable.

Exhibit 3   Interest-Rate Swap Transactions*

Year	Billions of U.S. Dollars	Annual Growth Rate
1982	3.0	
1983	17.0	467%
1984	55.0	224%
1985	100.0	82%
1Q 1986	39.9	
2Q 1986	48.4	
3Q 1986	51.2	
4Q 1986	51.0	90%
1Q 1987	57.4	**
2Q 1987	67.6	42%

* Notional Principal Amount
** Increase over first half of 1986

Sources: Globecon estimates and ISDA

Exhibit 4   The Product Life Cycle

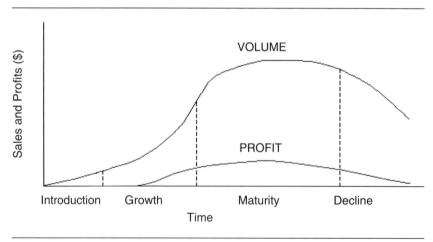

Rather than suffer a decline in relative profitability, many producers (including intermediaries in the swap market) attempt to alter the product in order to increase the total demand for the product (expand the size of the market). Ideally, this will not only increase total demand but enhance the market share of the innovator, until other market participants copy the innovation. Innovations are continually introduced and each one experiences its own complete life cycle. As a result, innovation tends to extend the life cycle of the basic product and thereby extend the period in which producers can achieve relatively attractive profits.

Innovation in the Swap Market

The first major innovation in the swap market was the use of asset swaps. An asset swap is nothing more than an interest-rate swap that is linked with specific financial assets. Because most swaps had been related to underlying debt transactions, the asset swap was viewed as a major step in broadening the potential application of swaps in general, which implied a significant expansion of the market.

The use of asset swaps appeals to a broad range of investors, allowing them to effectively lengthen or shorten the duration of their portfolios. Amplifying our previous example, the high credit quality bank could have elected to synthetically fix the rate on its floating-rate assets and match funding them with fixed-rate liabilities (see Exhibit 5).

The structure of this interest rate swap is exactly the same as in Exhibit 2, only the application is different. The most innovative concept in this transaction is the identification of a large segment of potential users not previously targeted. *One significant form of innovation in the swap market (and in markets for other financial products) is a much more intense focus on origination activities—matching an existing product with a new type of user.*

Exhibit 5   Generic Asset Swap

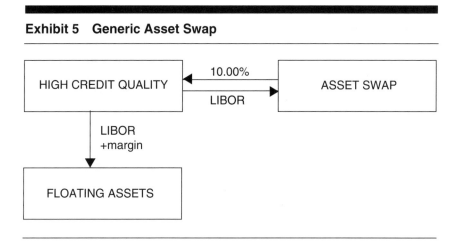

Another swap structure that has received a lot of publicity is the combination of various types of options with swaps. By providing either the end-user or swap arranger with the right to terminate or extend the transaction, this combination may result in putable, extendable, retractable, or callable swaps. There are many possible benefits to such a structure, including: limited opportunity loss, matching an uncertain time horizon, and the right to choose a different financing structure at some point in the future. In almost all cases, the option-based swap is matched with an underlying debt issue that contains a similar option. In this manner, the risk of the option is passed to the purchaser of the debt.

There were a large number of these transactions in the third quarter of 1987, when many financial institutions issued fixed-rate debt with a call option and swapped it for floating. The fixed-rate payer in the swap had an option to terminate the transaction (and paid a higher fixed rate in exchange for this option). If the swap was terminated, the financial institution would simply call the debt issue (see Exhibit 6).

While this structure provides significant benefits—the higher fixed-rate receipt on the swap for the financial institution and the option structure for the end-user—the financial institution would be highly exposed to market risk if it were not able to match the swap with the callable debt issue. The ability to sell the underlying debt issue is critical to engaging in this type of swap. For this reason, the distribution process is becoming increasingly important to swap market participants. *Another form of innovation is merely identifying a group of investors with a specific structural preference and then*

Exhibit 6   Option-Based Swap

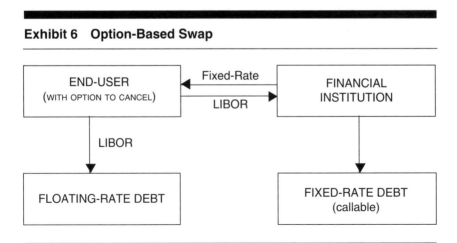

exploiting that preference. The distribution process continues to grow in importance.

The last type of innovation we will discuss is the use of swaps that involve "complex" cash flows. These involve amortizing swaps, forward swaps, zero-coupon swaps, and swaps with increasing notional amounts. In all these cases, the cash flows on the fixed-rate side of the swap are uneven in amount, although they are known for certain at the inception of the swap. The most commonly used method of "pricing" an uneven set of cash payments is the use of the internal rate of return (IRR). By using this approach, complex cash-flows can be transformed into a single, effective fixed rate.

From the standpoint of the swap arranger, the more important question is, how can the interest-rate risk inherent in such a transaction be managed? In almost all cases, this task is much less complicated than it appears. An interest-rate swap with complex cash flows (and indeed, most complex financial transactions) can be broken down into several simple components. Each component, in the case of swaps, is a simple fixed/floating swap with a "bullet" maturity. By using this methodology, the swap arranger is able to match the complex swap with several simple swaps in the market—in which case the position is closed more quickly and at a more competitive cost than if a particular, nonstandard structure was necessary.

Perhaps the simplest example of this approach is a situation in which a bank is asked to provide a swap on the following terms:

Exhibit 7   Terms of Amortizing Swap

Amount:	$50,000,000
Maturity:	2 years
Amortization:	equal annual notional principal
Bank pays:	LIBOR
Customer pays:	fixed rate (which must be determined), annual basis

Current market rates:

	One Year	Two Year
Treasury	7.50%	7.90%
Bank's swap bid	.70%	.75%
Bank's swap offer	.74%	.80%

Exhibit 7   Terms of Amortizing Swap (continued)

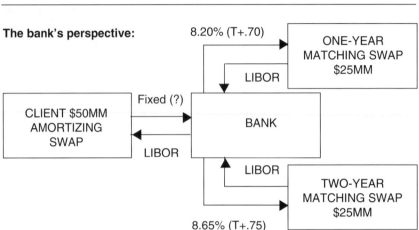

Using this structure, and identifying the cash flow implications for the bank, the IRR would be determined as follows:

The rate of 8.50% represents the cost to the bank of creating the amortizing swap. Any profit margin would be added to the 8.50%.

The most important point in this case is the ability to take advantage of a highly standardized transaction (the offsetting swaps) with a very liquid and efficient market to create "complex/value-added" transactions. *This is one of the most widely used forms of innovation—transforming the cash flows of a complex transaction into several sets of simple cash flows, then pricing each set independently.*

An excellent example of this application is the financing entered into by Kodak in May of 1987. Kodak issued zero-coupon, Australian-dollar (A$) denominated debt and, through the use of currency swaps, interest-rate swaps, and forward foreign-exchange transactions, converted the debt to U.S. dollars, with semiannual payments of fixed interest. The effectiveness of the A$ issue is a function of all the related transactions. Without the ability to combine the debt issue with interest-rate and currency swaps, each component of which is fairly simple, there would have been no reason to issue the debt in A$. In this case, the ability to combine all the products and present Kodak with a complete structure is probably what led to the selection of Merrill Lynch as lead manager.

Exhibit 8   Cash Flow Analysis

	Initial	End Year 1	End Year 2
Principal borrowing and repayment	−$50,000,000	$25,000,000	$25,000,000
Interest on 1-year swap (8.20% x 25,000,000)		2,050,000	
Annual Interest on 2-year swap (8.65% x 25,000,000)		2,162,500	2,162,500
Net cash flows	−$50,000,000	$29,212,500	$27,162,500

Using the HP-12C calculator, the keystrokes would be:

Keystrokes	Display
50000000 [CHS]	−50,000,000
[g] [CF$_0$]	−50,000,000
29212500 [g] [CFj]	29,212,500
27162500 [g] [CFj]	27,162,500
[f] [IRR]	8.495980

The Future

As the number of participants in the financial services industry continues to increase, or at least fails to lessen significantly, more and more products will become commodities. The product life cycle is becoming shorter and shorter, and innovation will play an ever-increasing role in extending the life of and enhancing the profitability of financial products. Rarely will innovation be in the form of a major technological development. Rather, it will be exhibited by one of three forms: an expansion of the origination function (as in asset swaps); enhanced distribution capability (the case with option-based swaps); or an alteration of the underlying cash flows by combining multiple products. The more efficient and liquid that markets become, the more important the last method will be.

7

The Bank as Intermediary

Futures and Options

The interest-rate volatility that characterized the 1980s, combined with the increased sophistication of banks and corporations, has spawned a broad array of rate risk-management products. In addition to swaps, forward-rate agreements (FRAs), caps, floors, collars, and other variations of option-related products have been heavily marketed to corporations by commercial and investment banks. Similar products have been developed in the currency-risk management field.

When swaps were introduced, many people questioned whether this type of activity was appropriate for commercial banks, and feared it was a radical departure from traditional business areas. What caused this period of new product creation? Do these activities represent a new business area for banks, and if so, does it expose them to a new type of risk? How can such risk be managed? What benefit are the banks providing?

The United States has experienced a period of high interest-rate volatility ever since the late 1970s when the Federal Reserve changed its emphasis from managing interest rates to managing the money supply. In the corporate marketplace—where a steady quarter-to-quarter increase in earnings is viewed as a sign of a well-managed company—this period of volatility has caused a

Exhibit 1   Historical LIBOR Rates

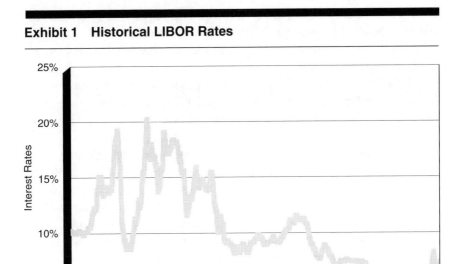

Interest Rates

25%

20%

15%

10%

5%

January 1979   January 1988

great deal of concern among corporate treasury staffs. This concern has been exacerbated by the increasing use of leverage by corporations. For companies with access to a variety of financing sources, the issue is how to obtain protection from the fluctuations without suffering the potential opportunity loss associated with fixed-rate debt. For corporations that do not have a variety of financial alternatives, the most important issue is simply to determine the appropriate degree of protection needed. In either case, the increasingly popular solution has been the acquisition of some form of rate-protection product from a bank.

The Role of the Bank as Intermediary

Disintermediation and competition have had a significant negative effect on the volume and profitability of traditional bank loan business. Banks have aggressively sought to offset some of this deterioration with fees from products such as rate risk-management transactions. Products such as swaps and caps were even more attractive before the recent action by regulatory authorities, which will require a capital commitment to support these activities. When providing risk-management products to a customer, thereby reducing the customer's exposure to interest-rate volatility, the bank effectively assumes the risk that the customer is trying to eliminate. If banks did not have the ability to manage this risk in some fashion, the level of exposure to interest-rate volatility would greatly increase the level of risk in the banking system.

While banks do "trade" these and other products among themselves, just as they trade funds among themselves, ultimately the risk is transferred to another party. This may take the form of finding an end-user of the product with needs complementary to those of the original customer.

In the traditional banking business of lending money, the matching of risk is analogous to having one customer that needs to borrow funds for 30 days and another wishing to invest the same amount for 30 days. The bank would intermediate this process and collect the difference between the rate at which it borrows funds and the rate at which it lends funds. If the bank can not obtain funds to match the specific amount, maturity, and pricing mechanism (prime rate versus certificate of deposit versus LIBOR) of the loan, it assumes some degree of liquidity and interest-rate mismatch. In addition, it assumes the risk that the loan it made will not be repaid.

The role of intermediary involves transferring risk among markets. Traditionally, this involves the transfer of liquidity risk between depositors and borrowers. In the role of intermediary, the bank has historically taken three major types of risk: liquidity, interest-rate, and credit risk. *By providing rate risk-management products to clients, banks are fulfilling their traditional role of intermediary. Specifically, banks are transferring interest-rate risk between different parties and, by standing between the parties, are providing a performance guarantee of credit or default risk.*

Offsetting Interest-Rate Risk

When a bank assumes interest-rate risk by entering into a transaction with a client, it has several alternatives for offsetting this risk. The bank can: match it with an asset/liability position (new or existing) on its balance sheet; match it with another counterparty; or offset the position in an exchange-traded market like futures or options. While it is also possible to refrain from offsetting the position (known as "going naked"), this is rarely done except for short periods of time. It is also possible to use combinations of these methods, for example, hedging in the futures market prior to finding another counterparty with which to offset the transaction. In many cases, a bank will explore all of these possibilities to find the least expensive and easiest method of creating the desired position.

Alternatives for Intermediaries

When swaps were introduced in 1981, many banks matched transactions on their own balance sheets. This allowed transactions to be offset quickly, at a reasonable cost, and also provided tangible benefits to the bank in its funding operations. As the volume of these transactions grew, other alternatives became more popular for several reasons. Practically speaking, there is a limit to the number of transactions that can be matched on a bank's balance sheet. As volume increased, it exceeded the amount that could be efficiently offset using the balance sheet. At the same time, the increasing usage of these products enabled banks to find offsetting transactions much more quickly, and the market continued to evolve into a more efficiently priced market—meaning the cost of offsetting risk was more reasonable and predictable.

At the same time that the use of swaps was increasing, development of the financial futures and options markets was accelerating. In the past year, the use of these exchange-traded instruments by banks to offset risk created by selling interest-rate management products has exploded.

The Use of Exchange-Traded Futures and Options

Financial futures were first introduced in 1972 when the International Monetary Market of the Chicago Mercantile Exchange introduced currency futures. Since then, many kinds of contracts have been added, with varying degrees of success. Each contract has specific terms relating to size, maturity, pricing mechanism, delivery terms, etc. By standardizing certain terms, the contracts serve to limit the number of variables, thereby concentrating trading into the remaining alternatives and enhancing the liquidity of those contracts. At the same time, however, there is a reduction in flexibility—forcing hedgers to accept "imperfect" hedges. The trade-off between flexibility and liquidity is an important one. Banks have been exposed to the problem of imperfect hedges for many years and, by using the skills that have been developed for traditional asset/liability management, have developed great expertise and complicated systems for use in managing the problem.

Banks can use futures, options, and other instruments to hedge a position (until a permanent offsetting transaction can be found), or they can use the futures and/or options market to "create" the permanent offsetting position. In this case, banks are using an exchange-traded product to create a transaction that is sold directly to a client (known as an "over-the-counter" or OTC transaction). *By intermediating between the exchange-traded market and the OTC market, banks are taking a small degree of risk but expanding their*

Exhibit 2   Alternatives for Intermediaries

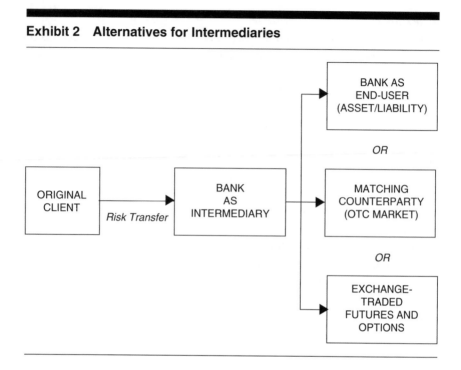

sources of fee income. For banks, the most important of the growing array of futures contracts for this purpose is the 90-day Eurodollar Deposit Contract (ED), which is essentially based on three-month LIBOR.

The Use of Eurodollar Futures Contracts

The trading volume and significance of the Eurodollar futures contract has increased greatly in importance since its introduction in 1981 for several reasons. One reason is the increasing role of U.S. dollar LIBOR as the "medium of exchange" in financial transactions, from interest-rate and currency swaps to floating-rate notes (FRNs) and interest-rate caps. Another important factor in the growth of the ED contract is its "cash settlement" (as opposed to physical delivery) feature. This allows gains and losses to be settled in cash during the life of the transaction, rather than based upon delivery of the underlying instrument. As a result, market participants find it easier to use, with less concern about the quality of the underlying instrument, than other futures contracts.

Contract Terms

The ED contract is based on a notional deposit of $1,000,000 for 90 days. The price is represented as an index determined by subtracting the current three-month LIBOR rate from a base of 100. Thus, a LIBOR rate of 8.50% implies an ED futures price of 91.50 (100 – 8.50). The ED contract, like many of the financial futures contracts, has four maturity dates (or contract cycles) per year. These contract cycles end in the middle of each March, June, September, and December (the specific date within each month varies slightly). Due to the nature of the ED contract, each change in LIBOR of one basis point (referred to as a "tick" in the futures market) results in a $25 change in the contract's value.

This is directly related to the size of the contract and to the assumed maturity of the underlying deposit, as follows:

$$\frac{\$1,000,000 \times .0001 \times 90}{360} = \$25$$

The easiest way to see how a futures contract can be used to create a product is to do so, starting with a relatively simple example, a forward-rate agreement (FRA).

Forward-Rate Agreements

Also known as a future-rate agreement, an FRA is really nothing more than an OTC futures contract. FRAs serve the same purpose as futures contracts, but are traded among banks and provided to corporations by banks. It is an agreement between two parties to fix an interest rate on a specific type of instrument and a certain notional principal amount at some time in the future. When the future date is reached, the specified rate is compared to the market rate for the appropriate instrument and any difference between the two rates is paid by one party to the other. It is a contract concerned only with changes in interest rates—no principal is ever exchanged.

Pricing the FRA

The bank will price the FRA by determining the rate available in the futures market. Because the dates are the same, this is easily accomplished by translating the futures price of 92.00 into its interest rate equivalent of 8.00%. If the bank wants to earn a profit of five basis points from its customer, it will enter into the FRA at a rate of 8.05%.

Exhibit 3   A Simple Forward-Rate Agreement

A company has borrowed $25,000,000 from a bank for a term of six months. The interest rate on the loan is 1.00% above three-month LIBOR. The rate for the first three months was set on the date of the borrowing, but the company is concerned that rates will rise before the next rate setting, three months from now. The company requests an FRA from the bank on three-month LIBOR, effective three months from today.

Assumptions

Today's date	March 15, 1988
Next reset date	June 15, 1988
Maturity date	September 14, 1989
Three-month LIBOR rate	7.00
June ED futures price	92.00

Because the dates of the FRA correspond to the dates available in the futures market, the bank is able to exactly offset the risk position created by the FRA by entering into a corresponding futures position.

If, on June 15, three-month LIBOR has increased to 8.50%, the company will pay total interest on the loan on September 14, 1989 of:

$25,000,000 × .0850 × 90/360 = $531,250

However, this will be partially offset by the proceeds of the FRA. The company will receive a payment from the bank based on the difference between the market LIBOR rate of 8.50% and the agreed rate of 8.05%.

If this payment were made on September 14, 1989, it would be:

$25,000,000 × (.0850 − .0805) × 90/360 = $28,125

This reduces the total cost to $503,125 ($531,250 − $28,125) for an annual rate of 8.05% [(503,125/25,000,000) × (360/90)]. However, the payment would actually be made on June 15, 1988. Therefore, it would be discounted for the three-month period at the effective three-month rate of 2.125% (8.50% × 90/360). The result is a total payment of $27,539.78.

Combining the calculation of the settlement amount and the discounting calculation into one equation produces the following formula to calculate FRA settlements:

$$\frac{(I_m - I_a) \times NP \times D}{(Y \times 100) + (I_m \times D)} = \text{Settlement Amount}$$

I_m = Market interest rate*
I_a = Agreed interest rate*
NP = Notional principal amount
D = Days in contract period
Y = Assumed days per year

* The interest rates used in the calculations are not in decimal terms (i.e., 8.50% = 8.50, not .085.)

At the same time, the bank will have realized a profit on the futures transaction. When it originally entered into the FRA, it sold 25 March ED futures, each with a notional principal amount of $1,000,000, and a price of 92.00. On June 15, with three-month LIBOR at 8.50%, the price would be 91.50 (100 - 8.50). At that time, the bank will close its position by buying back the futures contracts that it previously sold. Therefore, it sold contracts at a price of 92.00 and repurchased them at 91.50 for a gain of 50 ticks.

Because each tick has a value of $25, the bank's gain on the futures hedge will be:

25 contracts × 50 ticks × $25 per tick = $31,250

The gain to the bank of $3,710.22 ($31,250.00 - $27,539.78) provides the amount used to pay the customer, plus the bank's profit. Technically the bank will receive this gain, in the form of margin gains, throughout the term of the hedge. The actual timing and amounts of the cash flows cannot be predicted, however, as they depend on actual market-rate movements.

Comparing Futures and FRAs

This example was constructed to demonstrate the relationship between the futures market and FRAs. The company could have used either tool to eliminate its risk, and the bank was able to completely eliminate the risk of the FRA in the futures market. In this example, the bank made a profit by standing between its customer and the futures market. There are many corporations that feel more comfortable with FRAs and feel that this, combined with the less complicated implementation and administration associated with FRAs, is ample justification for including a bank as intermediary.

Other practical considerations include: unusual amounts, dates that do not match the futures dates, instruments that do not conform to the underlying futures contracts (i.e., six-month LIBOR versus three-month LIBOR),

etc. Each of these considerations makes structuring the hedge more complicated and significantly reduces the possibility of a "perfect hedge." The
intermediary is accepting the risk of these mismatches and the responsibility
of sheltering its client from them.

It is this type of situation that most effectively demonstrates the benefit of
FRAs relative to futures—the flexibility of alternatives. *For those corporations interested in a very close match, the FRA provides a much better hedge;
however, the bank acting as intermediary will price the FRA based on the
prices in the futures market and the perceived level of risk involved in
structuring the hedge.*

The final consideration involved in comparing futures and FRAs is the
issue of credit or performance risk. In the case of FRAs, the company is
subject to the risk that the bank will not perform. If that occurs, the company
will be exposed to market-rate movements. Similarly, the bank is exposed to
the risk that the company will not perform, if rates move against it. For this
reason, most banks treat FRAs as having a small degree of credit exposure.
Futures contracts, however, because of the margin system and daily price
change limits, have a mechanism to eliminate the concern about performance. Effectively, every buyer and seller of futures contracts is insulated
from every other buyer and seller by a "clearing corporation," which stands
in the middle of all trades and guarantees performance.

Short-Term Interest-Rate Swaps

The issues applicable to a comparison between futures and FRAs can also be
used to evaluate short-term interest-rate swaps. Short-term swaps generally
have a maximum maturity of three years. In such an agreement, it is most
common for the two counterparties to agree to exchange fixed-rate payments
for a floating rate based on three-month LIBOR (compared to the use of six-
month LIBOR for longer swaps). The effect of this agreement is to fix the
rate on three-month LIBOR until maturity of the swap. The three-year time
horizon reflects the ED futures contract cycle with the longest maturity that is
available on the International Monetary Market.

In many cases, the rate associated with an interest-rate swap can be
determined by referring to the futures market. In order to minimize any type
of mismatch between the hedge and the swap, however, some conditions
must apply, namely: the floating rate must be three-month LIBOR, final
maturity cannot exceed three years, and the rate reset dates must conform to
the ED contract cycles (mid-March, June, September, and December). Despite these limitations, the ability to synthesize swaps by using futures has

led to a huge increase in the volume of both futures transactions and short-term swaps. In the first half of 1987, the International Swap Dealers Association estimated that 50% of all new U.S. dollar interest-rate swaps had a maturity of three years or less. This suggests that more than $60 billion of short-term swaps were entered into during the first six months of 1987.

By providing intermediaries with the ability to offset risk in a liquid and efficient market, financial futures have enhanced the efficiency and competitiveness of swap pricing. In addition, the liquidity of the futures market has been transferred to the swap market, enhancing the ability of intermediaries to match transactions.

Once again, the easiest way to demonstrate the relationship between the two markets is to create a swap using futures.

Exhibit 4   A Two-Year Swap

A company has asked its bank to provide a swap in which the company pays a fixed rate for two years, beginning on March 15, 1988, and receives three-month LIBOR. The notional principal amount is $10,000,000. What is the fixed rate on the swap?

The fixed rate can be calculated, and the risk can be offset by the bank, using the futures market.

Assume that today is February 12, 1988, and futures prices are as follows:

Contract	Price	Yield
March 1988	93.03	6.97%
June	92.85	7.15%
September	92.56	7.44%
December	92.26	7.74%
March 1989	92.00	8.00%
June	91.78	8.22%
September	91.60	8.40%
December	91.44	8.56%

In the swap, the bank will suffer if LIBOR exceeds the specified fixed rate—and wants to protect itself. This is done by selling (or shorting) futures contracts. The June contract would be sold at 92.85: If interest rates rise, futures prices will fall (due to the nature of the price index) and the contract can be repurchased (to close the position) at a lower price. The swap amount ($10,000,000) is 10 times the value of one ED contract, so 10 contracts will be sold. Because the swap covers three-month LIBOR on a quarterly basis for two years, contracts corresponding to each quarterly cycle during this period will be sold. Selling contracts at each maturity is called "selling the strip" of futures contracts.

Pricing the Swap

By selling the strip of contracts, the bank will effectively fix the rate on LIBOR for each three-month period over the next two years. However, the customer wants one fixed rate, quoted on a semi-annual effective basis. This can be determined by compounding the quarterly effective rates associated with the futures prices.

Exhibit 5   Translating Futures Prices into Bond Yields

Contract	Price	Annual Money Market Yield (nominal) (100 − price)	Quarterly Money Market Yield (effective) (nominal + 4)	Quarterly Bond Equivalent Yield
March 1988	93.03	6.97%	1.7425%	1.7667%
June	92.85	7.15%	1.7875%	1.8123%
September	92.56	7.44%	1.8600%	1.8858%
December	92.26	7.74%	1.9350%	1.9619%
March 1989	92.00	8.00%	2.0000%	2.0278%
June	91.78	8.22%	2.0550%	2.0835%
September	91.60	8.40%	2.1000%	2.1292%
December	91.44	8.56%	2.1400%	2.1697%

The quarterly effective bond equivalent rate is then compounded to a two-year effective basis:

$$(1.017667) \times (1.018123) \times (1.018858) \times (1.019619) \times$$
$$(1.027800) \times (1.020835) \times (1.021292) \times (1.021697) =$$
$$1.1784 = \text{two-year effective cost (principal + interest)}$$

The two-year effective cost is then decompounded to a semiannual basis and the principal component is removed:

$$(\text{fourth root of } 1.1784) - 1 = .04189$$

Convert to nominal annual interest rate (multiply by 2 and 100)

$$.04189 \times 200 = 8.38\%$$

The rate of 8.38% (plus any profit margin for the bank) is the rate that would be quoted for the swap. If the bank had been trying to create a swap in which it paid the fixed rate, rather than receiving it, it would have bought the futures strip. In this transaction the cost of the hedge would also be a rate of 8.38%, but the profit margin would be subtracted from the rate (to reduce a payment). Therefore, if the bank plans on making three basis points on any swap, it must be willing to pay a rate (the bid rate) of 8.35% and receive a rate (the offer rate) of 8.41%.

Comparing Short-Term Swaps and Futures

ED futures contracts can create the same effect as a swap. This is possible for a swap of up to three years, with the limitations we mentioned. Economic effects are the same, but other issues should be considered. If a company enters into the swap, it is accepting the risk that the bank might not perform under the agreement. If futures are used, there is no such risk, for the clearinghouse guarantees all transactions. With futures, there is the need to post initial margin and variation margin (this mechanism eliminates performance risk in futures) the "cost" of the initial margin (if any) and uncertainty associated with variation margin should be examined.

The futures contracts may provide greater liquidity than the swap. If the company wants to terminate the transaction at a later date, it is assured of a "market price." From a cosmetic standpoint, the swap may be more attractive because it will provide one fixed rate over the entire time horizon, rather than eight different fixed rates that are economically the same as one fixed rate. From an operational standpoint, the swap may be less cumbersome, because of fewer accounting requirements, cash payments, etc. However, this may be offset by the more complex legal documentation required.

Conclusion

Active management of interest-rate and currency risk has become more widely practiced and important, and commercial banks have assumed their natural role as intermediary in these transactions. This role has many similarities to the traditional activities of commercial banks: credit risk, interest-rate risk, and risk transference. The ability of banks to effectively manage these activities has been greatly enhanced by the introduction and staggering growth of the exchange-traded futures and options markets.

As we have seen, financial futures are frequently used to create OTC products. Exchange-traded options can be used the same way. In many cases, the role of bank as intermediary of interest rate risk is very simple and straightforward. However, the presence of factors such as mismatched contract dates, unusual dollar amounts, basis risk, and liquidity risk demonstrate the value that banks provide in this area. Because many corporations prefer to avoid these risks, it is possible that the disintermediation that has affected the banks' traditional lending business will not infiltrate this product area, and there is no sign of such disintermediation as yet.

8

The Bank as Intermediary
Option-Based Products

Banks have been involved in the options business for many years, although many bankers may not have realized it. The fixed-rate retail loan (mortgages, automobile loans, etc.), a fixture of retail banking, includes an option: The loan can be repaid at any time prior to maturity. The ability to prepay is an option the bank grants to the borrower. In the same way, banks effectively issued options when they offered corporate loans in the late 1970s on a floating-rate (usually prime-rate) basis, and the loans had a ceiling on the floating rate. Essentially, this facility included an interest-rate cap.

Unfortunately, many options were granted by banks without an understanding of the nature and magnitude of the risks involved. In many cases, the result of these options was (and sometimes still is) a loss to the bank—either through an unmatched asset/liability position or foregone income. The important difference is that now most banks recognize that they are writing options and have developed sophisticated methods of pricing, hedging, and monitoring the option positions.

As with swaps and forwards, options-related products enable banks to enhance fee income, while using the basic skills and applications traditionally practiced by intermediaries. In the past few years, banks have introduced many option-related products for managing interest-rate and currency risk. A sampling of these products is listed in Exhibit 1.

Exhibit 1   Bank Risk-Protection Products

Interest-Rate Risk	Currency Risk
Caps	Options on currencies
Floors	Bearer exchange rate option (BERO)
Collars	Forward with optional exit (FOX)
Options on Treasuries	Shared currency option under tender
Cylinders	Currency exchange warrants

The Fundamentals

Prior to addressing the current uses of options and the role of banks in this process, it is appropriate to review some of the fundamental characteristics of options.

Despite the mistaken perception that an option is no more than a highly leveraged tool of speculation, use of options by all types of institutions continues to increase. The application that is growing most in popularity is the use of options to hedge risk positions. While it is true that options can be used as a leveraged tool of speculation, this application is not the fastest growing.

Over the mid-1980s, the number of corporations using options and derivative products (caps, collars, etc.) grew tremendously. Although the growth was interrupted by the market disruption of October of 1987, the current uncertain environment makes options hedging attractive again. The expanding use of options has been influenced by many factors: the increasing availability of exchange-traded instruments, more sophisticated financial management strategies, the role of banks as intermediaries, and increased market volatility.

Terminology

The most confusing aspect of options is the terminology. An option entails the right to buy or sell a specified asset (the underlying asset) at a predetermined price at some time in the future, without requiring the purchase or sale of the asset. An option to purchase is known as a call option, while the option to sell is known as a put. The predetermined price is referred to as the strike price, and the date (or dates) upon which the holder of the option can elect to buy or sell is known as the exercise date(s). The buyer or holder of the option has the right to exercise the option, while the seller or writer is subject to the decision of the buyer.

Varieties of Options

The first widespread use of options was on individual stocks. During the 1980s, several options—known as stock index options—were developed on baskets of equities. While this is the most popular use for individual investors and pension funds, corporations and banks use other types of options with different objectives. The increasingly popular tools for institutional hedging are currency and interest-rate options.

Currency options were first traded on an exchange in 1982, and now are traded in two primary forms: options on the actual currency and options on currency futures. While the mechanics are somewhat different, the effects of the two types of transactions are similar. Today, currency options are traded on several different exchanges, including:

The Montreal Exchange (ME);
The Philadelphia Exchange (PHLX);
The International Monetary Market (IMM);
The London International Financial Futures Exchange (LIFFE); and
The Singapore International Financial Monetary Exchange (SIMEX).

While currency options have been in existence for a longer time, the most visible area of growth for banks in exchange-traded options in recent years has been interest-rate options. Some of the more well-known instruments include options on Eurodollar deposit futures, Treasury bond futures, Treasure note futures, Treasury bill futures, and Eurosterling deposits.

As with exchange-traded futures contracts, one reason for the increase in popularity of interest-rate options has been the bank's role as an intermediary between the exchange-traded market and the ultimate user. The increase in the variety and liquidity of exchange-traded options contracts has enhanced the bank's ability to offset the risk of option-related products sold to clients.

The expanding use of options has also been evident in the over-the-counter (OTC) market, in which banks and corporations buy and sell various types of options to and from each other. Since the first well-known product, interest-rate caps, the number and variety of alternatives to manage interest-rate and currency risk introduced by banks has been incredible. (See Exhibit 3 for a more comprehensive list of exchange/traded futures and options contracts.)

Uses of Options

Option contracts are an advantageous way for banks and corporations to hedge many types of situations. Options are similar to insurance policies, providing worst-case protection with a potential for benefit if the protection is not needed. As a result, options are being used increasingly to:

- establish a maximum cost on floating-rate debt;
- limit exposure to exchange-rate fluctuations;
- hedge the issuance of future fixed-rate liabilities;
- hedge against uncertain (contingent) risk;
- protect the yield of investment portfolios; and
- generally increase financial flexibility.

The ability to identify a worst-case scenario, without forsaking possible benefits, is a strong incentive to many option users. This is best demonstrated by an example (see Exhibit 1).

Example 1: Hedging Currency Exposure

Situation
A U.S.-based company has agreed to purchase equipment from a supplier in Germany. Payment of DM1,000,000 will be due in mid-June. While the treasurer does not believe that the dollar will continue to depreciate (in which case the cost of the equipment—in dollars—would increase), he is aware of this possibility and wants protection.

Market Environment
Current exchange rate $.5920/DM1.00
Forward exchange rate (June) $.5970/DM1.00

June Call Options on DM

Strike Price	Premium*
$.58	$.0198
$.59	$.0133
$.60	$.0085

*Expressed on the basis of dollars per DM

Analysis
If the spot rate doesn't change between now and June, the equipment will cost $592,000 (DM1,000,000 × .592). If the company elects to purchase DM now, for value in June, the equipment will cost $597,000 (DM1,000,000 × .597).

An alternative would be to purchase call options on DM. These options would provide the company with the right, but not the obligation, to purchase DM at a predetermined price (the strike price). One possibility is to purchase the call options with a strike price of $.58/DM1.00. Using such an approach, the company can determine the maximum cost of the equipment.

Cost of purchasing options:	$1,000,000 \times .0198$ =	$ 19,800
Exercise cost of DM:	$1,000,000 \times .5800$ =	$580,000
Maximum cost of DM 1,000,000:		$599,800

While the maximum cost of the equipment using the call options is higher than the spot or forward rate, this may still be an attractive situation for many companies. For example, if the dollar appreciates relative to the DM between now and June, the company can ignore the option and purchase the DM on the spot FX market. If the dollar strengthens to $.577/DM1.00, the total cost would be:

Premium paid for options:	$1,000,000 \times .0198$ =	$ 19,800
Spot FX purchase of DM:	$1,000,000 \times .5750$ =	$575,000
Total cost of DM1,000,000:		$594,800

The Role of Banks

There are many logistical and cosmetic problems associated with using options. The role that banks are fulfilling, to an increasing extent, is to make the use of options less complicated and mystifying.

Repackaging

In some cases, simplification is accomplished by merely changing the terminology. Rather than sell puts and calls, banks market interest-rate "caps" and "floors"—terms that describe the objective in a logical/intuitive way. As with other products, banks combine several different types of options, in many combinations, to provide a package to clients that is easy to implement, cost-effective, and can sometimes be a "perfect hedge."

Any banker who has marketed financial products to corporations is aware of the reluctance of many corporate treasurers to pay fees in advance. This aversion has hampered the growth of options. However, bankers have found ways to make the option premium less burdensome. The first major step in this direction was the introduction of interest-rate collars. A simple interest-rate collar can be created by using exchange-traded options in which the underlying asset is the Eurodollar (ED) futures contract. These options are traded on the International Monetary Market (IMM), the London International Financial Futures Exchange (LIFFE), and other exchanges.

An interest-rate collar, which guarantees that LIBOR will not go above or below a certain level, can be constructed using put options on the ED futures contract (the maximum level) and call options (the minimum level). Creation of a simple, one-period collar is analyzed in Example 2.

Example 2: Creating a Collar on Three-Month LIBOR

Situation

A client anticipates borrowing US$25,000,000 in December. To reduce the exposure to rising rates without forsaking the benefit of level or falling rates, the company has requested a cap on three-month LIBOR. However, knowing the client is averse to paying fees, the bank suggests a collar. The desired level of the LIBOR cap is 7.75%.

To create this simple collar, the bank will use the exchange-traded market for options on ED futures, which are based on 90-day LIBOR. Because the borrowing will occur in December, the December options will be used. Prices are listed as follows:

Exhibit 2   Prices for Options on ED Futures

Strike Price	Put Premium*	Call Premium*
92.25	61	51
92.50	74	39
92.75	89	29
93.00	106	21
93.25	124	14

*Expressed in "ticks"—worth $25 each per $1,000,000 face value

Step 1: Creating a Cap

The company's borrowing cost will increase if interest rates rise; therefore, the objective of the hedge is to profit if rates rise—offsetting the increased borrowing cost. One alternative is to use futures contracts. The pricing mechanism of the ED futures contract (price = 100 – LIBOR) indicates that an increase in LIBOR will result in a decrease in the price of the futures contract. To profit from a rate increase (a price decrease), the ED contract would be sold immediately and repurchased in December. The price at which the contract is repurchased would be based on the three-month LIBOR rate in effect in December. If interest rates increase, the price would be lower than today, resulting in a gain on the hedge (sell high, buy low). However, if the futures contract is sold immediately, the hedge could also result in a loss—if interest rates fall.

This scenario does not meet the objective of limiting exposure to an increase in rates without forgoing the benefit of a fall. To accomplish this, an option must be used—specifically, a put option on the December ED futures contract. The put provides the option to sell an ED futures contract at a predetermined price. If rates rise above the level of the cap (futures prices fall below the strike price of the option), the option will be exercised, and the result will be a profit on the hedge.

If the desired cap level for $25,000,000 is 7.75% (futures price of 92.25), put options on 25 ED futures contracts (each with a $1,000,000 face value) would be purchased. The price of each option is 61 ticks.

Total cost of cap = 25 contracts × 61 ticks × $25 per tick = $38,125

Step 2: Adding a Floor

While the cap meets the initial objective, there is a way to reduce the cost if the client is willing to surrender some of the potential benefit of falling rates—the sale of a call option.

The strike price of the call is set at the "floor" level for LIBOR. The risk and profit profile of the call is the opposite of the put, but at a different level of LIBOR.

If a floor of 7.00% is used, the amount received for the call option would be:

Total value of floor = 25 contracts × 21 ticks × $25 per tick = $13,125

Step 3: The Result—A Collar

By purchasing the put options and selling the call options, the client (or the bank on behalf of the client) has created a collar. The maximum LIBOR rate will not exceed 7.75%, and the minimum will not fall below 7.00%. The cost of the hedge is the net amount of the two option premiums:

Cost of collar = $38,125 − $13,125 = $25,000

Imperfect Hedges

The variety of exchange-traded option contracts is not so great as with futures contracts. In addition, many of the contracts traded are not so liquid, or are not available more than three to nine months into the future. Therefore, the ability of banks to hedge option-related risk effectively is much lower than with futures and forward contracts.

Once again, one of the major roles banks play in this market is to shield their clients from the risk of imperfect hedges that may result from unusual amounts, dates that do not conform to exchange-traded alternatives, instrument mismatches, or illiquidity.

There are many other methods to hedge option-related risk. Most alternatives are extremely complex, requiring combinations of futures, options, and cash market securities. While these methods are usually effective hedges, there is a risk that such cross-hedges will not perform as expected. This was the case in October of 1987. There have been many horror stories about firms losing large amounts of money due to inferior hedging strategies.

The purchase of OTC options, specifically structured by a bank to meet a corporation's objective, is one method of eliminating this risk.

Conclusion

Banks' entry into option-related products has been a natural extension of their role as financial intermediaries. The growth in this activity, and the array of products in the OTC market, has greatly increased the ability of financial managers to hedge market risk. At the same time, this activity has enabled banks to strengthen client relationships by expanding their services and also increased fee income.

Despite all these benefits, the expansion of the OTC market would not have been possible without the parallel expansion of the exchange-traded markets in futures and options. As the following tables indicate, the range of instruments and the liquidity of many of these contracts provide hedgers with a variety of alternatives.

In addition, the fact that many instruments are traded on several exchanges around the world enables international banks to manage their exposure on a 24-hour basis. This ability has also been enhanced by the development of "mutual offset agreements" between exchanges (for example, the IMM and SIMEX), which allow positions opened on one exchange to be closed on the other. Factors such as these lead to increased liquidity and flexibility.

One issue that will be interesting to explore is the degree to which nonfinancial corporations are actually using these risk-management products, and their preference for OTC versus exchange/traded instruments. Ultimately, the question that arises is whether or not the disintermediation that has affected banks' lending business will also affect risk-management products.

Exhibit 3   Selected Futures and Options Contracts

Financial Futures	Exchange	Contract Unit	Contract Months	Offset Agreement
3-Month Eurodollar Interest Rate	IMM	$1,000,000	March, June, September, December	SIMEX
3-Month Eurodollar Interest Rate	SIMEX	$1,000,000	March, June, September, December	IMM
3-Month Eurodollar Interest Rate	SFE	$1,000,000	March, June, September, December	LIFFE
3-Month Eurodollar Interest Rate	LIFFE	$1,000,000	March, June, September, December	SFE
90-Day U.S. Treasury Bill	IMM	$1,000,000	March, June, September, December	None
90-Day U.S. Treasury Bill	Mid-America Commodity Exchange	$500,000 Face Value	March, June, September, December	None
U.S. Treasury Note	CBOT	$100,000	March, June, September, December	Soon on FINEX

Exhibit 3   Selected Futures and Options Contracts (continued)

Financial Futures	Exchange	Contract Unit	Contract Months	Offset Agreement
U.S. Treasury Note	New York Cotton Exchange	$100,000	March, June, September, December	Soon on CBOT
U.S. Treasury Bond	CBOT	$100,000	March, June, September, December	None
U.S. Treasury Bond	LIFFE	$100,000	March, June, September, December	None
U.S. Treasury Bond	Mid-America Commodity Exchange	$50,000	March, June, September, December	None
U.S. Treasury Bond	SIMEX	$100,000	March, June, September, December	None
Corporate Bond Price Index	New York Futures Exchange	$500 × Price Index	March, May, July, September, December	None
Long-Term Municipal Bond Index	CBOT	$1,000 × Bond Buyer Municipal Bond Index	March, June, September, December	None
3-Month Eurosterling Interest Rate	LIFFE	£500,000	March, June, September, December	None
Short Gilts	LIFFE	£100,000	March, June, September, December	None

Exhibit 3   Selected Futures and Options Contracts (continued)

Financial Futures	Exchange	Contract Unit	Contract Months	Offset Agreement
20-Year Gilt Interest Rate	LIFFE	£50,000	March, June, September, December	None
Japanese Government Bond	LIFFE	¥ 100,000,000 Face Value	March, June, September, December	None

Options on Futures				
3-Month Eurodollar Interest Rate	LIFFE	One LIFFE Eurodollar Futures Contract	March, June, September, December	None
3-Month Eurodollar Interest Rate	IMM	One IMM Eurodollar Futures Contract	March, June, September, December	None
90-Day U.S. Treasury Bill	IMM	One IMM T-Bill Futures Contract	March, June, September, December	None
Long-Term U.S. Treasury Note	CBOT	One CBOT T-Note Futures Contract	March, June, September, December	None
U.S. Treasury Bond	CBOT	One CBOT U.S. T-Bond Futures Contract	March, June, September, December	None
Long-Term Municipal Bond Index	CBOT	One CBOT Municipal Bond Futures Contract	March, June, September, December	None

9

The Bank as Intermediary

Disintermediation in Futures and Options?

In many situations, it is possible for corporations to accomplish their risk-management objectives by accessing the futures and options markets directly—bypassing the intermediary. Chapters 7 and 8 looked at the role of banks in the exchange-traded futures and options markets and at the creation of over-the-counter (OTC) products—like swaps and caps—using these vehicles. Here we will look at the possibility of disintermediation in the futures and options markets.

Many products (including commercial paper, junk bonds, and placements) have caused the disintermediation of banks in their traditional lending business. This results in increased competition, decreased profitability, and the need to accept greater levels of risk to maintain earnings. The opposite has occurred with risk-management products—the use of bank-provided products continues to increase. In order to understand the long-term implications of rate risk-management products, bankers must be cognizant of the degree to which disintermediation has or will affect futures and options. Many issues can accelerate or delay this process—they must be understood.

Since the early 1980s, several factors have combined to make this an important product area for banks and corporations. Interest rates and foreign-

Exhibit 1   The Use of Risk-Management Products

Percentage of Largest 500 Nonfinancial Companies Using Rate Risk-Management Products

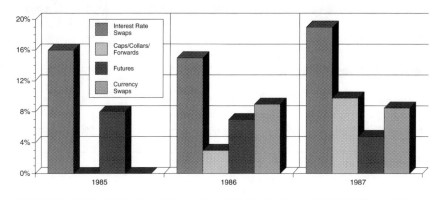

exchange (FX) rates have never been more volatile. The volume of international trade (leading to FX risk) and debt financing (interest-rate risk) continue to increase dramatically, and refinements in accounting rules and disclosure guidelines have increased the visibility of these risk components.

These conditions occurred during a period in which corporate earnings have been under pressure, and stability and predictability became major concerns. Corporate treasurers have demonstrated an increasing level of concern with these risks. As a result, treasurers have become much more sophisticated and demanding. Many banks, in turn, have focused their efforts on meeting the demand for hedging products and providing education and consulting services to their clients.

Increasing Usage of Products

Whether it is through the intermediation process or direct access, much of the increase in demand for rate risk-management products is ultimately transferred to the exchange-traded futures and options market. At the same time, the expansion of instruments and increased liquidity in these markets has facilitated the increased offering of OTC products. While the October of 1987 market crash has had a serious impact on stock-related futures and options, this has not been as evident in currency and interest-rate products. As Exhibit 2 demonstrates, the volume of transactions in this area has grown dramatically over the past several years.

Exhibit 2   The Growth of Rate Risk-Management Products

Percentage Annual Increase in Volume of Transactions

	1984	1985	1986	1987
Eurodollar Futures[1]	370.6%	112.3%	21.7%	88.6%
Long-Term Treasury Futures[2]	55.3%	36.9%	31.7%	26.4%
Currency Futures[3]	19.8%	25.9%	15.3%	6.5%
Interest Rate Swaps	223.5%	81.8%	90.5%	31.2%*

*First half data annualized

Notes
[1] Futures on 90-day Eurodollar time deposits, traded on the Chicago Mercantile Exchange (CME)
[2] Futures on 20-year Treasury bonds and 10-year notes, traded on Chicago Board of Trade (CBOT)
[3] Consists of futures on Pound Sterling, Canadian dollar, and Deutschemark, traded on CME

Sources: Chicago Mercantile Exchange, Chicago Board of Trade, International Swap Dealers Association, and Globecon estimates.

Use by Corporations

Despite the continuing growth in these markets, it appears as though most of the increase in exchange-traded volume is from financial institutions. Nonfinancial institutions do not use the exchange-traded markets to any great extent. While there are many large corporations that are active users of futures and options, surveys indicate that these firms are in the minority.

In general, firms that do use futures and options have a centralized treasury function, a large and sophisticated treasury staff that is managed in an aggressive fashion (often as a profit center) and is actively managing a large amount of exposure—either debt, assets, or currency.

A recent survey by Greenwich Associates indicates that the use of OTC products by the largest 500 nonfinancial corporations in the United States is more than six times as popular as accessing the futures and options markets directly. It is even more important to realize that over the past three years, the relative importance of OTC usage has increased, relative to direct market access.

Usage of Risk-Management Products

Percentage of Largest 500 Nonfinancial Companies Using Rate Risk-Management Products

	1985	1986	1987
Interest Rate Swaps	19%	18%	21%
Caps/Collars/Forwards	NA*	4%	10%
Futures	11%	8%	6%
Currency Swaps	NA*	9%	9%

*Not available
Source: Greenwich Associates

Strategic Implications

The previous data imply that risk management products are one area in which banks have been able to preserve their role as intermediary. In fact, other data compiled by Greenwich indicate that commercial banks are becoming increasingly important in this field (relative to investment banks). This gain is due primarily to a difference in strategy between the two types of institutions. Commercial banks have traditionally taken the approach of offering customized products to their clients, in hopes of providing incremental value and receiving a higher fee. Most investment banks, on the other hand, focus on commodity-type transactions in hopes of generating significant volume. This difference is often referred to as the "relationship" versus "transaction" or "trading" orientation.

In many situations (commercial paper, placements, etc.), the transaction perspective has produced significantly lower costs for corporations, without increasing the level of risk. However, in the case of risk-management products, because the primary differences between the exchange-traded and OTC markets are flexibility and ease of execution, the risk factor is a very important part of the decision.

Due to the limited number of alternatives in futures and options, it is rarely possible to structure a "perfect hedge." The inability to find the perfect solution increases the risk of using these products. In light of the degree of concern exhibited by most treasurers on this issue, this incremental risk is not acceptable to most. If banks are marketing customized hedging products, the client can significantly reduce the level of risk by using the bank product. As the exchanges introduce additional futures and options instruments, an increase in the degree of disintermediation is inevitable. However, it appears as though this will be a very slow process. Interest-rate and currency-risk management is likely to be a fertile activity for banks for several more years.

Marketing Implications

The greater willingness and historical ability of banks to offer customized solutions is a distinct marketing advantage in this area. At the same time, as the level of interest-rate and currency risk remains high or increases, and treasurers increase their attempts to manage the risk, the usage of these products will increase. In order to capitalize on these opportunities, bankers must understand the issues faced by corporate treasurers. Understanding these issues will enhance a banker's ability to target candidates and enhance their ability to act as consultants. This ability will become increasingly important as the range of products and competitors increases.

It is significant that, of the several factors identified by Greenwich as influencing the choice of providers of interest-rate swaps, one has consistently been the most important. *The most important factor is the expertise of the product specialist.*

In rate risk-management situations, expertise is demonstrated in several ways:

1. understanding the nature of the client's exposure
2. discussing alternative solutions (whether provided by the bank or by competitors)
3. analyzing the advantages and disadvantages of various alternatives—both quantitatively and qualitatively
4. assessing the client's risk profile, etc.
5. making and supporting a recommendation, based on all of these ways.

In reality, these issues must be addressed by both the relationship officer and the product specialist. Specifically, the relationship officer must be responsible for items 1 and 4 and, using this information, might work with a product specialist on the remaining items. In this process, bankers must be aware that they are competing with other commercial and investment banks and also with exchange-traded futures and options.

Understanding the Alternatives

Chapters 7 through 9 provide the basic framework for determining the cost of a hedge established using futures or options (transaction costs of approximately one basis point were ignored). In general, if an exposure can be hedged with identical results in either the OTC or exchange-traded market, the OTC market will be more expensive. However, the cost difference will probably be very small. In addition to cost factors, it is important to understand many subjective concerns.

Elimination of Exposure Versus Reduction of Exposure

While the standardization of exchange-traded contracts provides many advantages, there is one major trade-off—flexibility. Because contracts mature only at specific times during the year (e.g., March, June, September, December), a treasurer with an exposed position at some other time (e.g., May) would be forced to accept an imperfect hedge. Similarly, because contracts are for fixed amounts, a treasurer may be forced to overhedge or underhedge if the amount of exposure does not correspond to an increment of the contract amount. Finally, if an exchange-traded contract does not exist for the instrument being hedged (e.g., commercial paper), it might be necessary to hedge using a similar but different instrument (a cross-hedge). The cross-hedge may or may not perform as expected.

In all of these cases, the risk of an imperfect hedge usually can be eliminated by obtaining a customized bank product. This is one of the most important considerations to many corporate users.

Liquidity

One benefit of the limited number of alternatives in exchange-traded products is the high degree of liquidity in the available alternatives. While the importance of liquidity varies greatly among corporate users, this is a factor that should be considered. If a swap or cap is entered into with a bank, the corporate client must negotiate a termination or assignment to completely eliminate the transaction prior to maturity. However, a position established on an exchange usually can be reversed very easily and quickly.

Credit/Performance Risk

If a corporation enters into a transaction with a bank, there is some degree of credit risk. This risk might be borne by the corporation, the bank, or both. If the risk is accepted by the corporate client, there might be concern about the bank's credit rating. Obviously, this has implications for banks with anything but the highest credit rating when dealing with conservative clients. However, if the client is a borrower, some sort of "mutual offset" arrangement might serve to lessen the concern. When the risk is accepted by the bank, credit capacity is utilized. A corporation might view this as reducing its flexibility with the bank.

Alternatively, exchanges require that margin be posted in most cases. While the posting of margin almost totally eliminates credit risk, it leads to an increase in the administrative burden and makes the timing of cash flows uncertain. Depending on the manner in which margin is posted, there may be an opportunity cost involved as well.

Volume of Transactions

For clients with limited or occasional hedging needs, the cost and time involved in establishing a program to hedge on the exchanges will be overwhelming. The requirements include: the establishment of broker relationships (possibly with an affiliate of the bank), margin accounts, operating procedures, accounting procedures, and controls. In addition, the education required for members of the treasury staff will be significant. If a client anticipates significant volume, it may be appropriate to suggest establishing a program with a licensed Futures Commission Merchant (FCM). While many banks have affiliates that are FCMs, it might be possible to accomplish the same objective with the bank executing transactions on behalf of the client.

Cosmetic Factors

Many people continue to view futures and options as purely speculative transactions. While this is not true, this impression is a factor in the resistance to increased usage. Banks have already capitalized on the situation by assigning names to strategies that imply conservatism and stability, rather than gambling. Perhaps the best example of this is a "collar" on borrowing costs, rather than combining the purchase of put options with the sale of call options. Until the "average" corporate treasurer, CFO, and CEO become more comfortable with the risk characteristics of exchange-traded products, bank products will have a decided advantage in this category. The publicity surrounding the October crash has increased this factor's importance.

Accounting and Taxation

Accounting and taxation are very important issues that we will explore in greater detail in a subsequent chapter. However, some generalizations can be made. The accounting and tax treatment should be the same, whether exposure has been hedged using OTC or exchange-traded products. Accounting parameters established for hedges allow gains or losses on the hedge to be deferred and amortized along with the underlying asset or liability (similar to premiums and discounts on the issuance of debt). To receive this treatment, certain criteria must be met to qualify as a hedge.

Unfortunately, there have been three different sets of criteria established in different accounting pronouncements:

1. FAS 52—Foreign Currency Translation
2. FAS 80—Accounting for Futures Contracts
3. AICPA Issues Paper—Accounting for Options

Exhibit 3   OTC Versus Exchange Products: Understanding the Issues

Issue	OTC Products	Exchange-Traded
Cost	Slightly more expensive than exchange, depends on degree of customization required. May be influenced by pending capital proposal.	Less expensive
Flexibility	Very flexible. Almost any situation can be hedged —for the right price.	None. Standardized contract items
Liquidity	Limited due to difference of products and credit concerns, but improving	Highly liquid
Credit/ Performance Risk	Present	None
Volume Considerations	Single transaction or large volume	Only appropriate for large volume
Cosmetic	Bank product—relatively conservative	Perception of gambling
Accounting and Tax	Similar	Similar

Summary

In order to act as a consultant, a banker must understand several issues. These issues include: the nature of the client's exposure and risk profile, the alternatives available, the relationship of the products to each other, advantages and disadvantages of the various strategies, and the costs involved. Throughout this process, bankers must be able to identify subjective factors and evaluate their importance. Is the company concerned about accepting performance risk? Which is more important: cash flow, accounting, or taxes? Is liquidity an important consideration?

Conclusion

Since identifying this business segment, banks have become increasingly important—generating significant volume, creating new products, and hopefully increasing revenues. This activity is a natural extension of the traditional role of banks and provides significant benefits for the average treasurer. The most important of these benefits are flexibility and cosmetic issues, without a substantial increase in cost.

One factor that may affect this prediction is the current bank capital adequacy proposal. The proposal may significantly increase banks' costs of providing these products. This may result in an increased cost difference between OTC products and exchange-traded instruments. If this differential becomes too great, it will increase the usage of exchanges by corporations.

Current indications are that this activity will not suffer from a high degree of disintermediation within the next few years. However, the entrance of more banks and products into the OTC market will undoubtedly increase competition. Nevertheless, the growth potential of the market may be sufficient to support the increasing number of suppliers.

In order to fully exploit the opportunities, banks and bankers must be prepared to act in the capacity of consultant, helping treasurers identify exposure, evaluate alternatives, and identify and implement strategies. For some clients with large volume, this might involve working to establish a futures and options hedging program through an affiliate. Other clients might require ongoing consulting and customized transactions. To be a major force in this dynamic market, an institution must be prepared for both extremes.

10

Caps and Swaptions
Evolution of the Option Market

Any bank seeking to increase profit margins on the sale of options must find new ways to sell the same basic products. Two products that illustrate this trend are caps and, more recently, swaptions. Both represent attempts to tailor generic options precisely to the needs of end-users. Both enable the bank to raise prices higher than would otherwise be possible. Both are intended to expand the potential base of customers. Caps and swaptions are two of many examples of efforts to reconfigure basic products to attract new customers paying higher prices.

The customer is the ultimate arbiter in this ongoing process of product evolution. The customer decides whether the value added by the bank is worth the higher price. To help the customer make this decision, the relationship officer must understand how the bank's way of modifying the basic product provides value and reduces risk.

The Search for New Applications
Kicked off by the interest rate volatility of the early 1980s, the market for interest-rate options continues to grow. However, options are just as subject to the product life cycle as loans, swaps or any other generic financial

transaction. As competition increases, margins shrink and the product becomes a commodity, with the most profits going to the players with the highest volume and lowest costs. In this environment, any bank aiming to increase or even maintain profit margins needs to find new end-users, new applications, or both.

For example, straight fixed-to-floating interest-rate swaps became less profitable as the interest-rate swap market evolved. The swap market became more competitive and differentiated. Heightened competition forced banks to look widely for new end-users—not only to the liability managers who populate the traditional origination side of the bank's business, but to investors on the distribution side as well. Swap variations developed by the banks included zero-coupon swaps, amortizing swaps, and asset swaps. New customers included fixed-income investors, middle market corporations, and S&Ls.

The same process is taking place in the interest-rate options market. Growth and profits in interest-rate options depend on the bank's ability to find new customers and new applications on both the origination and distribution sides of the business.

For instance, the most generic interest-rate option is the option on Eurodollar futures traded on the Chicago Mercantile Exchange. This market for options on three-month LIBOR is quite liquid. But in straight, unmodified form, these options have only one hedging application: as a hedge of an anticipated three-month LIBOR-based payment or receipt on a date precisely matching that of the exchange-traded option.

The bank adds value to this generic product by tailoring it to suit a specific type of end-user. By doing this, the bank can both charge a higher price and widen the customer base. Examples of ways banks have customized interest-rate options include:

- Matching options to the precise maturities of a customer's cash flows.

- Developing options on floating-rate indices other than three-month LIBOR, such as six-month LIBOR, commercial paper, banker's acceptances, or the prime rate.

- Developing options on fixed-rate payment streams (swaptions).

- Selling options in strips matched to the timing of the customer's payments or receipts (caps and floors).

- Creating buy-write strategies to subsidize the cost of option purchases (collars and participating rate agreements).

Exhibit 1   Applications Utilizing Floating-Rate Receipts/Payments

Bank intermediation	Distribution (investors)	Origination (borrowers)
Interest-rate risk for customers	Falling	Rising
Puts*	Sell	Buy
Objective	Enhance yield	Cap payments
Calls**	Buy	Sell
Objective	Lock in minimum receipt	Subsidize borrowing rate

* When offered in strips to match a borrower's payment dates, this is a cap.
** When offered in strips to match a borrower's payment dates, this is a floor.

In addition, the bank finds new end-users by searching for applications among asset managers as well as the bank's traditional borrower client base. For every option buyer, there must also be an option seller. Customers on both the origination and the distribution sides of the bank can be potential option counterparties. Only by fully integrating distribution and origination can banks optimize the potential of option products.

These symmetrical applications are shown in Exhibits 1 and 2. The tables show distribution applications in the left column and origination applications in the right column. Exhibit 1 illustrates uses for puts and calls on a floating-rate index; Exhibit 2 shows uses for puts and calls on a fixed-rate index.

As an example, the top row of Exhibit 1 is labeled "puts." The row shows how investors can benefit by writing puts, while borrowers can benefit by buying puts.

Every investor holding a floating-rate asset is exposed to the risk that interest rates will decline. By writing a put on the asset, the investor receives a premium that increases his or her yield. On the downside, the investor gives up the potential for higher receipts if floating rates rise, for rising rates will trigger offsetting payments to the buyer of the put.

A floating-rate borrower, on the other hand, can protect against the danger of higher rates by buying a put. If rates rise, the value of the put will increase as well. The payment received from the put will offset the higher rate paid on the debt obligation.

Exhibit 2 Applications Utilizing Fixed-Rate Receipts/Payments

Bank intermediation	Distribution (investors)	Origination (borrowers)
Interest-Rate Risk for Customers	Rising	Falling
Puts*	Buy	Sell
Objective	Lock in minimum price	Subsidize borrowing rate
Calls**	Sell	Buy
Objective	Enhance yield	Benefit from fall in rates

* A payer swaption is a type of put; the right, but not the obligation, to pay a specified fixed rate and receive floating.

** A receiver swaption is a type of call; the right, but not the obligation, to receive a specified fixed rate and pay floating.

Investors and borrowers with offsetting option positions first came together in the early 1980s, when institutional investors were offered floating-rate notes (FRNs) with maturities of three to five years. In return for a yield of about 25 basis points over that of FRNs of similar credit quality, the investors accepted ceilings on their LIBOR-based receipts. Although many of the investors did not realize it, they received the extra yield because they had sold a series of puts that capped their interest receipts.

The issuers who had bought the puts sold them to the underwriters of the FRNs, who resold the puts at a profit to corporate borrowers with floating-rate debt. Part of this profit went to the issuers and helped to reduce the borrowing cost to below LIBOR. The rest went to compensate the investment banks that arranged the transactions. By finding matching applications on the investor and borrower sides, the intermediaries were able to maximize profit and minimize exposure.

A similar pairing of investor and borrower needs is the swaption arbitrage that gained momentum in the early months of 1989 (see Chapter 40 in *The Derivatives Engineering Workbook*). Investors are willing to write calls on bond issues. Issuers buy the calls from investors and resell them to fixed-rate payers in swaps, who are willing to buy the calls at a higher price.

End-users cannot be found for every application. Frequently option purchasers are plentiful and option writers are scarce. This is because option purchasers take on only limited risk, while option writers assume unlimited risk. FRN investors have been willing to sell puts to issuers in the past. However, these investors are unwilling to do so now. As a result, there is no natural source of supply for these puts, and banks wishing to offer them to borrowers are forced to create them in other ways.

Caps and Swaptions

Two products resulting from efforts by banks to customize options to client needs are caps and swaptions. Although caps and swaptions are fundamentally different products, both are used to protect a borrower from rising interest rates, and both can be used in many of the same customer applications.

Caps and swaptions appeared at different stages in the history of option-based products. Caps emerged early in the evolution of option products, while swaptions appeared more recently. In fact, swaptions can be seen as a product refinement that addresses certain problems inherent in caps. It is no surprise, therefore, that the growth of swaptions is outpacing that of caps.

A cap is a series of progressively longer and longer-dated puts on a floating-rate debt instrument. For example, a three-year cap on three-month LIBOR consists of a three-month option on three-month LIBOR, followed by a six-month option on three-month LIBOR, and ultimately extending out to a three-year option on three-month LIBOR. Each option matches a payment date on the customer's LIBOR-based liability. The strip of options and the premiums for each option are lumped together into one instrument, a cap, with one up-front fee.

Caps have value because they enable a borrower to lock in a maximum payment on floating-rate debt and still gain if rates fall. For instance, if three-month LIBOR rises, the customer's gain on the option will offset the higher interest payment; if LIBOR falls, the customer will reap the benefit if rates decline enough to offset the cost of the option premium.

In contrast to a cap, which is a series of puts, a swaption is a single option—an option on an interest-rate swap. The holder has the right, at a given time in the future, to pay fixed and receive floating (a payer swaption), or receive fixed and pay floating (a receiver swaption).

In effect, a swaption is an option on a fixed-rate payment stream. For example, a floating-rate borrower concerned about the possibility of higher rates could buy a receiver swaption. If interest rates rose, he or she could exercise the swaption, electing to pay fixed and receive floating. The swap would convert the borrower's floating-rate loan to fixed, protecting the borrower against rising rates.

Exhibit 3   Cap and Swaption Rates (December 1988)

Market Rates

Three-month LIBOR	9.5%
Six-month LIBOR	9.5%
Three-year coupon swap	9.75%

Three-year caps on three-month LIBOR

Strike price (MMY)	9.25%	9.50%	9.75%
Cap price	2.125%	1.875%	1.625%
	(in the money)	(at the money)	(out of the money)

Three-month payer swaptions on three-year swaps

Strike price (BEY)	9.5%	9.75%	10.00%
Swaption price	1.15%	0.80%	0.55%
	(in the money)	(at the money)	(out of the money)

From a customer's viewpoint, the fundamental differences between a cap and a swaption center on price versus flexibility. Exhibit 3 shows prices on caps and receiver swaptions with various strike prices in March of 1989. Although the two sets of prices are not directly comparable, it is clear that the caps are more expensive. Because a cap is a series of options with progressively longer maturities, and time value is the biggest component of an option's price, longer maturities are linked with higher prices. In return for paying more for the cap, however, the borrower receives the ultimate in flexibility: a ceiling on payments if interest rates rise and lower payments if interest rates fall.

The swaptions shown in Exhibit 3 also offer long-term protection, but at a lower cost—and with less flexibility to the borrower. The swaption costs less because it contains little time value. It is a short-term option on a long-term debt instrument. At the same time, the swaption offers less flexibility than the cap. Once the borrower exercises the swaption and swaps from floating into fixed, the borrower is locked into a fixed rate. There are no further gains if interest rates decline. In contrast, buyers of caps continue to enjoy the potential for opportunity gains from interest-rate declines for the life of the cap. This difference between the cap and swaption is shown in Exhibit 4.

Exhibit 4   Applying Caps Versus Swaptions

**Yield on
three-month
LIBOR**

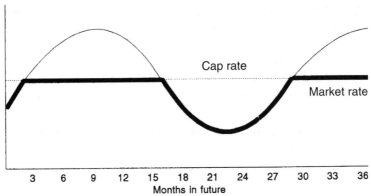

1. Cap is better:

    curved line shows change in three-month LIBOR
    dark portion is rate customer pays (capped on upside, floating on downside)

**Yield on
three-year
swap**

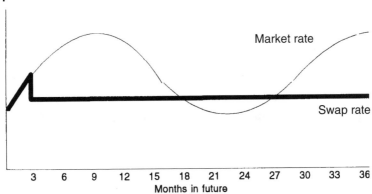

2. Swaption is better:

    curved line shows change in three-year swap rate
    swaption exercised three months from start
    dark portion is rate customer pays (fixed regardless of future changes in rates)

Choosing Between Caps and Swaptions

Caps are expensive and can be difficult to sell. In fact, the customer's gut feeling that cap protection is too expensive is often correct. A financing combined with an option purchase is always more expensive than a straight financing. And of all the option-based products, caps are among the most expensive. A customer who pays a high price for too much insurance is unlikely to remain loyal for long. One must know with precision the needs of the customer in order to recommend one rate risk-management vehicle over another.

The first decision the customer must make is whether to choose an option-based product at all. The first grid in Exhibit 5 shows one way of choosing between a swap (or other fixed-rate financing) and an option-based solution. The table applies only to customers who think interest rates will rise, and the choices in the table are limited to two: do a swap or buy an option. If the customer thinks rates will remain stable or fall, he or she will borrow at a floating rate or wait for lower rates.

If the customer is certain that rates will rise, he or she will use a swap to lock in a fixed rate. Because the customer is confident of the forecast, he or she is unwilling to pay extra for the opportunity to benefit from a decline in interest rates.

Exhibit 5   Swap, Swaption, and Cap Alternative

Customer's Alternatives Are:

Three-Year Interest-Rate Swap
Three-Month Swaption
Three-Year Cap

| | | Degree of Certainty | |
		High	Low
Forecast Rise in	**Sharp Rise**	swap	option
Interest Rates	**Slight Rise**	swap	swap

Timing of Interest-Rate Rise

Next three months	Swaption
Next three years	Cap

If the customer is uncertain of the forecast, but thinks that interest rates will rise only moderately, he or she is also likely to use a swap to lock in fixed rates. Because the risk is low, a swap is preferred as the cheapest solution.

In only one case—the customer forecasts a large rise in rates, but is only moderately certain of the forecast—will the option be the correct choice. The customer's lack of certainty, coupled with apprehension over a possible big jump in rates, translates into a situation in which the customer may be willing to pay a premium for a flexible option-based solution.

Once the borrower has decided on an option, the next choice is between a cap and a swaption. The second table in Exhibit 5 shows one key element in the choice: the time horizon of the customer's choice. In general, if the customer believes that interest rates will rise over the next several months, a short-term option such as the swaption is probably the most cost-effective solution. However, if the rise in interest rates is expected over a longer time horizon, the extra cost of the cap may be justified.

Conclusion

The future profitability of banks depends on finding new product applications, new end-users, or both. One way of doing this is modifying generic products to fit customer needs and taking a higher profit margin for doing do. This phenomenon has occurred in lending and in interest-rate swaps. It is also occurring in the area of interest-rate options.

Two option products that have resulted from this process of new product creation are caps and, more recently, swaptions. Caps and swaptions are fundamentally different products. A cap is a series of options on floating-rate payments, while a swaption is an option on a fixed-rate obligation. However, both are used to protect a borrower from rising interest rates, and both can be used in many of the same customer applications. Marketing caps, swaptions, or any other interest-rate option product requires an understanding of the trade-offs inherent in options. Specifically, it involves communicating to customers the flexibility they receive for the added premium they pay, and the market conditions that give this extra flexibility value.

11

The Swaption Market
Growth in Volume and Applications

Swaptions present bank customers with an attractive and flexible tool for customizing assets and liabilities. The cost of swaptions is usually lower than caps. Corporate treasurers who understand swaps are likely to be open to swaptions. The growth of the market has increased liquidity for both dealers and end-users. And a number of recent swaption structures have illustrated the many ways in which swaptions can be used to "monetize the indifferences" of borrowers and investors.

A swaption is an option to enter an interest-rate swap. A payer swaption gives the holder the right to pay fixed in a coupon swap and receive LIBOR; a receiver swaption gives the holder the right to receive fixed. Sometimes the terms put and call swaptions are used to refer to payer and receiver swaptions, respectively. However, these names can be confusing, and increasingly the terms payer and receiver swaption are becoming standard.

Advantages of Swaptions

The recent success of swaptions results in part from the comfort that corporate treasurers now have with swaps. Options are no more complicated to understand than the underlying instrument. If a treasurer is comfortable with the idea of using payer swaps to hedge future borrowing costs, he or she can easily be made comfortable with payer swaptions. The growing linkage of swaptions to the market for callable and puttable corporate bonds has provided a boon to the swaption market, but the product's acceptance by corporate treasurers was an essential prerequisite.

The emergence of swaptions as the basic product for hedging calls and puts on corporate debt obligations results from the superior liquidity of the interest-rate swap market. Indeed, swaps are the most liquid of "debt" instruments in the two- to ten-year maturities. Whereas the most efficient hedge for a call or put on IBM bonds would be an equal and opposite option position on IBM debt, such positions would have only limited marketability. The generic nature of the interest-rate swap overcomes this important liquidity issue.

Another reason for the emergence of swaptions is the fact that their exercise leads not to short and long positions in a security but rather to pay and receive positions in an interest-rate swap. The off-balance sheet nature of swaps is attractive from this standpoint: swaption buyers and sellers need not worry about taking or making delivery of a scarce asset upon expiration. The only possible result is a position in an interest-rate swap.

Credit Issues

The contingent interest-rate swap position gives rise to a credit-risk issue. A swaption will only be exercised when it is in the money—that is, when it has value relative to current market swap rates. The buyer of the swaption demands that the seller enter into a disadvantageous swap, paying a higher fixed rate or receiving a lower fixed rate than that prevailing in the market. Once the swaption has moved into the money, the buyer is at risk to the seller.

In certain conditions a swaption seller also takes on credit risk. When a swaption is exercised, the buyer is exposed to the credit risk of the seller. However, in the absence of cash settlement, the buyer and seller have now entered an interest-rate swap with one another. The mark-to-market value will change over the life of the swap. Depending on interest-rate movements, the seller of the swaption could easily be at risk to the buyer in the future. If the swaption is settled in cash, however, the seller takes on no credit risk.

Cash Settlement

Often the swaption buyer may not want to enter an interest-rate swap. In many cases, the swaption buyer's primary aim will be to generate cash to offset losses on existing positions. In these cases, it would be desirable to take the swaption gain in cash rather than enter a swap.

Summary Sheet: Swaptions

Writer	Issuers of and investors in fixed- and floating-rate debt in US$, £, ¥, C$, DM, SFr, ECU; interest-rate swap end-users
Buyer	Same as above
Intermediary	Commercial banks, investment houses, and brokers
How Bank Profits	Bid-offer spread on naked swaptions; fees on more complex transactions
Deal Size	Interbank is $25 million and up; for end-users, as low as $250,000
Credit Considerations	If settlement is in cash, writer has no credit risk; buyer at risk for mark-to-market value of swap.
Major Players	Same as major interest-rate swap players: U.S. commercial banks include Citibank, Chemical, Bankers Trust, MHT; major U.S. investment banks; in Europe, Midland Montagu, Midland, Barclays
Fees/Competition (Product Life Cycle)	Less competitive than swaps and caps, but increasingly a commodity product

The dealer community is in the process of addressing this issue by finding an acceptable way to mark swaptions to market. The main concern to swaption players is how the market swap rate will be determined on the expiration date of the swaption. This complication notwithstanding, cash settlement swaptions are growing in popularity and are likely to be standard in the future.

Sectors of the Swaption Market

The largest and most liquid sector of the swaption market is options on U.S. dollar coupon swaps. According to the only figures available—a survey by the International Swap Dealers Association (ISDA) published in the spring of 1989—U.S. dollars accounted for 61 percent of the notional principal of all swaptions written by the institutions surveyed.

The number two market in terms of size, and perhaps the most sophisticated in terms of applications, is in sterling. The third largest market is in Deutschemarks. According to the ISDA, swaption deals have been done in seven currencies—presumably Swiss francs, French francs, yen, and ECU in addition to the U.S. dollar, sterling, and Deutschemarks.

Liquidity is a problem in all swaption markets, including U.S. dollars. Although bid-offer spreads may be narrower in U.S. dollars and sterling than in other currencies, it is always expensive for end-users to actively buy and sell swaptions. Unlike interest-rate swaps, where bid-offer spreads are as narrow as 5 to 10 basis points in U.S. dollars, swaption bid-offer spreads are in the 15 to 50 basis-point range. Even among the most sophisticated end-users, swaptions tend to be bought and held rather than actively traded.

All swaption markets except sterling are capital markets driven. This means that the swaption writers who supply the market come from the ranks of bond investors who buy callable and puttable bonds—in effect, writing options to bond issuers, who resell them as payer or receiver swaptions. The existence of a large body of investors willing to write options has helped the swaption market to overcome the lack of supply that has hindered the growth of other option markets.

In the sterling market, option writers have more often come from the ranks of local authorities such as Hammersmith and Fulham, which over the past several years entered swaps and caps, collars and swaptions totaling about $9.5 billion. Seventy-seven other British local authorities entered contracts totaling another $1.5 billion. A ruling by Britain's High Court in November of 1989 ruled that Hammersmith in particular, and the other local authorities in general, were not liable for trading losses totaling about $800 million on the swap and option products. According to the court, the treasury officials entering the swaps and options were acting illegally. Now that the largest source of sterling swaption writers has been barred from participating in the market, the U.K. swaption market will probably become more capital markets driven.

Development of the Swaption Market

Interest-rate swaps have been around since 1981, when Citibank transformed the rate basis on a yen asset from fixed to floating for Japanese investors. Options on interest-rate swaps were introduced three years later, in 1984, when Solomon Brothers underwrote a callable U.S. dollar Eurobond issue by Bergen Bank. In this transaction, Bergen monetized the call by selling a receiver swaption. This transaction became the basis for the most common swaption application: the swaption arbitrage outlined in Chapter 31 of *The Derivatives Engineering Workbook*.

In 1984 and 1985, the U.S. dollar swaption market developed further when Morgan Stanley underwrote four U.S. dollar Eurobonds with debt warrants. The warrants effectively gave investors the right to extend the bonds beyond the original maturity. The issuer, an AAA-rated U.S. corporation, bought receiver swaptions to hedge against the exercise of the warrants.

Trading in U.S. dollar swaptions began in 1985, and the first swaption books were started. In 1986, the first swaptions were written on Canadian dollar interest-rate swaps. Swaptions began to be sold on sterling in 1986 and Deutschemarks in 1987.

Development of Swaption Applications

As the swaption market has grown, so have the number and variety of swaption applications. In the beginning, swaption applications tended to mirror traditional bond market structures such as callable and puttable bonds. More recently, however, swaptions have been used to create complex asset and liability structures.

One way to categorize swaption applications is as follows:

- Swaptions in isolation
- Swaptions in combination with swaps
- Swaptions in combination with debt (arbitrage/hedging applications)
- Applications involving multiple swaptions.

Swaptions in Isolation

Corporate end-users seldom take speculative naked positions in any options, including swaptions. However, swaptions are often bought and sold in isolation. The buyers and sellers are end-users or other banks that structure swaption-related products on their own. This is a result of the disintermediation of banks that have historically sold complex structures involving swaps, swaptions, and debt issues. Issuers are increasingly structuring simpler swap- and swaption-related transactions on their own, handing the pieces out to the lowest bidder.

Swaptions Plus Swaps

Exhibit 1 shows all of the ways that a swaption purchase can be combined with a swap. The four applications have one feature in common: All give the swapper the right to modify the original terms of the swap at his or her discretion. Because the swapper purchased the option, the right to exercise is his or hers.

The combination of a swaption and a swap yields two useful applications: an extendible swap and a cancelable swap. In an extendible swap, a corporate would buy the right to extend the swap by purchasing a swaption with an

---

Exhibit 1   Combining a Swaption Purchase with a Swap

Position in Swaption	Position in Swap	
	Pay Fixed	*Receive Fixed*
Buy Payer	Extendible (swaption exercise date coincides with swap maturity)	Cancelable (swaption exercise date is before swap maturity)
Buy Receiver	Cancelable (swaption exercise date is before swap maturity)	Extendible (swaption exercise date coincides with swap maturity)

---

exercise date matching the expiration date of the swap. A fixed-rate payer would buy a payer swaption; a fixed-rate receiver, a receiver swaption. By exercising the swaption, the corporate would be able to enter a new swap at the end of the old—in effect, extending the swap.

Creating a cancelable swap involves taking the opposite position. For example, a fixed-rate payer could make the swap cancelable by buying a receiver swaption. An end-user can create a cancelable swap by buying a swaption with an exercise date before the final maturity of the swap. The swaption should enable the end-user to take on a position precisely offsetting the existing swap. Upon exercise, the receipts and payments would perfectly match, canceling the swap.

Swaption Writing Applications

Exhibit 2 shows how a swaption sale can be combined with a swap. In these applications, the swapper receives an up-front premium in exchange for selling the right to exercise the swaption. The swap can still be canceled or extended, but it is no longer at the swapper's discretion. The decision on whether to cancel or extend is out of the swapper's hands.

What kind of corporate would combine a swap with the sale of a swaption? These positions would be taken by end-users indifferent between two maturities. The swaption market allows them to "monetize their indifference" by selling to someone else the right to make the choice between the two maturities. Similar examples are common in today's capital and derivatives markets. Issuers or investors may be indifferent not only between two maturities, but between other aspects of the debt as well: fixed- and floating-rate funds, for example, or U.S. and Australian dollar funds. Issuers are

Exhibit 2   Combining a Swaption Sale with a Swap

Position in Swaption	Position in Swap	
	Pay Fixed	*Receive Fixed*
Sell Payer	Cancelable at discretion of buyer; seller is indifferent.	Extendible at discretion of buyer; seller is indifferent.
Sell Receiver	Extendible at discretion of buyer; seller is indifferent.	Cancelable at discretion of buyer; seller is indifferent.

beginning to realize that every aspect of a funding decision contains some implicit or explicit choice. By selling this choice in the form of option, the issuer can collect premium income that can be used to reduce the cost of funds.

An example of a swaption-writing application in the swap market would be a fixed-rate payer indifferent between a three- and five-year maturity (see Exhibit 3). The payer could reduce the amount of his or her fixed payment by entering a three-year swap and selling a receiver swaption exercisable at the end of year three on a two-year swap. If interest rates fell and the swaption

Exhibit 3   Two Ways to Monetize Indifference to Tenor

Fixed-rate payer is indifferent between three- and five-year funds.

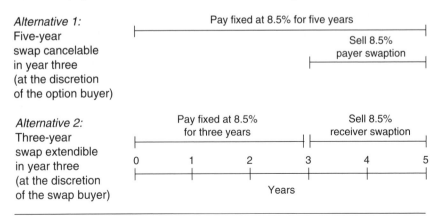

Alternative 1: Five-year swap cancelable in year three (at the discretion of the option buyer)

Alternative 2: Three-year swap extendible in year three (at the discretion of the swap buyer)

were exercised, the company would be forced to pay fixed to the buyer of the receiver swaption for another two years, extending the swap. A rise in rates would end the swap after three years.

The exhibit shows how the company could achieve the same end in an alternate way: by entering a five-year swap and selling a payer swaption on a two-year swap starting at the end of year three. A rise in interest rates would result in the exercise of the swaption and the cancelation of the swap at the end of year three—the same result as in the previous case.

Selling swaptions, like selling any options, exposes the seller to unlimited risk. The writer of a swaption receives premium income, but also always achieves a less than optimal result. In the previous example, the company that paid fixed in a five-year swap and sold a payer swaption would want to continue to pay fixed if interest rates rise and cancel if interest rates fall. Instead, the swaption buyer will exercise the swaption in a way that ensures the opposite result. For this reason, swaption writing applications are less popular than buying applications.

Arbitrage/Hedging Applications

Swaptions can be used to modify fixed- and floating-rate debt as well as swaps. The mechanics are similar; only the underlying positions are different.

The most prominent application involves an issuer selling a receiver swaption to offset the call on a callable bond (see Chapter 31 of *The Derivatives Engineering Workbook*). This was the first application and is still the most common, not only in the U.S. dollar swaption market but in other markets as well. The issuer of callable debt sells a receiver swaption with an exercise date and maturity matching that of the call. If interest rates fall and the swaption buyer elects to receive fixed, the issuer calls the debt. Instead of paying fixed to the original investor, the issuer pays the swaption buyer.

For the issuer to access below-market funds, he or she must receive more for the swaption than he or she pays for the call. Typically, the bond investor undervalues the call, the issuer takes on credit exposure, or both. For instance, if a BBB-rated investor sold a call to an AAA-rated issuer, who in turn sold a matching receiver swaption, credit reasons alone would dictate that the swaption carry a higher price than the call. The buyer of the receiver swaption is exposed to an AAA-rated credit, while the issuer (the buyer of the call) must accept a BBB-rated credit.

Another hedging application actively marketed by U.S. banks is the use of receiver swaptions by investors to hedge the call options embedded in bonds. A significant proportion of bonds—especially older bonds in the U.S. domestic market—carry call protection. Any decline in interest rates will trigger action by borrowers to call the bonds. Investors can hedge this risk by buying receiver swaptions. As the bonds are called, investors will receive fixed from the swaption sellers rather than the bondholders. This strategy is especially popular among insurance companies.

Multiple Swaption Applications

A final category of applications is complex blends of debt, swaps, swaptions, and other options that combine to create a structure that takes advantage of the preferences and indifferences of a particular customer. Marketing these complex packages can be difficult. Customers may be unaware of the choices they are implicitly making and unsure about the ultimate structure they want. Often borrowers must be bombarded with many possible bond, swap, and swaption combinations before they decide which provides the proper mix of reward and risk. Nevertheless, it is these complicated structures that provide the best returns for swap intermediaries.

One example was the $100 million Transamerica Finance issue in April of 1989. The structure required the issuer to sell callable debt, then write two swaptions∇one payer and one receiver swaption. This combination of swaptions allowed Transamerica to monetize its indifference to two aspects of the borrowing. One was the term, which would be either four or six years; the other was the rate basis, which could be either four years at the commercial-paper rate or two years at CP followed by four years at a fixed rate. In return for taking on this uncertainty, the cost of Transamerica's funds was reduced by the amount of the two swaption premiums.

Conclusion

Swaptions are the newest and fastest-growing generic interest-rate hedging product. But increasingly, swaptions, like swaps and caps before them, are becoming low-margin commodities. The life cycle of swaptions is apt to follow the course set by other options products, such as caps. The "easy" profits have probably already been made, but synergistic uses of the product are likely to continue to create profitable opportunities in a variety of applications.

Most successful large banks combine capabilities in both financial engineering and trading. Knowledge of financial engineering allows a bank to develop customized rate risk-management solutions and charge a premium for the value added. Trading capabilities enable the bank to become a low-cost producer of the generic cash, swap, and option products that are the building blocks of more complex packages. Superior hedging technology will likely separate the winners and losers in the long run, as spreads tighten and pinpoint pricing becomes essential.

A combination of financial engineering and trading permits a bank to appeal to a broad range of customers. For example, a single bank with well-developed financial engineering and trading capabilities could conceivably earn profits on swaption products offered to the World Bank, Transamerica Finance, and a $100 million dollar manufacturing company. The World Bank would simply unbundle the deal and bid out all of the pieces necessary to create the desired structure. The intermediary offering the low-cost swaption—probably the bank with the most well-developed trading capability—would win the bid. In the case of Transamerica Finance, the bank's financial engineering skills as well as the individual pieces would provide the return. The bank could draw profits from the underlying issue, the swap, and the two swaptions, as well as a fee for structuring the entire package. The middle market equivalent might simply be a cancelable swap, which would offer the intermediary more pricing flexibility than a straight swap.

The Swap Market

Reading the Signs

A relationship officer is charged with marketing dozens of products. How can he or she find the time and resources to follow a single specialized market? In the case of swaps, the answer lies in creating a simple system to monitor swap market trends—and developing the product knowledge needed to interpret trends in light of customer needs.

Bankers who know how to monitor and interpret interest-rate swap spreads can uncover opportunities to sell swap products. Every move in swap and credit spreads has marketing implications. Every shift favors certain swap applications and thwarts others. By understanding how market moves enhance or diminish the appeal of swaps, bankers can often create marketing opportunities even when the swap market is moribund.

This chapter answers three questions:

- What does a shift in swap spreads mean for your customer?

- What market conditions signal swap opportunities?

- Finally, what are the best sources of timely information on the swap market?

How to Read Swap Spreads

Swaps enable customers to change the interest-rate sensitivity of assets or liabilities. By receiving fixed in a swap, an investor who anticipates a fall in interest rates can transform a floating-rate asset into a fixed-rate asset; a borrower who anticipates the same fall in rates can use the same swap to switch from fixed to floating liabilities. (See Exhibits 1 and 2.)

Why would a customer use a swap to perform these transformations? The reason is simple: increased profitability. A customer will do a swap if it offers the highest-yield or lowest-cost route to a desired asset or liability. The challenge for bankers is knowing when this is the case.

The key to monitoring swap spreads is this: Whether the customer is an investor or a borrower, he or she wants to receive more and pay less. The swap spread is the rate over Treasuries a customer receives or pays. If the swap spread is high, he wants to receive it (receive fixed); if the swap spread is low, he wants to pay it (pay fixed).

Exhibit 1   Swap Terminology—Applications and Market Cues

	A Fixed-Rate Payer	A Fixed-Rate Receiver
Terminology	Pays (provides) fixed; receives floating	Receives fixed; pays floating
	Buys a swap; is long a swap	Sells a swap; is short a swap
	Is short the bond market	Is long the bond market
Product Application	Has used a swap to transform a fixed-rate asset into a floating-rate asset (investors)	Has used a swap to transform a floating-rate asset into a fixed-rate asset (investors)
	Has used a swap to transform floating-rate debt into fixed-rate debt	Has used a swap to transform fixed-rate debt into floating-rate debt
Market Cues	Thinks interest rates will rise	Thinks interest rates will fall
	Likes low swap spreads (relative to credit spreads)	Likes high swap spreads (relative to credit spreads)

A marketing opportunity exists when swap spreads are high and the customer thinks interest rates are coming down. Both investors and borrowers will be anxious to receive the high swap rate: the investor to create a fixed-rate asset, the borrower to create a floating-rate liability.

Similarly, an opportunity appears when swap spreads are low and the customer thinks interest rates are headed up. An investor will pay the low swap rate and receive floating, creating a high-yielding floating-rate asset. Borrowers will pay the low swap rate and receive floating, creating cheap fixed-rate debt.

The Role of Credit Spreads

What exactly do "high" and "low" mean? U.S. dollar swap spreads are expressed as basis points over Treasuries (quoted in terms of semiannual bond-equivalent yield). From a customer's viewpoint, however, a low swap spread is not always the same as a low spread over Treasuries.

The customer compares the return or cost of a swap to his or her own investment or borrowing alternatives. For an investor, a narrow swap spread is low relative to the credit spread on a bond he or she holds; for a borrower, narrow means low relative to the credit spread on a borrowing over the same maturity.

For instance, a borrower seeking fixed-rate funds would pay fixed in a swap. Because the borrower pays fixed, he or she likes low swap spreads. The total cost is the swap rate plus the spread over LIBOR. But if the borrower can borrow at an even lower rate by issuing a bond, he or she has no incentive to swap.

Similarly, an investor seeking to transform a bond into a floating-rate asset also pays fixed and likes low spreads. But if he or she can buy a higher-yielding floating-rate asset of similar quality through a direct purchase, the investor will do so.

Interpreting swap spreads always involves comparing two alternatives: a swap and a direct investment or borrowing. To know when a customer will be willing to swap, you must know the customer's investment or financing alternatives. The information needed for each type of customer is summarized in Exhibit 3.

Market Clues to Swap Opportunities

The only sure way to know whether a swap makes sense is to run the numbers. However, certain market signals precede any burst of swap activity.

A general rule: Swaps occur when bond yields are changing. Yields change when views of market participants diverge. Buyers think prices are

Exhibit 2   Swap Applications in a Rising Rate Environment

When customers expect the yield curve to rise...

...both fixed-rate investors and floating-rate borrowers...

...can pay fixed in a swap...

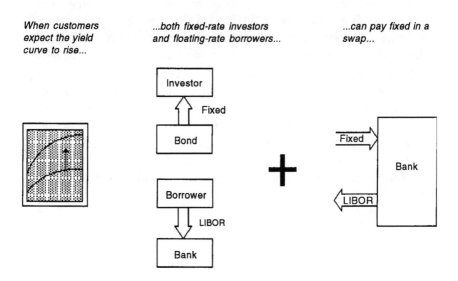

...and create a floating-rate asset or a fixed-rate liability.

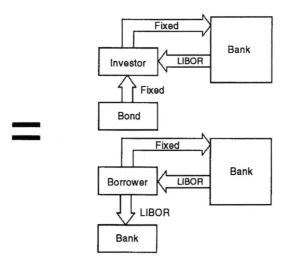

too low; sellers, too high. Substitute "fixed-rate receivers" for buyers and "fixed-rate payers" for sellers and the same two viewpoints create a two-way swap market.

A shift in the U.S. Treasury yield curve affects swaps in another way. Treasury bonds are far more liquid than corporate bonds. A price change in Treasuries does not always trigger the same price change in corporates. When U.S. Treasury prices change, swap and credit spreads may be temporarily thrown out of sync. This creates swap opportunities.

Although swaps occur when the yield curve is rising, swaps are more likely to occur when the curve is falling. In a rising yield curve environment, the volume of bond issues declines. No borrower wants to issue into a sinking market. The supply of receivers may dry up, while payers may wait for a rally to lock in fixed rates.

Swap opportunities will emerge from any sudden change in the price of a specific debt security, or specific class of securities, as opposed to an overall market change. The collapse of FRN prices created an entire new source of high-yielding synthetic fixed-rate securities. And the practice of stripping warrants from bonds—depressing prices and boosting yields—has prompted investors to pay fixed in a swap and create LIBOR-based assets with higher-than-market yields.

In the same way, any sudden change in a customer's borrowing cost will affect his or her decision to use a swap. The flight to quality immediately after 1987's equity crash pulled in spreads on the debt of top-class borrowers, but not on debt of lower-rated entities. In some cases, both high- and low-rated borrowers saw the difference between their borrowing costs and swap spreads increase. This provided a greater incentive to swap.

A high volume of dollar Eurobond issues implies swap activity. A good proportion of Eurobond issues is swap-driven. The issuers become fixed-rate receivers in a swap, often as the prelude to a swap from U.S. dollar LIBOR into another currency. A high volume of Eurobond issues suggests a surplus of receivers and narrowing swap spreads. This creates opportunities for payers—especially those who believe fixed rates are near a bottom.

Similarly, news of large floating-rate borrowings may signal the emergence of potential fixed-rate payers. To the extent that these borrowers wish to diversify the rate sensitivity of their debt, they may be waiting for a window to swap into fixed.

Changes in the absolute level of swap spreads (or the price of Eurodollar futures contracts in the shorter maturities) may indicate potential swap business as well. Swap spreads generally rise and fall with credit spreads. But not always. A surplus of receivers or payers may cause swap spreads to widen or narrow independently of credit spreads.

A typical situation: A borrower issues fixed-rate paper and seeks to receive fixed in a swap. No fixed-rate payer can be found. A swap dealer takes the position—agrees to pay fixed—and hedges himself or herself in the cash market. As more and more receivers seek to enter the market, swap spreads decline and opportunities for payers increase. However, there has been no change in credit spreads.

During 1989, all of the previously mentioned market conditions preceded swap activity. Uncertainty and a falling yield curve brought armies of fixed-rate payers into the market immediately after the equity crash. A high volume of Eurobond issuance during the February–March rally boosted the number of fixed-rate receivers and pulled in swap spreads. Although a rising yield curve has curtailed swap activity, narrow spreads and fear of rising rates have brought some fixed-rate payers into the market.

Sources of Information

There are three sources of information on the swap market: swap desks, terminal-based systems such as Reuters and Telerate, and print publications.

The best way to follow the market is to stay in touch with in-house swap personnel. The staff of a swap desk know the story behind the quoted swap spread. They know where the spread has been and have an idea where the spread is going. They know which side of the bid-offer spread is firm and which side is soft. And because they monitor the bond market as well, they know the level of credit spreads and may be able to point out specific swap opportunities.

Swap spreads are available on the Reuters and Telerate terminal-based systems. On Reuters, the page is EBSW; on Telerate, 6492 and 17440. These pages are provided by Eurobrokers and Tullet & Tokyo, two interbank swap brokers.

Coverage of swaps in the print media is sparse. Salomon Brothers' monthly *Review of International Financial Markets* contains swap and credit spreads. *International Financing Review (IFR)*, a weekly London-based financial magazine, publishes U.S. dollar interest-rate swap spreads and brief summaries of activity in each of the major swap markets. In a separate section, *IFR* contains credit spreads for new issues in the U.S. domestic and Eurobond markets. *Swaps Monitor*, a New York–based biweekly newsletter, also publishes swap spreads and commentary on the major swap markets. Finally, *Markets & Marketing* publishes a chart comparing swap and credit spreads each month.

Because swap market activity flows from bond market events, a good source of information is newspaper coverage of the bond market. Both the *Financial Times* and *The Wall Street Journal* offer daily commentary on the U.S. domestic and Eurobond markets, including credit spreads on new issues.

With a Standard & Poor's bond guide for maturity dates and a daily newspaper for prices, and using an HP calculator to compute yields, it is easy to calculate credit spreads on secondary market issues by specific customers. Combined with a knowledge of how swaps and bonds interact, this should be sufficient to draw general conclusions on potential swap opportunities.

Exhibit 3   Determining the Suitability of a Swap

	Fixed-rate payer	Fixed-rate receiver
Investor	Credit spread on bond held	Spread over LIBOR on floating-rate asset held
	Swap spread	Swap spread
	Spread over LIBOR desired	Credit spread on bond desired
Borrower	Spread over LIBOR on borrowing	Credit spread on fixed-rate issue
	Swap spread	Swap spread
	Credit spread on fixed-rate issue	Spread over LIBOR desired

13

Swap Spreads
Implications for Marketers

For much of the early and mid-1990s, U.S. dollar swap spreads—the spread above a benchmark Treasury rate at which end-users can enter into a swap as either the payer or receiver of a fixed rate—have been historically narrow. These low spreads are presenting bankers with good opportunities to arrange attractive financing rates for their customers. For liquidity reasons, the United States is currently the only swap market that routinely quotes swap prices as a spread over an underlying benchmark (i.e., Treasuries); most other swap markets continue to quote prices on an all-in basis. This is changing, however, particularly in Germany, Australia, France, and England. As futures markets develop and spread pricing becomes more prevalent in these countries, an understanding of the mechanics behind swap spreads will be useful in creating financial solutions for customers.

This chapter discusses some of the technical factors behind how swap spreads are determined, examines the market-driven reasons for the current level of swap spreads, and outlines several ways that relationship managers can capitalize on these spreads to bring value-added service to their customers.

What Drives Swap Spreads

What drives swap spreads depends on the maturity. One way swaps can be classified is by maturity: those swaps that fall within the futures market maturities (for instance, five years in the U.S. dollar market), and those swaps that have maturities longer than that of the futures market.

Inside the Futures Contract Dates

Most market makers can hedge a swap position in several ways. By far the most liquid, and therefore cheapest, method is to create an offsetting position in the futures market. In the United States, this means using the three-month Eurodollar futures contract, the most liquid and widely traded futures instrument in the world. These futures contracts incorporate all available market information and therefore represent the market's "best guess" as to where interest rates will be in the future.

Summary Sheet: Interest-Rate Swaps

End-Users	Companies that (1) seek to swap from fixed to floating, (2) want attractive synthetic fixed-rate financing, or (3) wish to lock in attractive swap spread levels
Intermediaries	Market-making commercial and investment banks
How Banks Profit	Bid-offer spread (5 to 10 basis points on "plain vanilla" swaps)
Major Players	Money center commercial and investment banks, large regional banks
Deal Size	Negotiable; average swap notional amounts of $10 to $50 million
Maturities	Very liquid out to five years, good liquidity in seven years, less liquid for longer maturities or highly structured deals
Fees	None unless associated with a structured transaction
Credit Considerations	Counterparty risk on all transactions. Many banks ask for collateral or margin accounts and periodic mark-to-market settlements.
Competition/ Life Cycle	Competition intense. As swap spreads and overall levels shift, marketing opportunities change and constantly repeat.

Importantly, the Eurodollar futures contract is a measurement of where LIBOR is expected to be. LIBOR, which stands for London Inter-Bank Offer Rate, is the rate at which banks are theoretically willing to do business with each other. LIBOR is also the benchmark rate for many corporate bank revolvers.

Because swap market makers can re-create a swap position with Eurodollar futures, for maturities within the futures contract dates, the quoted swap rate should be the same as (or very close to) quoted cash LIBOR, and this, in fact, is the case.

When quoting a swap rate as a spread over Treasuries within the futures contract dates, therefore, the swap spread simply represents the difference between LIBOR and Treasuries. This difference is known as the TED spread, or Treasury-Eurodollar spread. Exhibit 1 shows a graph of the TED spread, using recent market rates.

If Treasuries represent a risk-free rate, then the price of any instrument quoted as a spread over Treasuries represents a risk premium tied to the risk of default of that instrument. Because LIBOR is the rate at which banks can borrow, the TED spread and, therefore, swap spreads represent the market's perceptions as to bank risk.

Also contributing to the general level of LIBOR will be corporate demand for LIBOR-based funding. A heavy demand for LIBOR funding from corporates will increase the marginal demand for LIBOR from the banks, and the level of LIBOR will rise accordingly.

Exhibit 1   Typical TED Spread (August 1993)

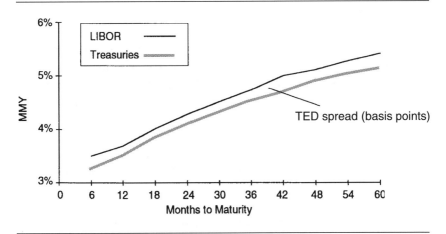

From this perspective, the graph in Exhibit 1 has two implications. Given the narrowness of the TED spread (30 basis points at its widest), we can imply that (1) the market perceives little systemic bank risk at this time and (2) LIBOR-based funding demand from U.S. corporates is low. Most major banks are currently comfortably profitable, and a prolonged recession has worked to reduce short-term capital demand from U.S. corporations. This is reflected in the narrow TED spread.

It should be noted that while Eurodollar futures contracts go out five years, liquidity drops off significantly in the fifth year. Swap spreads for five years begin to be more influenced by corporate bond spreads and other factors, as discussed in the next section.

In September of 1993, the Chicago Mercantile Exchange launched a three-month Eurodollar futures contract with a seven-year maturity. This contract is meant to fill the gap created when the U.S. Treasury announced that it would no longer issue or auction seven-year Treasury notes. As liquidity builds, the pricing of both five- and seven-year swaps should become more efficient.

Outside the Futures Contract Dates

Swap spreads outside the futures contract dates are affected by other market forces. Historically, swap spreads have tended to track a range with a general minimum and maximum of the spread over Treasuries where double-A and single-A corporations can issue public bonds of comparable maturity. This makes intuitive sense if swaps are thought of as a fixed-rate funding alternative to public bonds: If swap spreads were significantly different from bond spreads, the logic of comparative advantage would dictate that issuers would access the cheaper market.

Over the past few years, however, this relationship has fallen apart. Exhibit 2 shows five-year swap spreads compared to bond spreads for single-A and double-A corporate issuers over the past four years. As the graph illustrates, swap spreads are now tighter than those of double-A corporates and may even approach the level of triple-A issues. Three market-driven factors as to why swap spreads have dropped out of the single A–double A bond spread "band" may be: (1) the emergence of triple A–rated swap dealing vehicles; (2) the increased use of collateral, margin accounts and periodic mark-to-market settlement; and (3) a general increase in market competitiveness.

Supply and demand also significantly affect swap spreads. If there is heavy demand from corporates to pay the fixed rate, this will work to widen

Exhibit 2   Bond Spreads and Five-Year Swap Spreads

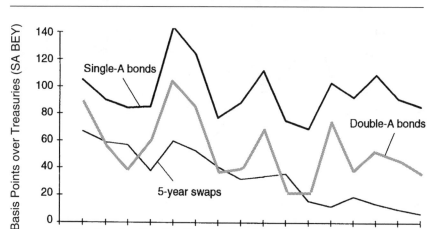

or increase swap spreads, and the reverse is also true (as is the case now). A further influence on swap spreads will be the cost of financing the swap for the market maker. This is a somewhat technical effect, influenced by the price of the underlying Treasury, which of the available benchmark Treasuries is being used to quote the swap price, and market conditions within the Treasury repurchase ("repo") market.

Current Market Conditions
As both Exhibits 2 and 3 show, swap spreads have declined significantly over the past several years and are currently trading at or near all-time lows. There are several reasons for this.

The Shape and Level of the Yield Curve
Interest rates in the United States, due to the prolonged recession, are very low. At the same time, the yield curve remains very positively and steeply sloped. In other words, there is a significant premium associated with lengthening maturities on liabilities (i.e., swapping from floating-rate debt to fixed). Because many corporates are currently unwilling to pay this premium, there has been little demand to swap into fixed, which has kept swap spreads narrow.

Exhibit 3   Historical TED spread levels

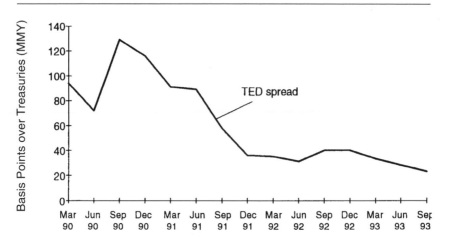

Expectations Regarding Future Rate Movement

The slope of the yield curve implies a fairly rapid rise in short-term rates over the next several years. Most corporations, however, do not believe this yield curve and are confident that rates will not rise quickly anytime soon. As a result, most corporations with the choice are choosing to continue funding themselves with short-term floating-rate debt. Because this means little to no demand to swap from floating-rate debt into fixed-rate debt, there is no upward pressure on swap spreads.

Attractive Corporate Bond Spreads

As Exhibit 2 shows, investment grade companies that do want to raise fixed-rate debt can do so at very attractive all-in rates as well as at attractive spreads over Treasuries. This has been reflected in the enormous amount of debt issuance over the past 12 months.

At the same time, although the all-in rate achieved through the bond issuance is attractive from an historical perspective, it still represents a significant premium over short-term borrowing rates. As a result, much of the corporate bond issuance has been swapped from fixed rates back into floating-rate debt. This means that market makers have seen a heavy demand for them to pay fixed—which in turn has resulted in swap spreads narrowing. (The more demand to pay fixed, the lower the fixed rate the bank will be willing to pay.)

Improved Efficiency in the Swap Market

A more general reason behind the decline in swap rates is the increased competition and efficiency in the swap market. The market in many countries has developed to the point that "plain vanilla" swaps have become a commodity product. This has worked to squeeze the bid-offer spread to around 5 to 10 basis points in most maturities and has put a general downward pressure on the overall level of swap spreads.

Marketing Opportunities for Relationship Managers

It is true that the shape of the yield curve and general market expectations have resulted in very low demand from corporates to swap from floating to fixed, which is the traditional corporate usage. The current narrowness of swap spreads, however, does provide several opportunities for other swap-related business.

Swaps from Fixed into Floating

The most obvious strategy that can be discussed with companies is that of "reverse swapping," or swapping from a fixed-rate liability to a floating rate. As discussed previously, this has been the most active swap market, driven mainly by new primary debt issuances. Though the narrowness of swap spreads dictates that the fixed rate the company will receive is lower than if swap spreads were wider, the attractiveness of being at the short end of the yield curve more than makes up for this.

Relationship managers should be examining the fixed/floating-debt mix of their customers and investigating whether there is interest in increasing the floating-rate percentage of debt. Although there are signs that the economy is slowly recovering, many corporations still do not believe that interest rates will rise quickly and prefer to borrow at short-term floating rates.

A number of variations on the fixed-to-floating swap are particularly relevant given the tightness of swap spreads. As Exhibit 2 implies, even double-A credits cannot routinely use swaps to obtain floating-rate funding at near-LIBOR levels, because the receipt on the swap is too low relative to the payment on the bond. For many borrowers, this may not matter. Although the swap may not offer arbitrage opportunities, it does offer flexibility and convenience, giving end-users the means to restructure the debt mix quickly in response to changes in market conditions and the borrower's own expectations. However, borrowers seeking ways of cutting floating-rate funding costs to the bone—even if it means taking on some risk—have used several structures to increase the receipt on the swap, decrease the payment on the fixed-rate debt, or both:

- *Mismatch the maturities of the swap and underlying debt to take advantage of the steep yield curve.* Here the swap can have a longer maturity than the underlying fixed-rate borrowing to increase the amount of the swap receipt. Because the yield curve flattens as maturities lengthen, the benefits of this structure diminish with the term of the debt. Moreover, once the underlying debt matures, the borrower is left with an unhedged swap, although the borrower could unwind the swap position as market conditions change.

- *Sell an embedded option to the investor.* Here the borrower obtains a narrower spread on the fixed-rate debt by selling, for instance, a put. The risk is that interest rates will rise and the investor will put the debt back to the borrower, leaving the borrower with an unhedged position in the swap. At this point the swap will also be registering a loss. This put position could be hedged, however, or perhaps even arbitraged in the swaption market.

- *Extend maturities in order to exploit anomalies in the relationship between swap and bond spreads.* In August of 1993 several borrowers swapped from fixed to floating at the 12- and 15-year maturities, where swap spreads were significantly wider (due to illiquidity) but bond spreads were little different from what they were in shorter terms.

Swapping into Fixed for Lower-Rated Companies

Bond spreads in the public debt market remain highly tiered. That is, lower-rated companies must pay noticeably higher bond spreads to place public debt successfully. While investors remain very yield-hungry due to the general low level of interest rates, the swap market, much like the bank loan market, does not differentiate for credit risk to the same extent as the public bond market. This means attractive financing opportunities for lower-rated companies, which happen to constitute a large percentage of the corporate customer base of most banks.

Exhibit 4 shows how a lower-rated company could achieve attractive fixed-rate funding. As a triple–B–rated borrower in the current market, XYZ can issue a public five-year fixed-rate bond at approximately 100 basis points over the five-year Treasury. It can also borrow under its bank revolver at six-month LIBOR + 0.25%. As shown in Exhibit 3, the five-year swap spread is approximately 25 basis points. By borrowing under the revolver and fixing via a swap, XYZ achieves an all-in fixed-rate of:

Exhibit 4   Achieving an Attractive Fixed Rate Via the Swap Market

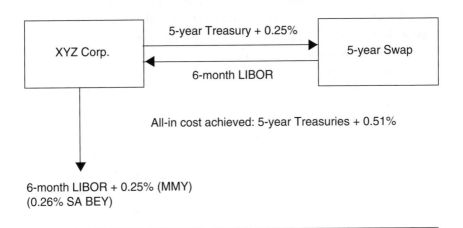

Pays on the revolver: (6-month LIBOR + 0.25%) (0.26% on SA BEY basis)
Receives on the swap: 6-month LIBOR
Pays on the swap: (5-year Treasury + 0.25%) (SA BEY basis)

All-in fixed-rate cost: 5-Year Treasury + 0.51% (Savings of 49 basis points over public market issuance)

In the current market environment, there may not be much demand for raising fixed-rate funding, but given the attractive levels available, relationship managers should be asking their customers to position themselves now in order to capitalize on this opportunity. Once rates do begin to rise and the market believes the rise is real, there will be an increased demand for swapping into a fixed rate, and this will widen swap spreads.

Purchasing Spreadlocks

Many banks can now offer customers swap spreadlocks. These enable customers to enter into a swap at a guaranteed spread over Treasuries for a predetermined period of time. In light of the current narrowness of swap spreads, this product has gained increased attention. Chapter 14 of *The Derivatives Enginneering Workbook* contains an example illustrating spreadlock usage.

For example, if XYZ Corporation ultimately wants a fixed-rate liability and likes the current level of swap spreads but believes that there is still room for Treasury rates to come down, it may be interested in purchasing a spreadlock that allows it to enter into the swap any time, say, over the next six months at a guaranteed spread over Treasuries that is set today.

With the spreadlock in hand, XYZ can now watch the underlying Treasury market over the next six months and, when it believes that rates have finally bottomed out, can enter into the swap at the predetermined spread over Treasuries.

This can be an attractive product to show to companies, but there are several aspects of spreadlocks of which relationship managers and their customers should be aware. The first is that the spread quoted in the spreadlock may not and probably will not be the current spread level. Rather, it will be a reflection of the current spread plus the cost of financing the Treasury underlying the swap on which the spreadlock is based. For example, although current five-year swap spreads are around 25 basis points, a six-month spreadlock might be quoted at, say, 30 to 31 basis points.

A second and more important factor is that many banks are reluctant to quote a spreadlock unless the customer guarantees that it will in fact enter into the swap prior to expiration. This presents two risks to the customer:

1. that spreads will actually narrow during the spreadlock period;
2. that Treasuries, which account for a far higher proportion of the swap rate than the spread, will rise during the spreadlock period.

Conclusion

The current narrow level of swap spreads is predominantly a market-driven phenomenon, dictated by the steep yield curve, low interest rates, heavy public bond issuance (which may then be swapped back to floating), and a lack of corporate interest in paying fixed. These market conditions may continue for some time. Nevertheless, relationship managers should be investigating the opportunities available in the current market for lower-rated companies seeking fixed-rate debt, for companies looking to increase the percentage of floating-rate debt on their books, and for companies that like the current level of swap spreads but believe rates will continue to fall. Understanding and tracking swap spreads is one way to stay abreast of these current market opportunities and bring value-added solutions to customers.

PART III

Foreign Exchange Derivatives

The management of foreign exchange risk following the collapse of Bretton Woods provided one of the first arenas for the development of modern derivatives. Rather than review the basics of currency futures and forwards, these four chapters discuss a range of more sophisticated and lesser-known currency risk management techniques.

The typical currency risk manager spreads purchases of foreign exchange contracts among several banks, holding mini-auctions to choose the low-cost provider in each case. Chapter 14 discusses an alternative, trigger swaps, which offers hedgers several advantages. First, these swaps offer a way to hedge separate but related exposures in one stroke. In doing so, hedgers can save on transaction costs by bundling several hedges into a single transaction. Finally, from the banker's perspective, these deals allow the bank to capture a large piece of the customer's business without bidding on multiple transactions.

Chapters 15 through 17 cover a wide range of end-user applications of currency options. Chapter 15 covers the basics. Chapters 16 and 17 explain the proliferation of customized options designed around the tradeoffs between cost and coverage: average rate, deferred-strike, barrier, lookback and installment options. Together with the applications in The Derivatives Engineering Workbook, *these chapters offer a comprehensive introduction to a wide array of currency option structures.*

14

Trigger Swaps
Combining Derivatives to Hedge
Multiple Exposures

*What Benefits Do Trigger Swaps Offer Bank Clients and
Relationship Managers?*

Many corporations face rate exposure in more than one market. Relationship managers often consider these exposures in isolation to each other—that is, they look at a company's foreign-exchange risk, interest-rate risk, and commodity risk independently. Treasurers may view these risks independently as well, and the hedging activities chosen often do not consider the overall strategic risk exposure.

As the derivatives markets have developed, however, banks and corporations are increasingly looking for ways to hedge more than one risk simultaneously. The advantages of doing so are obvious: The company can take a more strategic approach to its hedging activity (by making it easier to hedge the overall exposures of a company rather than each exposure separately), and there is significant potential for the reduction of documentation, counterparty risk, and transaction costs.

One of the more interesting techniques in multiple hedging is the trigger swap, also known as a semifixed swap. These swaps can be constructed in several ways and with many variations, but they have one common purpose:

Summary Sheet: Trigger Swaps

End-Users	Any corporation or financial institution with price or rate exposure in more than one market (e.g., interest rates, foreign-exchange rates, or commodity prices)
Intermediaries	Commercial and investment banks
How Banks Profit	Bid-offer spread; prices slightly higher than sum of plain vanilla derivatives deals combined to form the trigger swap
Spreads/Fees	Slightly higher than for plain vanilla deals in the individual markets; banks that can offer binary or digital option structures earn more due to less competition.
Deal Size	Customized to customer needs; average of $10–$50 million
Maturity	Typically two to five years; limited by illiquidity in commodity and long-dated FX forward markets
Major Players	Any financial institution with derivatives capabilities in multiple markets can be a competitive player.
Risk Factors	Same as for standard, single-market derivative transactions
Competition/ Life Cycle	Components are mature (except for binary options), but combining them to hedge multiple risks is still relatively new.

combining instruments from more than one market to create an instrument that hedges multiple exposures. The most common combine an interest-rate hedge with a foreign-exchange hedge, an interest-rate hedge with a commodity hedge, or a commodity hedge with a foreign-exchange hedge. The primary advantages from the relationship manager's perspective are that they are easy to structure, easy to understand, and easy to explain to clients.

How Can Corporations Use Trigger Swaps to Hedge Multiple Exposures?

Consider a corporation that generates a substantial portion of its revenues from exports—for example, an Australian beer producer with sizable export revenues from the United States. Most of the beer producer's costs are in Australian dollars. In this simple example, the Australian company has exposure to Australian interest rates and to the U.S. dollar/Australian dollar exchange rate. Specifically, when the U.S. dollar is strong, export revenues are high (in Australian dollar terms); when the U.S. dollar is weak, export revenues are low (in Australian dollar terms). If a bank could structure an instrument that tied the company's financing costs to the level of the U.S. dollar, that bank will have helped the company to hedge multiple exposures—interest rates and foreign exchange. This would result in a much smoother operating performance for the company. One instrument that would accomplish this would be a semifixed interest-rate swap with an FX trigger, or, more simply, an FX-trigger swap.

Extending this logic, any company with significant exposures in more than one market is a candidate for a trigger swap. Some examples are shown in Exhibit 1. In general, a trigger swap will be structured so that the gains in one market will offset losses in the other market. With the Australian beer company, the trigger swap would be structured so that the fixed rate on the swap increases when the U.S. dollar strengthens against the Australian dollar. The higher cost on the swap would be offset by the increased Australian dollar value of the U.S. dollar export revenues. Likewise, the swap rate would fall when the U.S. dollar weakens versus the Australian dollar, because lower export revenues would be offset by lower interest expense. In this way the Australian beer company could work to smooth its overall operating performance—a strategic advantage in making projections, allocating resources, and enticing prospective shareholders.

How Are Trigger Swaps Structured?

Trigger swaps are created by embedding forwards or options from one market (for instance, foreign exchange) into a swap in another market (for instance, interest rates). The gains or losses from the embedded forwards or options are then used to adjust the fixed rate on the swap. This adjustment is why these instruments are also called "semifixed" swaps: the fixed rate will adjust each reset period depending on the value of the embedded forward or option. An illustration of this is shown in Exhibit 2.

The simplest way to create a trigger swap is by using forwards. In the example of the Australian beer company, a "flat-rate FX forward" on the U.S. dollar/Australian dollar exchange rate would be embedded into an Australian dollar interest-rate swap. Suppose the company currently borrows on a floating, BBR- (Australian bank bills) based rate. The relevant swap and foreign-exchange rates are:

Exhibit 1   Multiple Exposures and Corresponding Trigger Swaps

Company Profile	Multiple Exposures	Appropriate Trigger Swap
German-based exporter	DM interest rates DM/US$ exchange rate	Semifixed DM interest rate swap with DM/US$ trigger
Australian aluminum producer	Aluminum prices US$/A$ exchange rate	Semifixed aluminum swap with US$/A$ trigger
U.S. airline	US$ interest rates Jet fuel prices	Semifixed US$ interest rate swap with jet fuel trigger
U.S.-based importer of Japanese electronics	US$ interest rates ¥/US$ exchange rates	Semifixed US$ interest rate swap with ¥/US$ trigger

---

2-year A$ plain vanilla swap rate   5.63% (quarterly, A/365)

2-year US$/A$ flat rate forward   US$0.7110:A$1

The swap rate is created from the Australian dollar forward-interest-rate curve, while the flat-rate forward is determined by taking the forward exchange rates every three months over the two-year period and determining an equivalent "flat rate" for the entire period. (It can be thought of as the foreign-exchange equivalent to an interest-rate swap, which is created by determining the equivalent "flat"-interest rate for a string of FRAs.) As an exporter with foreign-currency revenues, the company's natural exposure is "long" U.S. dollars. The company would therefore *sell* the flat-rate forward, guaranteeing a rate of US$0.7110:A$1 for a portion of its U.S. dollar revenues. The flat-rate forward is then embedded into the interest-rate swap. The results (also summarized in Exhibit 4) are:

- If the spot Australian dollar rate is above (weaker than) US$0.7110:A$1, the adjustment results in a lower financing cost as the client has made money on the forward contract.

- If the spot Australian dollar rate is below (stronger than) US$0.7110:A$1, the adjustment means a higher financing cost as the client has lost money on the forward contract.

A benefit of these types of structures is the leverage with respect to the flat-rate forward. It is not necessary to use a face value for the FX forward

Exhibit 2   A Generic Semifixed Swap

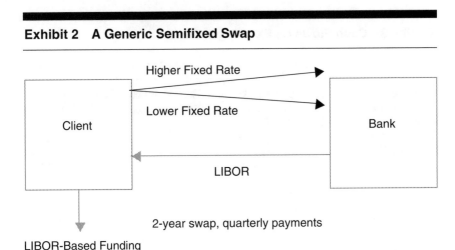

anywhere near as large as that of the underlying interest-rate swap. In this example, assume a notional swap face value of A$10 million and a flat rate forward amount of A$500,000 (that is, the company will be selling forward US$355,500, or A$500,000 × US$0.7110:A$1, at each of the eight quarterly forward dates at a rate of US$0.7110:A$1).

At each quarterly reset date, the spot U.S. dollar/Australian dollar exchange rate will be stronger, weaker or the same as the flat-rate forward rate of US$0.7110:A$1. Taking an example of each possible outcome, the resulting adjustment to the swap rate is shown in Exhibit 3. Relatively wide exchange-rate swings were chosen to illustrate the swap adjustment. If on a given reset date the U.S. dollar has strengthened (or the Australian dollar has weakened) to US$0.6000:A$1, then the Australian company has an increased borrowing cost of 5.63% + 3.70% = 9.33%. The company can afford this increased expense, however, because the stronger U.S. dollar means this exporter's U.S. sales are generating more Australian dollars.

Likewise, if the U.S. dollar weakens (or the Australian dollar strengthens) to US$0.8000:A$1 (thus reducing the Australian dollar value of U.S. export sales), the company will offset these lower revenues with a cheaper swap, in this case 5.63% − 2.23% = 3.40%.

This simple example shows how trigger swaps can be used to hedge not only the foreign-exchange transaction exposure (in this case, the value of the Australian company's U.S. dollar revenues), but also to hedge long-term competitive and economic exposure.

Exhibit 3   Cash Flows on FX-Trigger Swap

	US$ Strengthens	US$ Stable	US$ Weakens
Future Spot Rate	US$0.6000:A$1.00	US$0.7110:A$1.00	US$0.8000:A$1.00
Flat-Rate Forward	US$0.7110:A$1.00	US$0.7110:A$1.00	US$0.7110:A$1.00
Points Gain/(Loss)	(US$0.1110)/A$1.00	0	US$0.0890/A$1.00
A$ Face Value	A$500,000	A$500,000	A$500,000
US$ Gain/(Loss)	(US$55,500)	0	US$44,500
A$ Gain/(Loss) at	(A$92,500)	0	A$55,625
Future Spot Rate			
A$ Notional Principal	A$10,000,000	A$10,000,000	A$10,000,000
Interest Calculation	$\dfrac{(A\$\,92,500)}{(10,000,000)} \times 4 = -0.0370$		$\dfrac{(A\$\,55,625)}{(10,000,000)} \times 4 = -0.0223$
Adjustment	−3.70%	0%	2.23%

How Can Trigger Swaps Be Constructed Using Options?

Trigger swaps can also be constructed using options, and there are advantages to the customer in doing so. In the previous example, the Australian company faced a higher interest expense on the trigger swap when the U.S. dollar strengthened. The adjustment to the swap rate was unlimited, depending on how much the U.S. dollar rose. However, the use of options allows the company to reduce interest costs when the U.S. dollar weakens; it also puts a ceiling on the maximum cost if the U.S. dollar strengthens. This structure can be created using two different kinds of options: ordinary puts and calls, and binary or digital options.

ORDINARY PUTS AND CALLS

Rather than selling a flat-rate forward, the Australian company could have purchased a series of put options on the U.S. dollar (or call options on the Australian dollar), all struck at US$ 0.7110:A$1. Rather than pay an up-front premium, the company would amortize the premium and embed the payment into the fixed-interest rate on the swap.

Suppose the per-annum cost of the options is 1.25%. The company has now locked in a higher fixed-interest cost on the swap, in this case 5.63% + 1.25% = 6.88%, but knows in advance that its fixed cost on the swap will never be higher than this rate. Meanwhile, the company will still achieve a lower fixed rate when the U.S. dollar weakens. The resulting payout, which is illustrated in Exhibit 5, can be summarized as follows:

Exhibit 4   A Semi-fixed A$ Interest Rate Swap with US$/A$ Trigger

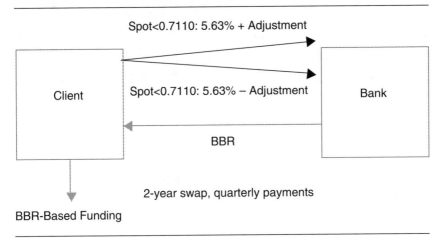

Spot<0.7110: 5.63% + Adjustment

Client

Spot<0.7110: 5.63% − Adjustment

Bank

BBR

2-year swap, quarterly payments

BBR-Based Funding

- If the U.S. dollar is below (i.e., is stronger than) US$0.7110:A$1, the company will not exercise its put options and will pay 6.88% on the swap.
- If the U.S. dollar is above (i.e., is weaker than) US$0.7110:A$1, the company will exercise its put options and use the gain on the option position to lower the interest rate on the swap.

Note that the option premium could also be reduced (thus lowering the maximum fixed cost on the interest-rate swap) by moving the strike price of the option further out of the money or by purchasing U.S. dollar call options (or Australian dollar put options) from the company, creating a collarlike structure.

BINARY OR DIGITAL OPTIONS

The trigger swap can also be structured using a more sophisticated option product known as a "binary" or "digital" option. Binary options are simply options in which the payout under the option, regardless of how deep in the money it may be on the exercise date, is fixed. In other words, the option is either "on" or "off" (thus the name "digital"), and if it is "on," the payout is a fixed amount.

In this strategy, the Australian company would buy a series of digital put options and sell a series of digital call options. The "at-the-money" flat-rate forward rate is used as the target strike price, but the strike prices for the puts and calls are adjusted slightly away from this target in order to achieve an

Exhibit 5   A Trigger Swap Using Put Options

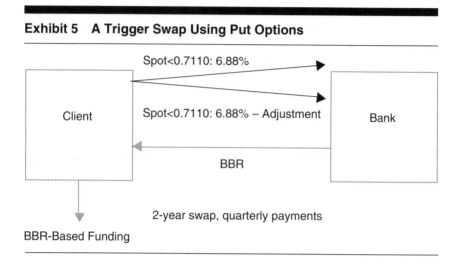

BBR-Based Funding

equal premium for both the puts and the calls. The company thus pays no net premium in structuring this deal. Assume for simplicity that the Australian company could construct a zero-premium deal in which both the digital calls and puts have a strike price of US$0.7110:A$1.

The payout on the digital options is known in advance, so the next step is to determine how wide a "range" the Australian company wants to pay on its swap. The notional amount of options can then be adjusted to achieve this range. For example, assume the company agrees to a 1.00% "swing" in its swap rate, depending on the U.S. dollar/Australian dollar exchange rate each reset date. Then the company's advisor can determine the number of digital puts and calls required to be sold to result in a 1.00% fixed payout upon exercise of the options.

The Australian company now has a situation that is illustrated in Exhibit 6 and can be summarized as follows:

- If the U.S. dollar is below (i.e., stronger than) US$0.7110:A$1, the company will not exercise its put options, but the call options it sold will be exercised. This exercise results in a fixed payout of 1.00%, and the company has a net interest cost for that quarter of 5.63% + 1.00% = 6.63% (remember that 5.63% was the plain vanilla market swap rate for two years).

- If the U.S. dollar is above (i.e., weaker than) US$0.7110:A$1, the call options that the company sold will not be exercised, but the company will exercise the put options it purchased. This exercise results in a fixed

Exhibit 6 Trigger Swap Using Binary Puts and Calls

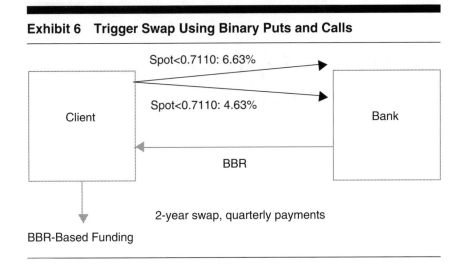

payment of 1.00%, and the company has a net interest cost for that quarter of 5.63% − 1.00% = 4.63%.

For a net premium of zero, the Australian beer company has linked its interest cost to the U.S. dollar/Australian dollar exchange rate (thus hedging multiple exposures) and knows in advance precisely what its interest expense will be for given exchange rates.

It is important to remember that regardless of the structure used (forwards, plain vanilla options, or binary options), the bank can adjust the strike prices and notional amounts in order to achieve exactly the payout profile desired by the company.

Summary: What Are the Key Points to Remember about Trigger Swaps?

Trigger swaps combine hedges of multiple exposures into a single instrument. Using trigger swaps, companies can hedge their overall exposures rather than each exposure separately, reducing documentation, counterparty risk, and transaction costs. Many companies already use interest-rate swaps and FX forwards separately to hedge interest rate and foreign-exchange risk. Trigger swaps simply package these products into one transaction, tailored by the banker to fit the exact payout profile desired. Doing so allows the relationship manager to charge a premium price while at the same time delivering to the customer a value-added hedge of multiple risk exposures.

15

Currency Options
Corporate Use Grows

An often neglected corporate hedging tool has experienced a surprising surge in popularity recently. Foreign-exchange options, considered by many an esoteric derivative of the highly active forward market, has emerged as a strong growth area within bank foreign-exchange departments. Hedging strategies that were formerly associated only with sophisticated treasuries have become standard. New strategies are being pioneered at a rapid pace.

The new life of the FX option has as much to do with its demystification as with any newfound usages. Bank foreign-exchange dealers have long insisted that FX options could enhance the practice of hedging without greatly complicating risk management. Resistance to the product has been attributable to the discomfort that many treasurers have had with the whole concept of options.

Growth of FX Options

In recent years, the use of foreign-exchange option transactions has grown among all classes of market participants. Options have gained not only in absolute terms, but also compared to spot, forward, futures, and other types of currency transactions.

According to a 1989 study by the Federal Reserve Bank of New York, the dollar value of options contracts traded in the United States rose more than sixfold between 1986 and 1989. The growth in volume was led by the surge in customized over-the-counter contracts, which grew to about 4% of turnover for commercial banks and 15% for other institutions (investment banks, insurance companies, corporations, etc.). In contrast, trading in FX futures declined by half between 1986 and 1989 for both classes of market participants.

Surveys focusing on corporate users of options show similar results. A Globecon survey of middle-market corporations published in 1989 showed that about 21% of U.S. companies with assets of more than $1 billion have bought FX options, while another 36% were open to the idea. Smaller companies used currency options less often. All companies were more likely to use currency options than interest-rate options, and all were more likely to buy options than write them.

Summary Sheet: Foreign Exchange Options

Writer	Intermediaries selling to hedgers; investors seeking higher returns on foreign currency-denominated portfolios
Buyer	Hedgers seeking protection against losses with potential for high gains; speculators seeking leveraged currency positions
Intermediary	Commercial banks, investment banks, brokers
How Bank Profits	Positioning, spreads; fees for more tailored products
Deal Size	On Chicago Mercantile Exchange, contract size is $60 to $100,000; on OTC market, transactions are generally $500,000 or more
Credit Considerations	For writers, none unless premium receipts are financed over life of options; for buyers, full premium plus future gains
Major Players	Market is fragmented; no banks dominate. Top tier includes First Chicago, Citibank, Bankers Trust, Salomon Brothers, Goldman Sachs.
Fees/Competition (Product Life Cycle)	Product is mature, competition strong except in niche businesses (long-dated options, options on exotic currencies).

A survey released in 1989 by Greenwich Associates focused on corporate use of exchange-traded currency options. According to the survey, 15% of European corporations expected to use exchange-traded options within the next 12 months; 7% used them at the time of the survey. The most active corporate users in Europe were in Switzerland, where 18% used FX options at the time of the survey and 31% expected to use them during the next year. Large companies tended to use these derivative products more than middle market firms did.

Option Basics

The growing corporate use of currency options has made it essential for bankers with FX product responsibility to understand the basic uses of options in the management of corporate foreign-exchange risk. Options are simply the right, but not the obligation, to do something. A foreign-exchange option is the right, but not the obligation, to exchange one currency for another at an agreed exchange rate at some time in the future.

The obvious advantage of options over forwards is that the option buyer can choose not to exercise the option if it is not beneficial to him or her. For example, the option to buy dollars for yen at a rate of ¥140:$1 will be valuable, and therefore exercised, when the yen at expiration is weaker than ¥140:$1. Conversely, that option will have no value when the yen is stronger than ¥140:$1, and the option holder will choose not to exercise.

The option right does not come free. Unlike a forward, the option costs money in the form of an up-front premium. Options are unique among risk-management products in this regard, and some of the traditional resistance to options results from the reluctance of treasurers to pay for something they might not use. However, the option premium is simply a fair payment for the expected return of the option position.

The benefit of the option right is a favorable asymmetry in the option return. Forwards are essentially "lock in" products; they create certainty by generating gains when the underlying position has losses, and losses when the underlying position has gains. Like forwards, options generate gains when the underlying position is losing money, but—unlike forwards—do not generate losses when the underlying position makes money. The option buyer will never lose more than his or her up-front premium. Option returns are, therefore, asymmetrical; losses are limited to the premium, gains are unlimited. Forward and option results are compared in Exhibit 1.

The less obvious advantage of options over forwards is their flexibility. Options can be flexibly combined to create myriad risk-return profiles.

Exhibit 1   Hedging with Forwards and Options

Underlying Hedge	Losses	Gains
Forwards	Gains	Losses
Options	Gains	No loss over up-front premium

Ironically, confusion about such combinations explains part of the past resistance to options by corporate treasurers. Fortunately, there has emerged a relatively small group of option strategies that treasurers have widely adopted. What these strategies have in common is that they provide an otherwise unattainable solution to a foreign-exchange risk-management problem. The following option combinations are the most commonly used ones. These combinations account to a significant degree for the surge in popularity of foreign exchange options among corporate risk managers.

Simple Option Strategies

Foreign-exchange transaction risk can be categorized into two types: foreign-currency payables and foreign-currency receivables. A payable leaves the company at risk to foreign-currency appreciation; a receivable, to foreign currency depreciation.

The traditional solutions for hedging foreign-currency payables and receivables are outlined in Exhibit 1. To hedge against the risk of appreciating foreign currency, the company should buy the currency in the forward market. To hedge against foreign-currency depreciation, the company should sell foreign currency in the forward market.

The simple option strategies that are alternatives to outright forward purchases and sales of foreign currency for domestic currency are also outlined in Exhibit 2. Rather than buying the currency in the forward market, the company can buy the option to buy the currency at an agreed-upon rate—for example, the corresponding forward rate—on a predefined date in the future. Rather than selling the currency in the forward market, the company can buy the option to sell. The option to buy foreign currency is a call; the option to sell, a put.

Exhibit 3 illustrates the difference between buying foreign currency in the forward market and buying a foreign-currency call option. The diagram compares a three-month forward purchase of foreign currency with the

---

Exhibit 2   Simple Hedging Solutions with Forwards and Options

Underlying	Risk	Forward Simple	Option Solution
FC Payable	FC up DC down	Buy FC Sell DC	Buy option to buy FC (Buy FC call)
FC Receivable	FC down DC up	Sell FC Buy DC	Buy option to sell FC (Buy FC put)

---

option to buy foreign currency three months forward. The forward rate for sterling is $1.50:£1, and the price of an "at-the-money" call option (i.e., the option to buy £1 at the forward rate of $1.50:£1) is $.02.

The graph plots the net purchase price of the currency against the spot exchange rate in three months. The forward locks in the purchase price at $1.50:£1. The option allows the holder to take advantage of a weaker sterling exchange rate should it be available in three months. If the pound is weaker than $1.50:£1, the option to buy at $1.50:£1 will be worthless and the option holder will choose not to exercise the option. Instead, he or she will buy the currency in the spot market. The only additional cost will be the two-cent option premium.

If the pound is stronger than $1.50:£1, the option holder will use the option to buy the currency at $1.50:£1, and the net cost will be $1.50 per pound plus the $.02 purchase price. This is why the graph flattens out above $1.50:£1. The break-even point—the point of indifference between a forward purchase and a call option—is $1.48:£1. The hedger would be better off with the option if sterling is weaker and better off with the forward if sterling is stronger.

The marketing implication of Exhibit 3 is clear, if somewhat counter-intuitive. If the customer is certain that the foreign currency will appreciate, he or she should buy the currency in the forward market. However, if the customer thinks the currency may not appreciate and, in fact, may depreciate, he or she should buy the option instead. Of course, if the currency does depreciate, he or she will have been better off not hedging at all.

The option will never turn out to be the best solution. But more importantly, it will turn out to be a pretty good solution in all circumstances. In summary, an option purchase will provide a great deal of protection in the event that the foreign currency appreciates, and will allow the holder to benefit to a great extent if the foreign currency depreciates.

Exhibit 3   Buy At-the-Money Call

Buy 150 call for $.02

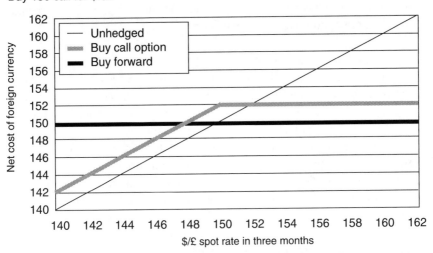

Exhibit 4   Buy At-the-Money Put

Buy 150 call for $.02

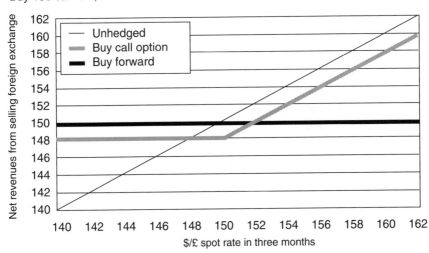

Exhibit 4 contrasts the sale of foreign currency in the forward market with the purchase of a put option. Again, a three-month forward sale at $1.50:£1 is compared with an option costing $.02 to sell the currency at $1.50:£1. Here the break-even rate is $1.52:£1; if the rate ends up lower, the forward will have been a better way to sell the currency, but if the rate ends up higher, the option will have been better.

IN-THE-MONEY VERSUS OUT-OF-THE-MONEY

Hedgers can obtain slightly different risk-return profiles by using option exercise prices different from the forward rate. When a call option's exercise price is above the forward rate, or a put option's exercise price is below the forward rate, the option is said to be out-of-the-money.

Out-of-the-money options can be characterized as lacking intrinsic value—that is, if the currency-exchange rate ends up at the current level of the forward, the option will expire worthless. In-the-money options are said to have intrinsic value—if the currency-exchange rate ends up at the current forward rate, the option will have value. Clearly, in-the-money options will cost more than out-of-the-money options. In-the-money and out-of-the-money call options are compared in Exhibit 5

Out-of-the-money options are especially beneficial for hedgers who will only be hurt by a large move in the exchange rate. The up-front premium is low, and protection is afforded for movements above the critical rate. In-the-money options more closely approximate the performance of the forward. They are, therefore, more appropriate for customers looking to lock in a result. The advantage they have over forwards is that they allow the user to benefit from a very favorable move in the exchange rate. In instances where failure to benefit from such favorable moves will be viewed very negatively, the in-the-money option will be the best solution.

RANGE FORWARDS

The range forward was invented as a response to the often heard complaint that foreign-exchange options are expensive. It represents the simplest of the option combination strategies.

The strategy of buying a range forward using out-of-the-money calls and puts is illustrated in Exhibit 6. Note that the net cost of the strategy is zero: The cost of buying the calls is equal to the revenue from selling the puts. This special case is known as a zero-cost range forward. Choosing other exercise prices would lead to net payments or net revenues in implementing the strategy, but the result would be similar to that shown in Exhibit 6.

Exhibit 5 In- Versus Out-of-the-Money Calls

Buy 145 call at $.054, 155 call at $.004

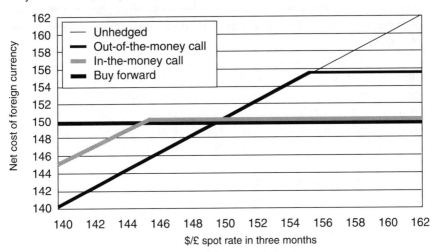

Exhibit 6 Buy Range Forward

Buy 155 call, sell 145 put

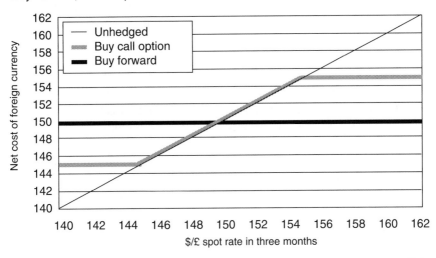

The range forward guarantees that the net cost of the foreign exchange will fall within a predefined band. For this reason, the range forward is sometimes called a cylinder. Such a hedge would be attractive to a customer who wanted some protection against a rise in the exchange rate but who could also live with some downside risk. Most important, the strategy would be interesting to anyone who objected to the cost of the simple option strategies.

Note that the width of the band in Exhibit 6 is determined by the difference in the exercise prices on the call and the put. Bringing these closer together narrows the band; widening the difference between the call and put exercise prices widens the band. Interestingly, a range forward using the same exercise price on the call and the put is equivalent to buying a forward; the band is narrowed to the point of being a straight line.

PARTICIPATION FORWARDS

In its simplest form, a participation forward combines elements of the simple forward and the simple option strategies. Clients who like the unlimited upside potential of options but who object to the cost can construct participation forwards customized to their needs.

The strategy requires simultaneous purchases of forwards and calls to hedge payables, and sales of forwards and purchases of puts to hedge receivables. Forwards and options can be used in any ratio adding up to 100% coverage. For example, a typical participation forward might be constructed with 50% of the hedge in forward contracts and 50% in option contracts. While providing full downside protection, the ratio allows for partial participation in favorable moves in the exchange rate. Remember, the range forward limits such participation to the edge of the band.

Exhibit 7 shows the purchase of a participating forward to hedge FX payable risk. In this case, the hedger buys equal amounts of forwards and call options to hedge the risk of an appreciating foreign currency. The participating forward costs half that of a simple call option strategy, provides full protection against a rise in the exchange rate, and provides some participation in a favorable decline in the FX rate.

In this illustration, the forward and option are used in equal parts, and the option's exercise price is the same as the forward's. More complex participation forwards can be constructed by varying these assumptions.

Exhibit 7　Buy Participating Forward

Buy 1/2 forward, 1/2 150 call

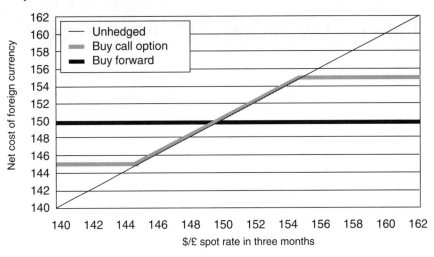

Conclusion

The complexities of hedging are made easier by the use of options. Today's corporate banker needs to be comfortable with options terminology, concepts, and strategies. Most people are confused by the theoretical world of option pricing and analysis; nevertheless, a focus on the simple strategies outlined in this chapter has helped many overcome the problem of technical overload.

16

Exotic Options
Tailoring Derivatives to Customer Needs

A few years ago, "exotic" options referred to simple combinations of conventional options such as range forwards and cylinders. Introduced in the mid-1980s, these combinations are now as integral to corporate hedging as swaps, caps, and floors.

The new exotic options are tailored option products that, unlike their 1980s predecessors, cannot be replicated by combinations of straight options. When matched to a corporate hedger's organizational structure and hedging objectives, they provide a superior hedge at a lower cost than conventional options.

These options, which include average-rate, barrier, deferred-strike, and compound options, can be difficult for banks to create and hedge. However, they are easy for customers to use and are tailored to provide solutions to very specific customer problems.

Most exotic options offer less protection than do straight options. But this is by design, not by accident. Straight options often provide more protection than a customer needs or wants. Banks can take apart straight options and sell the customer only what is needed, monetizing what the customer doesn't need and offering a precisely tailored solution at a lower price. This is not

---

Summary Sheet: Exotic Options

Writers	Intermediaries selling to hedgers; investors seeking higher returns on investment portfolios
Buyers	Hedgers seeking lower-cost insurance against adverse price moves or increased potential for gains; investors seeking yield enhancement
Intermediary	Commercial banks, investment banks, brokers
How Bank Profits	Spread between hedger's cost and bank's cost to construct position
Deal Size	Generally $1 million and up
Major Players	Market is fragmented; no banks dominate. Major players include Bankers Trust, Citicorp, Continental, Goldman Sachs, Merrill Lynch, Swiss Bank Corporation.
Competition	Margins may be greater than on straight options, but most buyers solicit multiple bids, so prices must be competitive.

---

always easy to do, but banks capable of doing it can do a better job of meeting the needs of their customers—and simultaneously collect higher margins than are available on generic derivatives.

Types of Exotic Options

Exotic options likely to have broad appeal include average-rate, barrier, deferred-strike, and compound options. Average-rate and compound options are bought by companies seeking a better hedge on specific risk exposures than can be achieved with conventional options. That these exotic options also typically cost less than alternative hedge instruments is secondary. However, barrier options are attractive primarily because they offer a lower premium than conventional options.

Corporate applications of exotic options are generally limited to foreign-currency hedging, but interest in exotic options on interest rates and commodity markets is growing. A number of exotic option structures can also be applied to portfolio management. Barrier options on equities, for example, have traded in U.S. securities markets since 1967 and are used internationally to enhance yields on investment portfolios.

Average-Rate Options (AROs)

Sometimes called Asian options, average-rate options were developed in Japan. The primary difference between an ARO and a conventional option is that the expiration value of the ARO depends on the average price of the underlying instrument or commodity over the life of the option. AROs typically cost significantly less than comparable straight options because average prices are less volatile than day-to-day prices.

AROs may be either fixed strike or floating strike. In fixed-strike AROs, the strike price is specified at inception. At expiration, the value of the option is the amount that the strike price is above (puts) or below (calls) the average price of the underlying commodity as determined by an agreed-upon sampling of periodic market prices.

Fixed-strike AROs hedge exposures that are either valued at an end-of-period average price or incurred throughout the period at the prevailing spot price, such as a stream of cash flows. By fixing the value of the option strike price less the option premium to a budgeted rate, a corporate hedger establishes a floor or ceiling equal to the budgeted rate while retaining the potential for price appreciation.

These options are particularly useful in hedging budgeted foreign-exchange translations, such as costs or revenues of foreign subsidiaries, which are translated at the average exchange rate for the measurement period. In the United States, under Financial Accounting Standard No. 52, income-statement items are translated at an average exchange rate.

The expiration value of floating-strike AROs is determined by the difference between the average price over the life of the instrument and the end-of-period spot price. At expiration, the strike price is set equal to the average price. The option is in the money if the strike price is below the spot price for calls or above the spot price for puts.

Floating-strike AROs hedge exposures to end-of-period spot prices. Because the strike price is not known in advance, floating-strike AROs are less effective for hedging a budgeted price than conventional options or forward-price agreements. But where a company has neither a market outlook nor a budget constraint, floating-strike AROs guarantee the average price (less the option premium) or better.

Compound Options

A compound option is an option on an option. The holder of a call option on an underlying call or put has the right to purchase the underlying option at a predetermined time for a specified premium amount, called the premium strike.

The initial premium paid for the first option depends on how far in or out of the money the premium strike is. The initial premium is generally substantially below the premium required on the underlying option. Upon exercise, the purchaser pays the premium strike and assumes the underlying option. The sum of the initial premium and the premium strike is always greater than the cost of a conventional option.

Compound options are particularly useful in hedging uncertain exposures such as contract bids. If a bid is not accepted, the most a company would lose on the hedge is the initial premium paid. However, if the first option finishes in the money, the company would exercise into the underlying option at a below-market cost, either to hedge the exposure created by the accepted bid or to sell the option at a profit in the market. The use of a compound option to hedge a contract bid is shown in Exhibit 1.

Exhibit 1   Compound Option Outcomes

Situation: Company buys a call on a Singapore dollar put to hedge revenues should it win the bid on a Singapore contracting project.

	Singapore dollar moves	
	below strike (in the money)	*above strike (out of the money)*
Company wins bid.	Company exercises right to buy S$ put at known cost.	Company rehedges at market price.
Company loses bid.	Company closes position and takes profit.	Company allows option to expire and loses small initial premium.

Barrier Options

Barrier options can be used to extinguish or establish a hedge automatically when a price objective is achieved. The purchaser specifies both a strike price and a barrier price in the underlying market at which the option is to be extinguished (known as a "knock-out" option) or established ("knock-in").

The low premiums associated with barrier options are attractive to companies that seek to minimize hedging costs. Corporate treasuries that operate as profit centers can also net higher returns using barrier options as an alternative to conventional options. However, purchasers of barrier options that extinguish when the barrier is reached run the risk of being whipsawed in volatile markets, because there is no protection should the exchange rate then reverse course.

Deferred-Strike Options

The deferred-strike option allows a purchaser to establish the strike price according to an agreed formula within a specified time prior to maturity.

The formula for determining strike price is based on the behavior of the spot rate. For example, the strike price may be set to the average spot rate during the interim, the maximum, or minimum spot rate occurring during the interim, or a fixed percentage over or under the spot rate at the end of the interim period.

Deferred-strike options also allow treasurers to time the hedging of volatility levels separately from rate levels. The option is purchased today, locking in the volatility level; the strike price is set in the future, deferring the hedging of the rate level.

Lookback Options

Lookback options guarantee the holder the most favorable rate occurring during the period hedged. At expiration, the spot price is marked to the maximum or minimum price in the underlying market over the life of the option. Because these options eliminate all opportunity costs, the premium is substantially higher than those on conventional options.

Corporate Applications

U.S. companies that have begun using exotic options during the past year include Union Carbide, the Interpublic Group of Companies, and Eaton Corporation.

These companies routinely use forward contracts and conventional options on foreign exchange to capitalize on their market outlook while limiting

Exhibit 2   Exotic Options Summary

Type	Definition	Application	Cost*
Fixed-strike ARO	Expiration value is difference between strike price and average market price over option life.	Hedging balance sheet or budgeted income statement items translated at an average rate	Significantly below straight option due to low volatility of average price
Floating-strike ARO	Expiration value is difference between average rate over life and end of period rate.	Guarantees best of average rate or ending spot price, smoothing volatility of cash flows	Above fixed-strike ARO but less than straight option
Compound Option	A call option on call or put	Hedging bid risk	Low initial premium, but exercise results in payment of second premium
Barrier	Option is extinguished or created when spot price touches barrier price.	Same as straight option, but user pays lower price, takes on more risk	Depends on distance of barrier rate from strike; cheaper than conventional option
Deferred Strike	Strike price is determined after inception but before maturity.	Same as straight option, but user has lower opportunity cost	Depends on formula used to determine strike; costs more than straight option
Lookback	At maturity, strike is set to most favorable price occurring over option life.	Speculation on large price swings	About twice as expensive as a comparable at-the-money straight option

All else equal

downside risk. Exotic options enable them to fine-tune these hedges, adding value to the hedge program.

Deferred-Strike and Average-Rate Options

For the Interpublic Group of Companies, an international association of advertising companies, deferred-strike options take some of the uncertainty out of timing a hedge.

Interpublic hedges cash flows and net translation exposure using a disciplined trader's approach to market timing. A significant portion of its risk-management effort is spent in evaluating market trends and identifying trend reversals. Once the company decides to hedge or weather an exposure, stop-loss orders are placed at critical price levels to minimize losses and capture profits.

Interpublic measures its performance in two ways. First, it compares its effective foreign-exchange rates to what it would have achieved by simply hedging everything with forward contracts. Second, it measures its opportunity costs. Although the company is not concerned with selling at the absolute top of the trend and buying at the absolute bottom, it does not want to miss significant profit opportunities. Based on this performance record, Interpublic found that the additional premium it invested in deferred-strike options would very likely pay off.

To hedge against a strengthening U.S. dollar, Interpublic bought six-month foreign-currency put options where, at the end of the first month, the strike price was set equal to the most favorable exchange rate occurring during that period. The company's minimum effective rate with this strategy is the spot price at inception less the premium. Subsequently, if instead of strengthening the dollar continued to decline, the company would realize a higher effective rate (strike price less premium or better) than with conventional options and reduce its opportunity cost.

Interpublic has also experimented with average-rate options. Fixed-strike AROs are appropriate instruments for hedging the company's recurring cash flows and translation risks. The company was less pleased with its results using AROs, however, in part because the opportunity cost incurred was higher than the company would have otherwise achieved by actively managing the position.

Barrier Options

Union Carbide began using barrier options in the summer of 1991. The company has used knock-out, knock-in and double-barrier combinations to hedge foreign-exchange exposures. It also considered using these options to hedge commodity-price exposures such as natural gas.

A multinational company operating on a local-currency basis, Union Carbide has a long position in foreign currencies by virtue of revenues and cash flows generated by foreign subsidiaries. The company hedges transaction and economic foreign-currency exposure over a one-year horizon.

While not a profit center, Union Carbide's treasury seeks to maximize gains from foreign-currency fluctuations by selecting strategies, which may include writing options, consistent with its market outlook. Performance is measured against a forward-market benchmark. Union Carbide uses barrier put options as an alternative to conventional options to provide potential price appreciation plus downside protection at lower cost.

In one instance, the company compared a conventional DM/US$ put struck at DM1.65:$1 to a barrier put that would extinguish if the spot rate moved to DM1.60:$1. Because the premium on the barrier option was 40% less than that of a conventional option, the barrier put provided better downside protection. The company would achieve a minimum effective rate of DM1.68:$1 with the barrier put versus DM1.70:$1 with the conventional put.

However, if the Deutschemark strengthened to DM1.60:$1, the barrier put would extinguish, leaving the company exposed to further-exchange rate fluctuations. To mitigate that exposure, the company was prepared to lock in at the more favorable forward rate if the barrier was reached, effectively capping its profits at five pfennigs (DM1.65 – DM1.60) less the option premium. By undertaking this additional execution risk, the company achieved a risk profile consistent with its profit objectives.

At first glance, it may seem that Union Carbide traded away profit-appreciation potential on the barrier put in return for a lower cost. With a conventional option, the company would, theoretically at least, enjoy unlimited profit potential throughout the life of the option. However, because Union Carbide actively manages its positions, it is unlikely that the company would hold the conventional option to maturity unless it had to. Once the spot market met the company's price objective, the company would sell the put at market and again lock in its profit by selling the underlying receivable in the forward rate.

In effect, the barrier put monetized the value of the company's intention to close out the hedge when its price was reached. The company was able to buy only what it wanted and no more, reducing the all-in cost of the hedge.

In another example, Union Carbide combined the knock-out put with the sale of conventional options—a put with a strike price above that of the barrier option and a call with a strike price below that of the barrier option—to reduce further the premium cost and create a range of outcomes the company would monitor through the life of the options.

The sale of the call limits price appreciation but at a ceiling against which the company would be happy to sell Deutschemarks. The barrier put provides price protection against a decline in the U.S dollar rate down to the level of the sale of the conventional put.

Union Carbide also uses barrier options to create a hedge once the barrier price is reached—for example, a knock-in put struck at DM1.65:$1 that becomes effective only if the spot rate reaches DM1.70:$1. This position is consistent with a bullish market view. By pushing down the rate at which the put becomes effective, the company limits the cost of the hedge and therefore increases the profit potential should the Deutschemark strengthen as expected. On the other hand, the company remains exposed when the Deutschemark trades between DM1.65:$1 and DM1.70:$1.

Union Carbide's treasury has pricing capabilities for several exotic option structures, including barrier options. After first pricing an option internally, the company solicits bids from banks with which it has a relationship. It considers the pricing and execution capabilities of counterparties as significant as credit risk. Because of the increased volatility of forward market prices more than one year out, the maturity of its barrier options is less than one year. The typical transaction size is $5 to $10 million face amount.

Compound Options

Cleveland-based Eaton Corporation seldom bids for contracts invoiced in a foreign currency. When it does, however, it is likely to use a compound option to hedge foreign-currency exposure.

The strike price of the underlying option is selected to protect the company's projected revenues if the bid is accepted. The premium strike of the initial option will depend on the initial premium the company is willing to risk. If the company specifies an out-of-the-money premium strike, the initial premium will be less. But if the option is exercised, the total outlay will be more than if the premium strike is set in the money.

Consistent with its overall profit-oriented hedge program, the company's choice of premium strike can be influenced by its short-term market outlook.

Conclusion

Corporate use of exotic options is growing rapidly. Many companies not yet using them are undergoing management reviews that will enable them to do so in the future. As treasurers become more familiar with the unique risk profiles exotics offer, new applications are likely to develop. For banks that offer these products, the inevitable growth of exotic options will lead to increased price competition and, in turn, narrower margins. However, corporations do not transact solely on price. Banks that can develop innovative solutions to corporate problems and provide efficient execution will make up much of the margin decline through increased volume. Moreover, these banks can presumably continue to develop new hedging structures that can be priced at a premium, at least during the early stage of the product life cycle.

17

Exotic Options

Shifting the Timing of Premium Payments

A new type of hedging instrument that has enjoyed considerable success in recent months is known as the contingent option, capitalized option, or break forward. These agreements offer customers the payoff characteristics of options while addressing the reluctance of many customers to paying up-front premiums. As with a forward or swap contract, no up-front payment is required; as with an option, gains are unlimited should exchange or interest rates move in the customer's favor. This combination of forward and option characteristics has proven attractive to large and medium-sized corporates unable or unwilling to construct these types of positions on their own.

The contingent or capitalized option is based on the combination of an "off-market" forward or swap with an option on a currency, commodity, or interest rate swap. The customer can pay for the position as a future value or annuity. These transactions illustrate how basic cash flow engineering techniques can be used to distinguish generic products, tailoring them to the preferences of a customer. The result can be new business and possibly higher margins as well.

Mechanics of the Contingent Option

A contingent option on a foreign-exchange purchase or sale combines two previously separate contracts: a forward contract and a call or put. The forward rate, however, is not the market forward rate; it is different from the market rate by the amount of the future value of the call or put premium. By bundling the two contracts, the option premium, which is normally visible, effectively disappears.

What really happens is that the bank finances the premium rather than receiving it up-front. This financed amount is then built into the forward rate. Banks have always been willing to finance option premiums, given an acceptable credit. This variation simply incorporates the financing charge into the forward contract, simplifying the transaction from the customer's viewpoint.

In the interest-rate variation, a customer typically buys a contingent payer swaption to hedge against higher interest rates. If interest rates fall, the payer swaption expires unexercised; the customer walks away with no premium payment, free to refinance at lower rates. But if interest rates rise, the customer *must* exercise the payer swaption. This commits the customer to paying fixed at a rate higher than had he or she simply entered a forward

---

Summary Sheet: Contingent Options

Buyers	Large and middle market corporate hedgers seeking to avoid up-front premiums; typical users are unable or unwilling to construct these positions for themselves.
Sellers	Commercial and investment banks
How Bank Profits	Bid-offer spreads
Deal Size	As with other OTC options, transactions are generally $500,000 or more.
Credit Considerations	When financing option premiums, banks take on credit risk of option buyers.
Major Players	Market for all FX and interest-rate options is fragmented; no banks dominate.
Competition/ Life Cycle	Early in life cycle; higher-than-average margins may be available for a limited time.

Exhibit 1   Bundling Options with Forward Contracts

Purpose	Hedge foreign-currency payable	Hedge foreign-currency receivable
Instrument	Contingent call	Contingent put
Forward Position	Purchase	Sale
Option Position	Put	Call

Exhibit 2   Payment Profile of Contingent Swaption

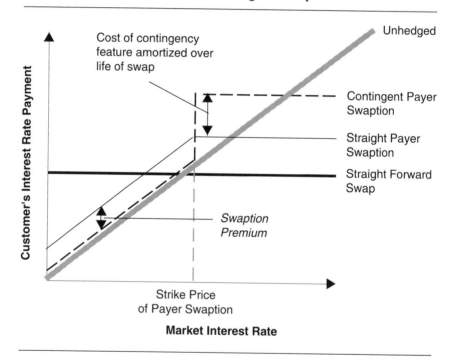

swap or purchased a straight at-the-money payer swaption. As Exhibit 2 illustrates, the fixed rate is higher by the cost of compensating the intermediary for the contingency feature.

As always, the customer's decision on how to hedge depends on his or her interest-rate forecast. If interest rates rise, the customer will have been best off with a straight forward swap. The next best alternative will have been a straight payer swaption, while the highest fixed rate is associated with the contingent payer swaption. If interest rates fall, however, there is no difference between the cost of remaining unhedged and the cost of a contingent payer swaption.

In both the FX and interest-rate variations, the contingent option can be structured in an infinite variety of ways. The customer can pay nothing up-front and the future value of the option as a one-time payment at expiration. In the swaption variation, the customer can pay for the option as a spread over the swap payment. The customer can pay any amount up-front and the rest at the end via any combination of one-time payment and spread. Specific exercises illustrating contingent option structures can be found in Chapter 19 of *The Derivatives Engineering Workbook*.

Market Conditions and Contingent Options

These hedging structures are used primarily as disaster insurance—as a static hedge when the outcome of market events is expected to be favorable but the customer still wants to guard against unexpected market events. Because the option is "free," the customer can take on protection and simultaneously receive the full benefit from favorable market movements. The trade-off is a higher cost should the unexpected occur and the option or swaption be exercised.

For instance, contingent options—known as break forwards in this context—have been widely used in recent months by Canadian exporters. The Canadian dollar has weakened against the U.S. dollar throughout 1992, falling from about C$1.12:US$1 in November of 1991 to C$1.20:US$1 in June of 1992. Because most market participants expect the unit to continue to decline, there appears to be little reason to hedge. At the same time, the U.S. dollar has been so weak, and the possibility of further declines in U.S. short-term interest rates is so clear, that many exporters are wary of leaving U.S. dollar receivables completely open. This is a classic option situation—except that the expected outcome (a weaker Canadian dollar) may discourage customers from paying an up-front premium for protection. In this case, the customer's expectations make the contingent option more attractive.

Conclusion

Contingent or capitalized options can be an attractive hedging alternative for many customers. The lack of a visible premium, and the prospect of no premium payment should the option expire out of the money, can be very appealing. These options are especially attractive as disaster insurance, for the customer sees them as "free" protection that will probably be unnecessary. As with all options, strike prices and maturities can be customized to meet the customer's specific requirements; in this case, however, the structure and timing of the premium payment can be customized as well.

From the intermediary's perspective, the contingent option is still a fairly new product, and the ability of customers to break it into its component costs and see the true cost structure is still minimal. That is, the market is still inefficient, and thus banks can add more "juice" into the final price. As contingent options become more widely utilized and traded, the cost will come down—as has occurred with every other derivative product.

PART IV

Commodity Derivatives

Although exchange-traded commodity futures predated most financial futures by at least a decade, commodity derivatives were slow to develop in the over-the-counter market. Nevertheless, the need for more stable cash flows among commodity producers and consumers—oil companies, utilities, airlines, film manufacturers, even governments—led to the development of a $50 billion market by early 1994.

The following three chapters chronicle the development of the commodity derivatives market, from unadorned swaps that simply extend the maturities of exchange-traded futures contracts to the "not just plain vanilla" intricacies of commodity-linked financings with yields enhanced by embedded options. For the most part, these chapters focus on hedging applications; capital markets applications of commodity derivatives appear in the following section.

18

Commodity Swaps
A Growing Risk-Management Product

In the past year, more and more banks have been moving into the growing commodity swaps business. For banks, the commodity swaps arena represents a natural extension into another risk-management market. Managing commodity price risk involves many of the same skills and systems required to manage interest-rate and currency risk. However, unlike interest-rate, and currency swaps, commodity swaps are still in their infancy, with few players and little interbank price quoting. For this reason, commodity swaps can be extremely profitable: With the market small and relatively illiquid, banks able to put together the transactions can command wide spreads.

Nobody knows the precise size of the commodity swap market because few deals are publicized. However, recent estimates have pegged the size of the market at no larger than $10 billion. This is only about 1% of the total interest-rate and currency-swap market, but the volume of commodity swaps is growing much faster than that of financial swaps.

In the United States, several banks recently began setting up commodity swap units due in part to a decision by the Commodity Futures Trading Commission (CFTC) not to claim regulatory authority over the swaps. Before the decision, the development of the U.S. commodity swap market had been stalled for nearly two years as U.S. banks moved or established commodity swap units abroad while waiting to see whether the CFTC would claim jurisdiction.

Another reason for the increasing popularity of commodity swaps has been a growing awareness among commodity producers of a need for a long-term hedge of commodities that have swung widely in price. Commodity swaps allow both commodity producers and consumers to control fluctuations in revenues and expenses.

However, establishing a commodity swap unit also requires expertise in the particular commodities targeted for swaps. Long lead times are frequently necessary. Mitsubishi Bank, for example, recently set up an operation at a London-based subsidiary to trade oil and precious metals commodities. The bank does not expect to offer commodity swaps until sometime next year.

Until 1988, commodity swaps were mostly written on oil and precious metals. The product is now applied to oil derivatives, such as jet and bunker fuel, naphtha, gasoline, and heating oil; base metals, such as copper, zinc, aluminum, and nickel; building supplies, such as cement; and timber derivatives, such as pulp.

Summary Sheet: Commodity Swaps

Counterparties	Companies with operations relying heavily on production or use of large volumes of commodities
Intermediaries	Commercial and investment banks
How Banks Profit	Arrangement fees in the range of 1% to 5% plus bid/offer spread on swap
Deal Size	$25 million to $250 million
Credit Considerations	Counterparty risk is greater than in interest-rate swaps because replacing counterparty is more difficult.
Players	Chase Manhattan, Phibro Energy, Banque Paribas, Bankers Trust, Goldman Sachs, Continental, First Chicago, Chemical
Competition (Product Life Cycle)	Competition limited; early in product life cycle

The Product

Commodity swaps are similar in purpose and structure to interest-rate swaps. In an interest-rate swap, the two sides to the transaction exchange obligations to pay a fixed or floating rate on a notional principal amount, effectively transforming a fixed-rate loan into a floating one and vice versa. But in a commodity swap, no exchange of commodities occurs; instead, cash flows are exchanged based on different prices for the commodity.

One party—usually a commodity buyer—agrees to pay a fixed price for the product and receive cash flows indexed to the market price. The other party—a commodity producer—agrees to pay an index and receive a fixed price. The index is usually pegged to a commodities index price on a particular exchange; in the case of oil, West Texas Intermediate is the most common index. Thus, the commodity producer avoids losses from a price decline and the buyer avoids losses from a price increase.

Banks serve as the intermediary between at least two commodity swap counterparties. As shown in Exhibit 1, on one side of the bank is the commodity producer and on the other is the commodity buyer. In most cases,

Exhibit 1 Cash Flows in a Commodity Swap

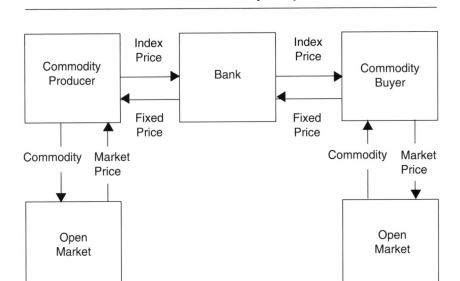

the commodity producer doesn't actually sell the commodity to the commodity buyer counterparty in the swap. In fact, the producer generally sells the commodity to a party unrelated to the swap transaction. The same is true with the swap's commodity buyer, which purchases the commodity from a different producer.

The diagram in Exhibit 1 shows the producer selling its product to an unrelated third party. The producer pays the bank an amount based upon a notional amount of the commodity and index price, while the bank pays the producer an amount based upon the fixed price of the commodity. The bank maintains an opposite arrangement with the buyer and profits on the spread between slightly different fixed prices for the two counterparties.

From the customer's perspective, the bank passes along the difference between the index and fixed prices. At the end of each period in the swap, either monthly or quarterly, the difference between the fixed and index rate is paid by the party owing the balance. Thus, if the floating price exceeds the fixed price, the producer pays the bank the difference. If the fixed price exceeds the index, then the bank pays the producer the difference. The arrangement is the same with the buyer. If the index price is greater than the fixed price, the bank pays the difference to the buyer. But if the index price is less than the fixed price, the commodity buyer pays the difference to the bank (see Exhibit 2).

At this stage in the growth of the commodity swap business, most banks match counterparties rather than assuming the risk of commodity price swings. One reason is that banks don't manage a commodity book in the same way that they manage an interest-rate or currency book. Therefore, there are few opportunities to hedge commodity price risks in the normal course of bank business. Although the commodity futures market can be used to temporarily hedge positions, futures have many limitations.

Benefits of Commodity Swaps

Commodity swaps allow both producers and users to hedge commodity price changes over the term of the arrangement, which can carry maturities of two to seven years. Swaps enable commodity producers to more accurately estimate future revenue and commodity buyers to more accurately estimate future raw-materials costs.

Much of the growth in commodity swaps can be attributed to the changing attitudes of commodity producers and buyers. Until about 20 years ago, few companies were willing to enter into such transactions. In the past, both sides preferred to take their chances on benefiting from favorable moves in

Exhibit 2   Payments in a Gold Swap

Notional amount: 1,000 ounces
Index: New York Commodity Exchange (COMEX) gold price
Swap rate: $400 for producer
                   $402 for buyer

Month	Producer	Bank	Buyer	
1	25,300 ◄———	2,000 ◄—	27,300	*Arrows show*
2	11,600 ——►	2,000 ——►	9,600	*direction of*
3	5,000 ——►	2,000 ——►	3,000	*cash flows*

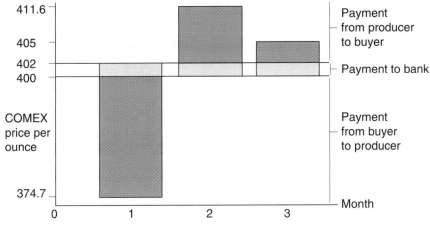

commodity prices—the buyer from a price decline, the producer from a price rise. However, the 1970s and 1980s have seen prolonged periods of rising and falling prices: the inflation-fueled increases of the late 1970s, the commodity price depression of the early 1980s, and the rebound and subsequent collapse before and after the stock market crash of October of 1987. These sustained price trends have pushed many unhedged commodity producers and consumers into bankruptcy or near-bankruptcy. After decades of extreme volatility, producers and buyers have grown more willing to settle on a price that enables both to profit.

Commodity swaps need not be used solely as a hedge. They can also be used by companies as a way to raise cash and can be linked to traditional types of bank lending, such as project and acquisition finance. Some banks may require a commodity producer to employ a swap before committing to a loan. Swaps can diminish credit risk by ensuring that the commodity price the borrower receives will provide enough revenue to adequately service its debt.

In 1989, Mexicana de Cobre (Mexcobre), a Mexican copper mining subsidiary of Grupo Mexico, obtained a $210 million loan from a syndicate headed by Banque Paribas. A three-year commodity swap involving Mexcobre, Paribas and Sogem, a Société Générale subsidiary that agreed to buy the copper, ensured an adequate cash flow to service the amortizing loan. The deal was the first copper swap, the first loan secured by a commodity swap and the first major voluntary, new hard-currency loan to a Mexican company since the country's 1982 debt crisis.

Swaps Versus Futures

Futures have long been used to hedge commodity risk. However, swaps are more attractive to many bank customers than futures.

First, commodity futures contracts rarely extend more than two years into the future. This represents a major obstacle to a company needing to hedge for more than two years. For example, maturities on copper futures extend only to 15 months on the London Metal Exchange and 24 months on New York's COMEX. And even these maturities are misleading, for the longest maturities tend to be illiquid. However, banks are offering commodity swaps out to seven years.

Second, no futures contracts exist for many commodities, forcing companies to hedge with substitutes. Such hedges result in the company taking on basis risk. For instance, because there are no futures contracts for jet fuel, an airline wanting to hedge its price risk needs to open positions using crude oil futures. This represents a risk because prices on the two products don't necessarily move in tandem. Citicorp reportedly pulled out of the commodity swap market in Japan after losing $13 million, in part, because naphtha commodity swaps were hedged with West Texas intermediate crude and prices of the two commodities failed to move together.

Selecting Swap Candidates

From a bank marketer's perspective, the most challenging aspect to structuring a commodity swap is finding commodity producers willing to act as counterparties. The inclination of many business managers in commodity industries has been to accept price fluctuations rather than to adopt methods for eliminating them. Companies with active risk-management strategies, such as oil firms, have sought to profit from short-term market movements.

As a result, bankers have found it easier to convince commodity buyers than producers of the value of swaps.

Adding to commodity producer reluctance to enter into swaps has been the attitude of stockholders. Many equity investors buy stock in commodity producers—for instance, gold mining companies—as a proxy for investments in the commodity itself. A commodity swap hedges the downside risk of a commodity price decline, but it also removes the upside potential that these investors seek.

The most desirable commodity producer counterparties are those with excellent credit histories. Banks, whether they match counterparties or assume commodity price risk themselves, are still exposed to the credit risks of the counterparties. If a counterparty defaults, finding a replacement is more difficult than in the case of interest-rate or currency swaps, which have large, liquid secondary markets.

The best producer counterparties also produce more of the commodity than they hedge in the swap. The higher the percentage of a company's commodity production earmarked for a swap, the greater the risk of nonperformance, particularly if the company has unstable labor relations or has shown an inability to produce the commodity at steady levels in the past. A company run by management that is generally risk averse in its business strategies and philosophy is more likely to be a potential buyer of swaps than a company run by managers who thrive on risk taking.

Firms with a mismatched balance sheet tend to be more receptive to swaps. An example might be an oil producer with assets in the form of proven reserves and liabilities in the form of bank debt and bonds. If oil prices fall, the value of the assets decline and the left side of the balance sheet shrinks. However, the effect of falling prices is not matched on the right side of the balance sheet.

Which Commodities Are Best?

Most swap candidates come from particular commodity industries. These industries produce commodities with the following characteristics:

1) *A well-established benchmark.* One of the major elements needed in a commodity swap is a reliable price index. Commodities with prices fixed by well-functioning markets are easiest to work with. A widely recognized index provides an objective and easily observable standard for the floating price in a swap. With oil, for example, there are three principal indices that can be used, depending upon the particular type of crude: West Texas Intermediate, Brent, and Dubai.

2) *A deep futures market.* Futures enable bank intermediaries to cover their position when counterparties are unavailable. Although hedging swap positions with futures market is frequently less than perfect, it can provide some protection. For example, a commodity swap involving Alaskan oil would have to be hedged with West Texas Intermediate because futures on Alaskan oil are not available on the exchanges. This hedge results in basis risk in the same way as using a Treasury futures contract to hedge a corporate bond.

3) *The lack of adequate substitutes.* If a commodity buyer can merely purchase a lower-priced substitute when commodity prices rise, there is no need to hedge.

4) *Volatility.* Unless commodity prices fluctuate, there is no need to hedge. Volatility also helps to trigger opposite price expectations among different participants in the commodity market. These institutions are potential swap counterparties. When the commodity is midway through a price cycle, commodity swaps are of the greatest value to both sides considering a transaction.

Exhibit 3   Comparing Commodity Futures and Swaps

	Futures	**Swap**
Contract amounts	Standardized	Customized to needs
Maturity	Up to 18 months	Up to 7 years
Payment dates	Standardized; possible date mismatches	Customized to needs
Margin requirements	Yes	No
Cash flows	Marked to market on daily basis settlement	Net cash on monthly or quarterly basis
Basis risk	Yes; hedges must often be done with substitute	In general, no substitution necessary
Default risk	Low; exchange guarantees contracts	Greater than futures
Liquidity	Liquid	Illiquid

U.S. Regulatory Issues

Commodity futures contracts are also effective hedging tools. They are widely used by companies involved in farming, food processing, and metals. Until commodity swaps became available, the futures market offered the only way to hedge price risk. In the United States, the Commodity Futures Trading Commission (CFTC) thought that commodity swaps were so similar to futures that it prevented banks from offering the product. In the late 1980s, commercial banks that wanted to develop commodity swap programs, such as Chase Manhattan, received approval from the Comptroller of the Currency to offer the product.

However, that go-ahead proved to be short-lived when the CFTC in August of 1987 subpoenaed Chase Manhattan for information on its swap activities. CFTC staff members expressed concern that commodity swaps might be futures transactions and therefore should be regulated by the CFTC. In an advance notice of proposed rules, the commission put a temporary stop on all hybrid and related instruments that it deemed to be off-exchange traded futures contracts, including transactions that resembled, but did not contain all the elements of, futures contracts.

Under pressure from the Federal Reserve Board, the CFTC backed off in July of 1989 and decided not to regulate the interest-rate, currency or commodity swaps and options businesses of U.S. commercial banks. However, the damage had been done. Banks that had been offering commodity swaps had already moved their operations overseas and those that were considering entering the market had suspended their plans. For example, Chase Manhattan, which is recognized as the pioneer of commodity swaps, concentrated its commodity swaps business in London while the CFTC was considering regulating swaps.

At present, CFTC supervision over swaps remains an active issue. In June of 1990, legislation was introduced in Congress that would permanently settle the matter by specifically excluding swaps from CFTC regulation as long as they were not offered to the general public. Until the bill becomes law or the issue is resolved another way, banks considering offering commodity swaps are best advised to structure their transactions to meet CFTC guidelines.

The CFTC listed five criteria that would be used to determine whether a particular commodity swap would be exempt from CFTC regulation. Banks that structure commodity swaps to fall within the guidelines will not draw a regulatory challenge from the agency. Even swaps that fail to meet the criteria will not necessarily be challenged, however. Instead, they will be reviewed on a case-by-case basis. The five criteria are:

1) The commodity swap must be individually tailored, unlike futures contracts, which are highly standardized, maturing on particular dates and carrying rights to specific amounts of commodities.

2) Performance obligations must be entered with the expectation that performance be carried out. The swap can only be terminated, absent a default by one of the counterparties, with the consent of the counterparty.

3) The commodity swap cannot contain margin requirements or use a settlement system designed to eliminate individual credit risk. These are features contained in futures contracts.

4) The commodity swap must be used by the counterparty as part of its general line of business.

5) The commodity swap must not be offered to the retail public.

Conclusion

By buying expertise in particular commodities and combining it with existing capabilities in structuring and marketing financial swaps, bankers can stake a claim to a growing and profitable new derivatives business. Many banks got into the financial swap business too late, after the product became generic and margins came under pressure. However, commodity swaps are still at an early stage in the product life cycle. The number of players is small and margins are high. For banks with mature interest-rate and currency swap businesses, commodity swaps represent a natural way to leverage and broaden their risk-management product portfolio.

19

Commodity Derivatives
A Market Grows and Matures

For the corporations that use them and the financial institutions that market them, commodity derivatives are an increasingly important aspect of risk management. Long familiar with the use of derivatives in foreign-exchange and interest-rate risk management, intermediaries and end-users are applying the same techniques to manage exposure to changes in commodity prices.

The 1991 war in Iraq, and the ensuing wild price fluctuations in oil and oil-related products, brought home to many corporations the importance of managing oil price exposure. Energy consumers that failed to hedge suffered as prices rose; British Airways, for instance, reported an earnings drop of £215 million in fiscal 1991 largely as a result of a 46% increase in jet fuel costs during the Gulf crisis. The Mideast crisis also highlighted the difficulty in using exchange-traded, as opposed to customized and bank-intermediated, hedges to cover the exposure. Airlines that used heating oil or gasoline futures were badly burned when the price of jet fuel spiked sharply higher than the prices on exchange-traded heating oil and gas.

Benefits of Commodity Derivatives

The positive side of this difficult lesson is that corporations have become more aware that managing exposure to commodity price changes means better control of costs, margins, and budgeting, and have become more open to the use of commodity derivatives. In addition, institutional investors are realizing the benefits of commodity-linked assets as a means of diversifying portfolios. Finally, banks and commodity-oriented financial institutions are seeing opportunities to bring value-added and wide margin (at least for now) techniques to customers, as well as ways to increase the credit quality of those customers by stabilizing production costs and sales margins. The result has been a rapid growth in the commodity derivatives market and expectations of further growth for the future.

Transaction Sheet: Commodity Derivatives

Counterparties	Heavy producers, refiners, or users of commodities
Intermediaries	Commercial and investment banks, commodity-oriented financial institutions, subsidiaries of heavy producers or users
How Banks Profit	Bid-offer spread on swaps, up-front premiums on options, arrangement fees
Deal Size	$25 million to $250 million is typical in bank-intermediated transactions; smaller deals often done on commodities exchanges; maturities of OTC deals are 2 to 7 years, although transactions of 15 to 20 years have been done.
Credit Considerations	Default can entail high costs to intermediary, especially when markets are illiquid.
Major Players	Phibro Energy, Chase Manhattan, Bankers Trust, First Chicago, Banque Paribas, CSFP, Banque Indosuez, Barclays, Société Générale
Competition	Participation limited to intermediaries with strong credit ratings; swap market maturing, option market still young

Growth of the Market

In August of 1990, the size of the commodity swap market was estimated to be $10 billion. By early 1994 the market for commodity swaps and options was estimated to be between $40 and $50 billion, with as much as 85% of that total comprised of oil swaps. The rest of the market is mainly precious- and base-metal-related.

Although a variety of companies use commodity derivatives, the biggest concentration is still among primary producers, refiners, and end-users of the commodities, including mining and metal production companies; oil producers, refiners, and retailers; transportation/travel companies; public and private utility companies (particularly if a high percentage of the electricity produced is from oil-burning plants); natural gas producers and pipeline companies; municipalities and other heavy users of heating oil; and project financings, particularly those for cogeneration plants.

In response to the proliferation of end-users, the number of financial institutions willing to be intermediaries in these transactions has also grown. Commercial and investment banks are the primary intermediaries, and the major players include U.S. banks such as Chase Manhattan, Bankers Trust, First Chicago and Continental; European banks such as Barclays, Banque Indosuez, Société Générale, BNP, Banque Paribas, and Credit Suisse (through its derivatives unit CSFP); and investment banks such as Salomon (through Phibro Energy) and Morgan Stanley. On the investment front, the market has seen the advent of such vehicles as the Goldman Sachs Commodity Index, allowing investors an alternative to buying commodities or the equity of a commodities company in order to add the asset class of commodities to their portfolios.

Benefits of OTC Transactions

The New York Mercantile Exchange (NYMEX) has listed futures and options on futures on crude oil, heating oil, gasoline, natural gas, and propane since the late 1970s. These contracts are viable hedging instruments for many companies. However, the increasing sophistication of end-users in identifying and quantifying actual exposure has highlighted the shortcomings of using exchange-traded products.

These shortcomings led to the development of an OTC commodity derivatives market. The techniques—swaps, caps, collars, and swaptions— have the same names and general characteristics as those used for foreign- exchange or interest-rate hedging. However, users of financial derivatives can generally be defined in terms of issuer/borrower or investor/lender; in the commodity derivatives market, the users are more appropriately defined as producers or consumers.

Following are the most popular commodity derivatives techniques and examples of how and when they can be used to manage commodity price exposure.

Swaps

Swaps represent the largest portion of the commodities derivatives market, and oil-based swaps account for most of the volume.

Following the Gulf crisis, most major oil producers either started a hedging program or expanded an existing one. Sovereigns such as Mexico (which reportedly hedged 60 million barrels), Brazil (45 million barrels), and Canada (10 million barrels) entered the oil swap market for the first time, receiving a fixed rate in order to guarantee a minimum return on oil production. The former Soviet Union has been an active player in the gold swap market, using it to lock in hard currency receipts.

Corporate end-users have also been active. Enron Corporation, the largest integrated natural gas company in the United States, has used natural gas swaps both to hedge purchase and transportation costs and to devise long-term, guaranteed-rate contracts with its customers, thereby obtaining a competitive advantage. Though the market is relatively new, many European and U.S. airlines have used jet fuel swaps to hedge one of their largest and most volatile cost components. There have been examples of paper, copper, and cement swaps as well. Any commodity for which spot and forward prices can be monitored through an accessible and respected market index is capable of being swapped.

Commodity swaps are similar to interest-rate swaps in that the two sides of the transaction agree to exchange floating- and fixed-rate cash flows, based on some agreed-upon market index. Unlike futures contracts, commodity swaps do not involve any exchange of the underlying commodity. The structure of a typical commodity swap is illustrated in Exhibit 1. A typical index for the floating side of the swap might be the West Texas Intermediate (WTI), Dubai, or Brent crude for an oil swap, the London Metals Exchange (LME) for base metal swaps, or the recently introduced Continental Elgin Jet Index (CEJI) for jet fuel.

In a typical commodity swap, the producer of the commodity receives the fixed rate, ensuring a minimum price level for the commodity. Likewise, the user of the commodity pays the fixed rate, setting a maximum cost. Rarely do the producer and user swap directly; rather, both sides enter into the appropriate swap with a commercial or investment bank intermediary. As with any swap, counterparty credit risk is a major factor in the transaction. This is why only major banks with strong credit ratings have been active in the intermediation role.

The floating-rate payment on an interest-rate swap is typically measured on a specific reset date. In commodity swaps, this floating-rate payment is determined by an average of daily spot prices over a specified period of time (monthly or quarterly) rather than the spot price on a specific date. Because producers constantly produce and end-users constantly use commodities, the use of an average rate helps to smooth timing exposure and provides a more effective hedge for both parties.

Commodity Options

The commodity options market is less developed than that for swaps, but a growing number of participants are considering caps, floors, collars, and swaptions. FMC Gold, a subsidiary of FMC Corporation, is the fourth-largest gold producer in the United States With exposure as both a user and producer in a variety of metals and chemicals, FMC has used commodity options on

Exhibit 1   Cash Flows in a Commodity Swap

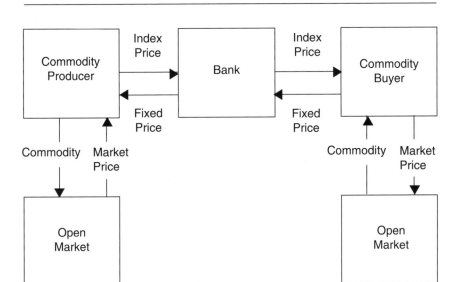

London Metals Exchange indices. Phelps Dodge is the world's second largest copper producer and in 1991 used both caps and floors to hedge about 25% of its expected copper production.

CAPS AND FLOORS

In a commodity cap, the purchaser pays an up-front premium for protection against a rise in the commodity spot price above the strike level of the price. As with swaps, average-rate spot prices are often used, and the strike rate on the cap will be compared at agreed-upon reset dates to an agreed-upon index. In a floor, the purchaser pays a premium for protection against spot prices moving below the floor strike rate, thereby ensuring a minimum price for the commodity.

In contrast to swaps, caps, and floors allow full benefit from favorable commodity price movement. The trade-off is the up-front premium paid, which can be expensive in times of high commodity price volatility, such as during the Gulf War. Becasue there is no up-front premium involved with swaps, they are often seen as a more attractive hedging tool when end-users expect large price increases or declines. Historical commodity prices, however, have shown long periods of stable prices, and during these times option prices may be lower and swaps less attractive.

Although end-users can earn premiums by selling options, the seller takes on potentially unlimited exposure. There are also some uncertainties, at least in the United States, regarding the classification of option sales as a hedge for tax and accounting purposes. For this reason, most end-users focus on option purchases.

COLLARS

A collar is a combination of a purchased cap that sets a maximum price level and a sold floor that sets a minimum price level. A collar may be used by a company that wants to hedge its upside price exposure but is willing to give up some of the benefit of a favorable price movement in exchange for a lower up-front cost. The premium earned by selling the floor can totally or partially offset the cost of the cap; the specific strike levels and cost are determined by the needs and views of the corporation.

SWAPTIONS

While still new to the commodity derivatives market, swaptions are gaining importance as potential users become more sophisticated. A commodity swaption is an option that gives the purchaser the right, but not the obligation, to enter into a commodity swap at a specified point in time as either a payer or receiver of the fixed commodity price. In periods of great price uncertainty, a swaption can be a viable hedging alternative. For example, just prior to an OPEC meeting where new production volumes are expected to be set, a company might consider purchasing a swaption giving it the right to enter into an oil swap as a payer of the fixed price. Should the OPEC meeting result in a spike in oil prices, the swaption purchaser can enter the swap at below-market levels. If oil prices drop following the meeting, the option will expire unexercised and the purchaser will be out only the premium price while still benefiting from lower market prices.

Multiple Hedging Strategies

A U.S.-based aluminum producing company has calculated that roughly 35% of the production cost of its aluminum is electricity, and that most of its electricity comes from oil-fired plants. Consequently, the production cost of its aluminum can be greatly affected by changes in oil prices. Furthermore, a

Exhibit 2   An Oil-Aluminum Swap

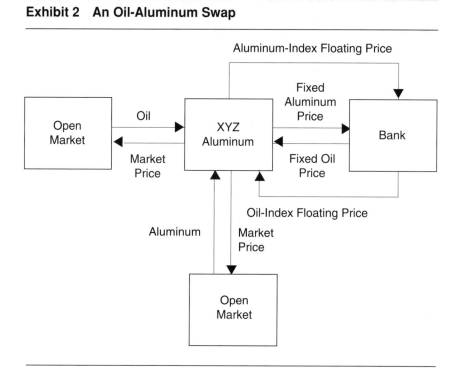

rapid rise in oil prices may not be able to be passed on via higher aluminum prices, because there are other aluminum producers that are not so dependent on oil-derived energy. The competitiveness and profitability of the company, therefore, is affected not only by supply and demand in the aluminum markets, but also by changes in oil prices.

With the help of its bank, the company structured an "oil for aluminum" swap, which is actually two separate swaps with the bank standing as the counterparty on both deals. On one side is an oil swap, where the company pays a fixed rate and receives an oil index–based floating rate. On the other side is an aluminum swap, where the company receives a fixed rate and pays an aluminum index–based floating rate. By using both swaps, the company hedged its exposure both as a commodity user (oil) and as a commodity producer (aluminum) and can therefore maintain competitive prices in the open market. A diagram of the probable structure of the transaction is shown in Exhibit 2.

This simple, but by no means unusual, example shows how different factors can affect a company's competitive position. The example illustrates that corporations, and therefore bank relationship managers, need to look at all components of the company's cost/margin structure, and not just the most obvious ones, in determining appropriate hedging strategies.

Marketing Commodity Derivatives

Commodity derivatives provide relationship managers with a value-added technique that can differentiate their banks from competitors. In addition, because the number of intermediaries is limited and the market tends to be illiquid (particularly for longer-dated transactions), these techniques can be quite profitable.

When discussing commodity derivatives with customers, relationship managers should focus on the benefits of a well-thought-out hedging program. Commodity hedging gives companies more control over costs and margins, allowing for increased accuracy in budgeting and planning. In addition, a hedging program can result in enhanced creditworthiness and more access to other capital markets. Appropriate hedging programs are often viewed favorably by ratings agencies, so a company that can demonstrate that its assets, costs and margins are less subject to commodity price fluctuations will be looked upon more favorably by banks and investors.

Once the customer understands how hedging can help his or her company, the next step is selling the benefits of the OTC market and the bank's capabilities. Because OTC commodity swaps and options involve no physical delivery of the commodity and are usually done through an intermediary, confidentiality is ensured and the hedges do not interfere with the supply or delivery of the commodities. Moreover, the over-the-counter nature of these products allows for customization of the hedge with respect to commodity, size, maturity (two to seven years is normal, though longer transactions have been done), and structure.

Certain steps need to be taken prior to initiating a hedging program, and the astute relationship manager can play an advisory role in these steps, which may lead to a higher probability of being awarded a mandate. The steps are:

1) *Define and quantify exactly the company's commodity risk exposure.* Although not an exact science, the process generally starts with a breakdown of production raw materials and the percentage of overall production cost allocated to each raw material, the lead time between changes in the price of production materials and changes in the price of end products, and the elasticity of end-product prices to changes in production costs.

2) *Establish specific financial objectives with regard to those exposures.* Cost containment, protection of revenues, stabilization of cash flows, certainty of planning and budgeting—what is it that the company wants to achieve?

3) *Select the hedging products that best meet the company's goals and objectives.* This will be determined by the company's overall exposure, its willingness to pay up-front premiums, the maturity sought, the degree of cash flow certainty required, and the company's views on price movement.

Conclusion

Commodity derivatives can be a welcome addition to a corporation's overall risk-management program and can offer relationship managers a new and potentially profitable product to market. The market is growing rapidly and will continue to grow as awareness of commodity price exposure increases and the means to quantify that exposure develop. As volume and liquidity increase, prices will fall and new products will develop. Although regulatory, tax and accounting issues complicate the use of commodity derivatives for end-users, the market will continue to grow as end-users demand the means to control exposure and investors seek commodity-linked investment products. Banks willing to assume the credit and market risks of these derivatives will gain increasing revenues and the ability to offer more complete client service.

20

Commodity Derivatives
No Longer Just Plain Vanilla

Products for hedging commodity risk have existed on regulated exchanges for many years, but it was only in the late 1980s that banks began to offer clients over-the-counter commodity hedging products. Since then, the commodity derivatives market has evolved beyond the "plain vanilla" stage to structured deals designed to meet specific client needs. Despite this evolution, the market is still less mature—and therefore less competitive—than interest rate or foreign exchange derivatives. Compared to other sectors of the derivatives market, commodity-linked transactions tend to offer banks greater opportunities to distinguish themselves and the possibility of earning higher margins. Moreover, for a given amount of exposure, commodities pose greater risk to customers, with annual volatility of 20% to 50% compared to interest rates (15% to 20% annual volatility) or foreign exchange (8% to 12% annual volatility).

The perceived importance of commodity hedging ebbs and flows with world events, particularly events that affect commodity prices. In 1991, when Iraq invaded Kuwait, energy-based commodity derivatives exploded as companies looked to hedge energy risk. In contrast, 1993 has been a stable year for commodities, with a worldwide economic downturn helping to keep commodity prices in check. In late 1993, crude oil prices dropped to below $14 a barrel, the lowest price in almost four years. Gasoline prices are also at five-year lows. Analysts expect gasoline prices to drop even further because there is a lag between a drop in crude prices and the refined product such as gasoline. Although it is often volatility that triggers hedging activity, depressed prices or rates can also be seen as a reason to hedge too, as participants in the U.S. interest-rate swap market have recently learned.

Users of Commodity Derivatives

Users of commodity derivatives are producers seeking to manage revenues or consumers hoping to manage costs. Both exchange unknown changes in

Summary Sheet: Commodity Derivatives

Investors	Retail and institutional investors looking to enhance yield through commodity price movements and reduce credit exposure through the use of commodities as collateral
Borrowers/ Counterparties	Producers and users of commodities, including airlines, utilities, mining companies, energy companies, manufacturers
Intermediaries	Commercial and investment banks, commodity-based financial institutions.
How Bank Profits	Bid/offer spreads on swaps and options; fees on structured deals
Deal Size	$15 to $300 million are typical sizes of bank-intermediated transactions. Most have maturities from one to seven years. Smaller transactions and shorter maturities are done on regulated commodity exchanges.
Credit Considerations	Intermediaries face credit risk from both sides if structures are hedged. This could entail high cost in certain illiquid commodity markets.
Major Players	Chase Manhattan, Citibank, Bankers Trust, Banque Paribas, Standard Chartered Bank, Westpac, First Chicago, CSFB
Competition/ Life Cycle	Less competition than in more developed sectors of derivatives market

commodity prices for a known risk (a fixed price in the case of swaps or a worst-case price in the case of options). Public and private corporations have become increasingly aware of market risks and their effects on company performance. Any corporation that buys or sells physical commodities faces exposure to commodity price risk. Commodity consumers include airlines and various types of manufacturers; typical commodity producers include mining and energy companies. Some companies are both consumers and producers, facing commodity risk on both the cost and revenue sides. Utilities consume oil and produce electricity; both can be hedged with commodity swaps.

Banks are increasingly using commodity derivatives to structure asset-backed loans. The asset securitization piece is used to reduce credit concerns while the commodity derivative is used to control price risk. Corporations with commodity reserves but weak credit can use commodity-backed financing to obtain funds at attractive levels. Investors like the slightly above-market returns these structures offer coupled with the reduced credit risk.

One nonstandard user of commodity hedging has been the state of Texas. In 1986 to 1987, tax revenues on oil production and refining declined. This condition added to an enormous state budget deficit. Texas now hedges part of its $500 million dollars in annual oil tax revenues, buying out-of-the-money put options for West Texas Intermediate (WTI) crude oil. These options trade on the New York Mercantile Exchange (NYMEX). Out-of-the-money options are purchased in order to hold down hedging costs. In addition, Texas hedges only for the next three months. These options are the most liquid and tend to have tight bid/offer spreads.

Another user of commodity derivatives targeted by banks is the investor with a portfolio of stocks exposed to commodity prices. For example, if an investor is exposed to firms that buy oil and energy products, these companies have exposure to rising energy prices. If the firms are not hedging this exposure, the investor can hedge that exposure through the energy derivative market.

Exchange-Traded Products

Commodity futures and options on commodity futures trade on regulated exchanges throughout the world. Futures offer the opportunity to lock in a price for a commodity, while options on futures can either protect the producer from downside risk while allowing participation in higher prices, or protect the commodity user from higher prices while allowing participation in a lower price environment.

While exchange-traded futures and options offer end-users a liquid market to trade or hedge commodity exposure, several features restrict their usefulness as well. Futures and options on futures are limited in terms of how far into the future they trade. The contracts that trade the farthest into the future are the West Texas Intermediate crude oil futures contract and the copper contract. Both trade out to about 18 months. Options on futures trade for shorter periods of time than the corresponding futures contracts. For instance, when the state of Texas chooses to use options to hedge its exposure to oil prices, it is limited in how far out it can hedge.

For many users, futures contracts also present basis risk. Many users are exposed to risk from a specific commodity. The exchanges may offer a contract on a similar but not identical commodity. Basis risk is the risk of a change in the price relationship between the exchange-traded commodity and the commodity the user wants to hedge. Basis risk can also arise from differences in the specific grade or delivery location of a commodity. For example, exchange-traded futures for natural gas are based on prices at a specific delivery point in Louisiana. Because natural gas is physically pumped to a location, prices differ based on delivery point. Using the exchange-traded contract to hedge the purchase of natural gas delivered at another location can generate substantial basis risk.

Exchange-traded futures contracts can also result in the possibility of taking delivery of the underlying physical commodity. Although this situation rarely occurs, it is a consideration for the exchange-traded futures user.

The factors that complicate a customer's use of exchange-traded products also make it difficult for banks to hedge the risk of over-the-counter commodity derivative products. This may be one reason why, in terms of volume and exposure, the commodity derivative market lags the interest-rate and foreign-exchange derivative markets. Value-added products are those that hedge a client's specific commodity risk for the precise period of time desired. These are often the same products that are difficult for the bank to hedge.

Plain Vanilla Commodity Swaps

A commodity producer uses a swap to fix revenues that are based on the sale price of a particular commodity. A fixed price over the swap period replaces the risk of falling commodity prices. However, the producer gives up any gains in price appreciation. A commodity user fixes the costs that are based on commodity prices through a fixed price swap. The user exchanges the risk of rising commodity prices for a fixed price, but gives up the benefit of lower

Exhibit 1   Plain Vanilla Commodity Swap

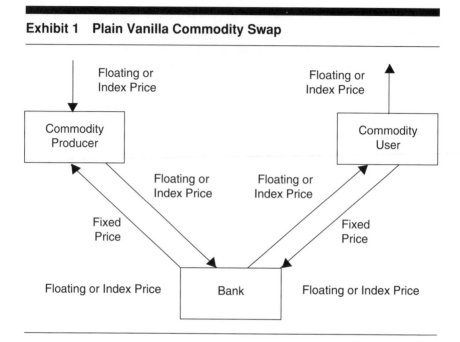

commodity prices. The bank stands in the middle, making a market for both user and producer and making a profit on the bid/offer pricing for both sides (see Exhibit 1).

Most commodity swaps are structured with the floating side resetting monthly and based on the average price of the commodity for that month. This structure is useful for a user that has commodity price risk throughout the period. The fixed payments are the notional at risk applied to the swap rate, and the floating payments are defined by the notional at risk applied to the average price over the particular period.

Other floating price reset structures include taking the average over the final three or five days. This structure mimics the price risk for a user where that risk is defined over a short period. The notional amounts at risk every month could be equal or could fluctuate depending on the exposures that are being hedged. Therefore, even the "plain vanilla" structure has several variations designed to offset the client's risk more precisely.

Structured Commodity Deals

Much activity in recent years has been directed toward designing deals to meet specific client needs. These deals tend to be highly structured, and overall activity and liquidity are limited. Part of the reason is the lack of major players willing to price and execute highly structured transactions. Just as hedgers have a hard time using the futures market to hedge their positions, banks have had a difficult time hedging their deals in the futures market. This cuts down on the liquidity in the market as banks come to terms with hedging their commodity books. However, clients demanding more precisely tailored commodity-based deals will drive banks to offer them, thereby increasing competition and driving up liquidity.

One feature of recent structured deals is the increasing use of commodity options and options combined with swaps. Commodity hedging used to mean plain vanilla swaps for producers to fix revenues and for consumers to fix costs. Put and call options on commodities are now very common. The first commodity swaptions were done in 1991. Now these types of structures are commonplace. Exotic options such as knock-out and knock-in barrier options are frequently seen in the market. Companies now look beyond standardized products to structures explicitly designed to offer a solution to their problem.

Double-Up Swaps

Airlines have always had a large exposure to changing energy and/or jet fuel prices. Historically certain airlines have hedged this exposure and certain airlines have not. Because of deregulation and increased competition, airlines that hedged came out ahead when fuel prices rose, and airlines that did not hedge benefited as fuel prices dropped. This is because in the competitive airline environment it is difficult to adjust ticket prices as fuel costs rise and fall.

Some airlines have recently entered into double-up swaps, which use the sale of an option to reduce the fixed cost of a swap. The airline enters into a traditional commodity swap to pay a fixed price on jet fuel and receive the floating index price. In order to lower the fixed commodity price on the swap, the airline sells the bank a put option. The pricing for the put option is embedded in the original swap rate (see Exhibit 2).

Double-Up Swap

Regular Fixed-for-Floating Jet Fuel 1-Year Swap Rate	$200/ton
Double-Up 1-Year Jet Fuel Swap Rate	$197/ton
Strike Price on Embedded Put Option	$197/ton

If the original notional amount of the swap is 100,000 tons, the airline pays

Exhibit 2   Double-Up Jet Fuel Commodity Swap

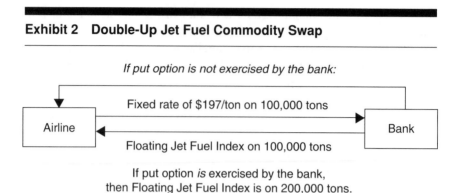

If put option is not exercised by the bank:

Airline — Fixed rate of $197/ton on 100,000 tons → Bank

Bank — Floating Jet Fuel Index on 100,000 tons → Airline

If put option *is* exercised by the bank,
then Floating Jet Fuel Index is on 200,000 tons.

$197 per ton fixed rate on this amount. If the jet fuel price falls below $197 per ton, the airline pays a fixed rate of $197 per ton, not on the original 100,000 tons but on 200,000 tons, or double the original amount.

The airlines' goal was to match their budgeted fuel costs over a particular period that they had assumed in pricing their tickets. These swaps were originally executed in March/April of 1993 when jet fuel was trading at about $200/ton. In June of 1993, the price had dropped to about $170 per ton, and airlines with this structure found themselves paying out about $30 per ton more than the market price, not on the original notional amount but on twice the original notional amount. The real danger to airlines executing this trade is if the original swap is based on a notional amount of more than one-half their fuel requirement. If the put option is exercised, the swap notional amount is "doubled," and the airline will find itself paying out a fixed amount on more jet fuel than it actually uses. Some airlines may have done just that as they came into the market in the summer of 1993 to buy put options to offset their exposure.

Zero-Cost Collars and Participating Swaps

Taking their cue from the interest-rate derivative market, intermediaries have completed several zero-cost (premium) option structures and participating swap structures. These structures focus on reducing the amount of up-front cash premium.

Major oil companies, including Mobil, Chevron, and Texaco, have been involved in hedging energy risks with these structures. Amax Energy, a supplier of natural gas, used a participating swap structure to hedge natural gas revenues. In this participating swap structure, a swap hedged a portion of the risk and an option (in this case a synthetic put option on natural gas) hedged the rest. Amax entered into a swap to receive a fixed price on natural gas for 50% of the amount that the company sought to hedge. On the other 50%, Amax entered into a swap to receive a fixed rate and also bought a series of call options, thus creating synthetic put options that would hedge against a fall in natural gas prices. The call strike was at the same level as the swap rate. Amax paid for the calls by reducing its fixed receipt on the swap. Thus, Amax received a slightly below-market minimum rate on natural gas sales while participating 50% in any price appreciation.

Commodity-Linked Financing

Banks are looking toward offering financing in which the structure is based in some way on commodity price movements. Asset securitization has been the mechanism whereby companies were able to raise funds using their assets. Layering on commodity derivatives takes this structure one step further by removing certain price and credit concerns/risks.

One of the first deals of this type was a copper-linked three-year loan structured by Banque Paribas. The $210 million loan was from a group of 11 European banks to a Mexican copper mining company. The deal allowed the mining company access to capital at competitive fixed rates. Normally a company of this type would not have been able to access the capital markets at such attractive rates. The deal was structured as follows:

- The full proceeds of $210 million go to the Mexican mining company.

- Every month for the three-year term of the loan the Mexican mining company delivers 4,000 tons of copper to Sogem, a subsidiary of Société Générale.

- Sogem deposits the proceeds from the sale of copper into an offshore escrow account. This account is assigned to the syndicate of banks as collateral for the loan.

By having funds in the offshore account, the bank syndicate avoids the risk that Mexico might impose restrictive exchange controls. However, the syndicate still runs the risk that the sale of the copper will not generate sufficient funds to repay the loan. Therefore, Banque Paribas executed a copper swap with the escrow account paying fixed into the escrow account and receiving floating proceeds based on the price of copper each month. To eliminate the risk of a cash shortfall, the fixed amount of funds deposited into the account must cover the interest and principal payments on the loan.

Exhibit 3   Oil-Linked Enhanced Yield Loan

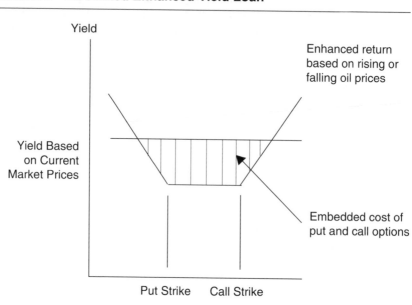

This structure fixes copper prices for the mining company, preventing participation in any price appreciation of copper. The deal provided attractive fixed-rate financing while reducing political and country risk for the lenders. The main risks now are copper production risk (from the Mexican company) and default risk on the commodity swap (from Banque Paribas). A transaction diagram appears in Chapter 26 of *The Derivatives Engineering Workbook*.

Enhancing Returns on Loans

Commodity options can also be used to enhance returns on loans to commodity producers. An example is the seven-year loan structured by Chase Manhattan Bank for the Algerian state-owned oil producer Sonatrach. If oil prices fall, the lender has a higher repayment risk and receives a higher rate of interest to compensate. The twist on the deal is that if oil prices rise, the lender also receives a higher interest rate.

This loan is structured using a fixed-price commodity swap that will lock in a fixed payment for oil production. These fixed payments are translated into an effective interest rate. In order to produce the enhanced return when oil prices rise or fall, call options and put options on oil are purchased. As oil prices rise or fall, the options are exercised and the payout passes through in the form of a higher interest rate to the lender. The lenders need to pay for the premiums on the call and put options, for they are ultimately the beneficiaries of these options. The premium can be structured as an up-front fee or passed through to the lenders through a below-market fixed rate that will be in effect between the put and call option strike rates (see Exhibit 3).

The strike prices on the options relative to the fixed rate on the commodity swap determine the payout profile. The closer the options strikes are to the option, the more sensitive the return is to rising or falling oil prices. However, the options also become more expensive as the strikes move closer to the swap rate. The notional amount of each affects the yield enhancement to the lender. The larger the notional size of the options purchased, the greater the yield enhancement for a given move in the oil price. The more sensitive the structure is to rising or falling oil prices, the more expensive the put and call options become.

Conclusion

Since its beginnings in the mid-1980s, the commodity derivative market has changed and grown. At first, most deals were plain vanilla, fixed-for-floating commodity swaps. While the plain vanilla swaps are still a large part of the market, an increasing number of structured transactions are being executed. These transactions are combining swaps and options and also blurring the line between commodity derivatives and interest-rate derivatives.

Commodity-linked financing offers the borrower access to funds at competitive rates that normally may not be available. This is accomplished by combining asset securitization methods with commodity derivatives to eliminate credit risks (i.e., political, country, or company-specific) and pricing risks. Adding options creates loans that give investors the opportunity for enhanced returns while offering borrowers the chance for submarket funding. Banks can put together financing packages that are attractive to both the borrower and the investor.

The commodity derivative business has developed and will continue to develop into a market that allows banks to satisfy investors while providing borrowers funds at an attractive level. For banks, this can mean structuring deals on commodities that cannot be easily hedged on regulated exchanges because an index on the exact commodity is not available and/or the maturity of the deal extends beyond the last traded futures contract. These are the types of transactions that add value for the client and profit for the bank.

PART V

Capital Markets
Applications

The year 1981 could be viewed as the most important in the history of derivatives. Throughout the 1970s, derivatives remained simple tools for hedging short-term risks. But when the World Bank and IBM exchanged simultaneous U.S. dollar and Swiss franc bond issues in 1981, the transaction opened a new world of longer-term applications and set the tone for the innovations of the next decade.

In the early years, these innovations were driven by the quest for lower financing costs through comparative advantage. Essentially, a borrower finds his market of comparative advantage, issues in that market, then exchanges the liability into a generic alternative like U.S. dollar LIBOR. In doing so, both sides win: the investor who buys the desired asset and the borrower who receives below-market financing even after the cost of the original issue and the swap. These swaps of primary issues also accelerated the globalization of financial markets by arbitraging the inefficiencies between different markets and sectors.

As derivatives technology became more sophisticated, it became possible to devise structures that very precisely reflected the desired positions of investors. It is these structures, most of which are also methodically dissected in The Derivatives Engineering Workbook, that form the core of the capital markets section:

- Chapters 21–23 discuss a variety of structured interest rate plays, including yield curve notes, SURFs, reverse floaters and range floaters.

- Chapters 24–27 focus mainly on investor-oriented applications of equity index swaps and options (Chapters 24–26), but also examine a classic corporate finance application: the converting preference shares of Coles Myer, an Australian retailer (Chapter 27).

- Chapters 28–30 cover cross-currency capital markets deals. Starting with a general introduction to currency swaps (Chapter 28), the section moves into cases on the mechanics of dual-currency private placements (Chapter 29) and dual-currency notes (Chapter 30).

- Chapter 31 examines the use of embedded commodity options in financings, including Kodak's gold-linked notes and SEK's silver-linked liabilities.

Each chapter in the capital markets section provides a slightly different perspective on the ways that derivatives can help bank customers gain increased access to global capital markets and investors, better manage assets and liabilities and widen the range of investment alternatives. All of these factors helped to drive the phenomenal growth of derivatives in the 1980s and early 1990s.

21

Yield Enhancement
Creating New Asset Structures

Bank distribution teams around the world face the challenge of providing U.S. dollar floating-rate assets with enhanced yields. A number of structures have been created to address this need. All involve a series of swaps or the purchase or sale of options to transform potential future income into a higher current yield. For investors who understand the risks, these structures can represent attractive alternatives to straight floating-rate assets.

Chapter 21of *The Derivatives Engineering Workbook* examines a sophisticated structure used to enhance (or reduce) yields: the switch swap. Also called cross-currency or LIBOR-differential swaps, these structures are driven by the gap between forward interest rates in different currencies. Switch swaps allow U.S. dollar-based investors to index floating-rate assets to the higher yields available in European currencies.

The Market Environment

Yield-enhancement structures can be sold in any market environment. However, the current U.S. interest-rate environment is uniquely suited to them. First, the Federal Reserve's lax monetary policy has pushed U.S. dollar LIBOR to about 3.5%, the lowest level since the 1970s. Second, despite 18

Exhibit 1   Three Yield-Enhancement Structures

Name	Structure	Customer Trade-off
Floored (minimum-coupon) FRN	Investor buys in-the-money floor.	Coupon cannot go below a floor set above current LIBOR; floor paid for by adjusting spread.
Collared FRN	Same as floored FRN, but investor sells out-of-money cap to cut cost of floor.	Investor gives up potential income from higher rates.
Switched FRN	Intermediary uses multiple swaps to "switch" rate.	Investor receives US$ at DM LIBOR (currently 9.5%).

months of steadily declining interest rates, the gap between short- and intermediate-term interest rates remains relatively high: 65 to 200 basis points between three-month LIBOR and one- to five-year single-A corporate debt.

The combination of low short-term rates and a steep cash yield curve has pushed up the forward-rate curve—the market's prediction of future short-term rates. Individual investors may not agree with this prediction of a sharp rise in LIBOR. Certainly this forecast, which has prevailed since the yield curve began to steepen sharply in 1990, has failed to hold true during the following two years. Indeed, a study from U.S. investment bank First Boston recently found that forward interest rates are a very poor predictor of future cash interest rates.

All of the yield-enhancement structures listed in Exhibit 1 operate on a similar principal: Potential future income resulting from the expected rise in LIBOR can be extracted and brought into the present in the form of a higher spread over LIBOR.

In the case of a floored (minimum-coupon) floating-rate asset, the investor buys a floor and pays for it by adjusting the spread on the coupon. The floor is in the money at the beginning (i.e., LIBOR is lower than the floor rate), increasing the investor's yield for the first (and perhaps subsequent) periods.

In the case of the collared floating-rate asset, the investor buys an in-the-money floor but also sells an out-of-the-money cap to help pay for the floor. The sale of the cap puts a ceiling on potential coupon income.

The third and most complex alternative is the "switched" FRN, which involves combining a floating-rate asset with a switch swap. Switch swaps allow bank customers to denominate assets or liabilities in one currency while indexing the interest receipt or payment to LIBOR in another currency. Borrowers can use switch swaps to take on European-currency liabilities at U.S. dollar LIBOR (plus a switch spread). Investors seeking enhanced yields can take on U.S. dollar assets at LIBOR (minus a switch spread) in Deutschemarks, Swiss francs, sterling or any other currency.

Switch swaps are examined in detail in Chapter 21 of *The Derivatives Engineering Workbook*. Briefly, switch swaps work because the yield curve in Germany is steeply inverted, implying lower short-term rates in the future. This is the opposite of the steep U.S. dollar yield curve, which implies higher short-term rates in the future. By pulling the potential income from higher U.S. interest rates into the present and transforming it into a "switch spread," the switch swap enables a U.S. dollar-based investor to index his or her coupon to Deutschemark LIBOR.

Conclusion

Floored, collared, and switched FRNs represent three solutions to the same problem: the low level of U.S. money market rates. Relationship officers who understand the dynamics of forward rates, the views of their customers, and the ways cash can be redistributed across the term of an investment, can offer customers a variety of ways to enhance the yields on floating-rate assets.

Despite a widening of the gap between U.S. and European money market rates, switch swaps have not been used much in recent months. However, every purveyor of a complex derivative product early in its life cycle faces a similar dilemma: The education of customers often poses a bigger obstacle than any problem inherent in the technique.

22

Reverse Floaters

Capitalizing on a Window of Opportunity

Wherever borrowers or investors have strong market views, bankers can creatively apply financial skills and market knowledge to create relatively straightforward but highly value-added solutions to financial problems. One recent result of this creative process is the rise of reverse floater structures in Germany. Currently the hottest debt structure in the German capital market, reverse floaters accounted for more than DM2.7 billion (US$1.68 billion) in transactions in January of 1993 alone.

The appeal of reverse floaters to investors lies in the steeply inverted shape of the shorter maturities of the Deutschemark yield curve and in the ability to "leverage" the expected drop in Deutschemark interest rates over the next 18 to 24 months into higher returns. The appeal to issuers is a strong investor demand and attractive market rates. To banks, the appeal is the ability to please both issuers and investors while skimming off a healthy bid/ offer spread.

Reverse floaters illustrate a broad principal applicable in any financial market: Structures that allow investors to take positions based on their market views can also often yield low-cost funds for borrowers. If the structure is innovative, the intermediary is likely to be able to collect relatively high fees and spreads as well. The key to these transactions is an understanding of the financial engineering techniques necessary to structure an instrument that will reflect investor views sufficiently to persuade investors to pay a premium.

Reverse floaters have also been done recently in other European countries, including France, Sweden, Switzerland and the UK. There is nothing to prevent them from being done in the United States, Canada, Australia, and other countries when market conditions and investor views are appropriate. This chapter examines the reasons behind the surge in reverse floater transactions, reviews the typical structure of several types of different reverse floaters, and discusses opportunities for bankers presented by these transactions.

Reverse Floaters: A Pure Yield Curve Play

Exhibit 1 lists the reverse floaters issued in Germany in January of 1993. Of particular interest was the DM500 million issue done by the Republic of Austria. This was the first reverse floater ever launched for a sovereign

Summary Sheet: Reverse Floaters

Sellers	Mainly banks in the form of deposits and/or corporations as a primary debt issuance. Can also be done in the secondary markets through swaps.
Buyers	Pension funds, portfolio managers, retail investors, institutional investors
Intermediaries	Mainly German and U.S. banks
How Banks Profit	Bid/offer spreads
Risk Considerations	Investors must have strong view on rates, and banks must hedge transactions properly, or else risk can be considerable.
Major Players	Trinkaus Burkhardt, Deutsche Bank, Morgan Stanley, JP Morgan
Competition/Life Cycle	Still fairly early, with good profit potential available. Key to winning mandates is an investor base.

Exhibit 1   Reverse Floaters Launched in January of 1993

Issuer	Amount (in DM millions)	Lead Bank
Rabobank NV	200	Morgan Stanley
Republic of Austria	500	Trinkaus
Nordic Investment Bank	100	DG Bank
EBRD	100	Morgan Stanley
DG Bank	150	DG Bank
Helaba	200	Helaba
Westfälische Hypo	75	Morgan Stanley
Daimler Benz	300	Deutsche Bank
Council of Europe	200	Trinkaus
European Investment Bank	300	Trinkaus
Nederlandse Gasunie	75	JP Morgan
Bayerische Vereinsbank	100	Bayerische Vereinsbank
General Electric Capital Corp.	200	IBJ
Deutsche Bank	200	Deutsche Bank
TOTAL	DM2,700 million	

borrower, as well as the first issue more than DM200 million in size. This list shows only the public issuances of reverse floaters and does not include any private (though much smaller) deals that may have been done.

The reason behind this rush of reverse floaters is fairly straightforward—a steeply inverted Deutschemark yield curve, which implies a fall in Deutschemark interest rates that many German investors find difficult to believe.

The Deutschemark yield curve is driven by two very disparate forces. In the short end of the curve (out to two and a half years), the yield curve is largely determined by the trading of Euro-Deutschemark futures contracts traded on the LIFFE in London. These market participants are expecting a continued decline in Deutschemark interest rates due to a deepening recession and political pressure from other European countries, which lay at least part of the blame for their own economic woes on a stubborn Bundesbank keeping Deutschemark rates too high. The Bundesbank is well-known for its anti-inflationary policies, and the inflationary pressures of a unified Germany have until recently kept short-term rates very high in comparison to other currencies.

Exhibit 2   Recent Cash and Forward DM Yield Curves

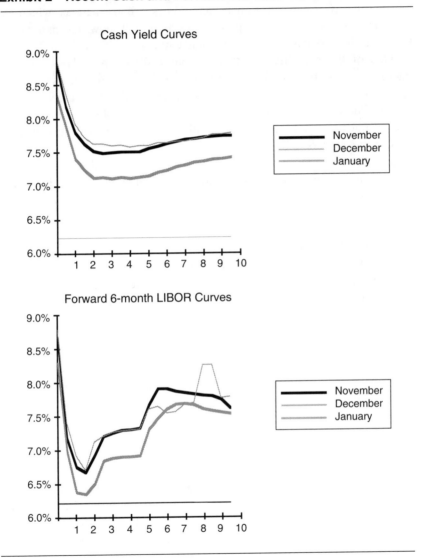

Inside Germany, the perception is very different. The Bundesbank's anti-inflationary stance is respected and accepted by most Germans. Many simply cannot believe that interest rates will fall as rapidly as the Euro-Deutsche-mark futures market implies. The result is a decided "hinge" in the yield curve, with yields in the three- to ten-year maturity actually showing a slight upward slope. Beyond two and a half years, Deutschemark yields are driven by the Bund (German government) and domestic bond markets, which are dominated by internal German participants. Exhibit 2 shows recent trends in the Deutschemark cash and forward yield curves.

One of the main reasons that the future direction of Deutschemark interest rates is so uncertain is the action of the Bundesbank itself. It has shown enough of a willingness to cut rates (though still not so much as some outside Germany would like) to make many of those in London believe that interest rates may still have room to fall—movement increasingly difficult for German players to believe.

It is the inverted shape of the early part of the curve that has led to the investor interest in reverse floaters, and the "segmentation" of the yield curve (its positive slope in later maturities) that has led to variations of the basic reverse floater structures.

The Investor's Perspective

Despite debate as to how fast and how far, most investors believe that Deutschemark interest rates will indeed fall. For these investors, who would like to capitalize on falling rates, the structure of the reverse floater is extremely compelling.

Suppose an investor holds a floating-rate note. With this investment, the investor is exposed to falling rates, since the yield on the FRN will decline as interest rates fall. To hedge this risk, the investor could use a plain vanilla floating-for-fixed swap and lock in a return of the swap rate. If the swap rate is 7.50%, then the investor has locked in his or her return at 7.50% over the life of the swap. But while this strategy protects the investor from a decline in rates, it does not allow the investor to *benefit* from a decline in rates.

Structuring the Reverse Floater

Getting the investor from the locked-in rate of the swap to a position where his or her return will increase as rates fall is relatively straightforward. If the payout profile is thought of as a "swap clock," then hedging the investor with one swap moves the payout line from one that is positively sloped to a flat line. By "rotating" the "swap clock" once more, a payout profile can be created that will show interest income rising as rates fall (see Exhibit 3).

To achieve this payout profile, the investor simply enters into another floating-for-fixed swap (see Exhibit 4). If, as mentioned before, the market swap rate is 7.50%, then the investor has achieved a return of:

Exhibit 3   Rotating the "Swap Clock" to Alter the Payout Profile

To a fixed-rate instrument:

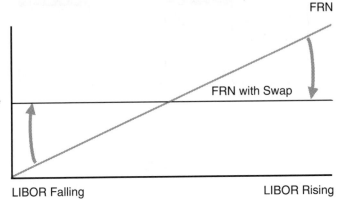

To a reverse-floater instrument:

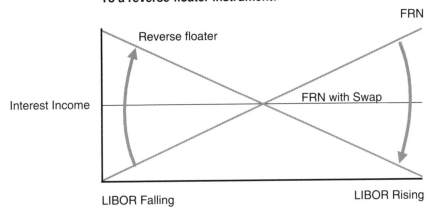

Receive on the FRN:	LIBOR
Receive on Swap 1:	7.50%
Pay on Swap 1:	– LIBOR
Receive on Swap 2:	7.50%
Pay on Swap 2:	– LIBOR
Net:	15% – LIBOR

Exhibit 4   Floating-Rate Note with Two Swaps

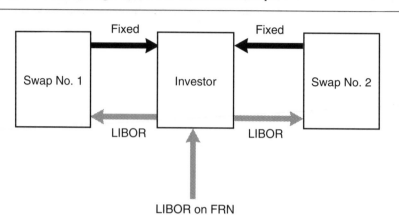

The investor now has exactly what he or she wanted: an instrument in which return increases as rates fall. This structure would give the exact payoff profile shown in Exhibit 3.

The beauty of this transaction is that as many swaps can be added as necessary in order to "leverage" the investor's view of how far rates will fall. For example, entering into a third swap at the market rate would result in a net return of:

Receive on Swaps:	$3 \times 7.50\%$
Pay on Swaps:	$-3 \times \text{LIBOR}$
Receive on FRN:	LIBOR
Net:	$21.50\% - (2 \times \text{LIBOR})$

As rates fall, the investor's return will increase by 50% more than in the straight reverse floater. This second structure is known as a double LIBOR reverse floater. There is obviously no limit as to how many times the structure can actually be leveraged, but a triple LIBOR reverse floater is about as far as the market has actually seen.

Variations on a Theme

Once the basic structure of reverse floaters is understood, it can be adjusted in a variety of ways to fit the investor's view on the Deutschemark yield curve. One of the most common variations is called a fixed/reverse floater.

This simply means that the investor receives a fixed rate of interest during an early period of the swap (usually one to two years), and then receives a reverse floating return for the remainder of the transaction.

Why receive fixed for the first year or two? The answer is that many investors do not believe the shape of the Deutschemark yield curve, either in the shorter maturities or in the longer maturities. Many investors do not believe that rates will fall as quickly or as far in the short end of the curve (the end driven by the Euro-Deutschemark futures market in London), nor do they believe that once rates start to rise they will rise as quickly or as high in the long end of the curve (the end driven by German bond investors).

The fixed/reverse floater fits this rate view perfectly. With a plain vanilla reverse floater, the investor benefits as rates fall. If the investor does not believe rates will fall as fast as expected, then a fixed rate is preferable to a rate with a return pegged to a reverse floating structure. Conversely, if the investor believes that rates will not rise as quickly as the yield curve suggests, then receiving a reverse floating return is desirable over a straight fixed return. This is the logic behind the fixed/reverse floater: It simply gives the investor the preferred return in each segment of the yield curve, based on the investor's view of future rate movement.

Structuring a fixed/reverse floater is relatively straightforward. By adding a plain floating-for-fixed swap for the first year or two of the reverse floating structure, the arranging bank can create a fixed rate of return for the investor for the life of that swap. Furthermore, with some simple rearrangement of the cash flows, the arranging bank can offer a higher than market fixed rate for that first year or two, and then make up the "loss" by lowering the fixed-rate portion of the reverse floater over the remaining life of the deal. These structures have enormous appeal for investors, particularly in light of their strongly held view of future yield curve movements.

Benefits for Issuers and Arranging Banks

Issuers of reverse floaters can persuade investors to pay a premium for two reasons. First, the issuers are offering a debt security that their investors want. Second, they are doing so at rates that appear attractive to the investors.

Assume, for example, that a German corporation could issue fixed-rate debt at the prevailing swap rate—7.50% in the previous example. The cost of pricing and hedging the reverse floater structure, as described, was 15% minus LIBOR. However, this is not the return offered to the investor. In this example, the investor might be offered 13.50% minus LIBOR. In the example of the double-LIBOR reverse floater, where the market rate was

21.50% minus twice LIBOR, the rate offered to the investor might be, for example, 20% minus twice LIBOR. From the investor's perspective, these offered rates may still seem very attractive, but the all-in cost for the issuer is well below market rates.

For example, assume an issuer issued a reverse floater security based on the structure shown in Exhibit 4 and offering a rate to investors of 13.50% minus LIBOR. On an unhedged basis, this would leave the issuer exposed to a downward movement in rates. However, examining the reverse floating structure diagrammed in Exhibit 4 from the issuer's perspective, it can be seen that the issuer has in essence entered into a fixed-for-floating swap with the investor, whereby the issuer pays the investor a fixed rate of 13.50% and the investor pays the issuer LIBOR.

The issuer may not want this exposure to a downward movement in rates. To hedge this risk, the issuer simply enters into a plain vanilla floating-for-fixed swap—at the prevailing swap rate of 7.50%—and the final result is fixed-rate funds at below market rates:

Issuer pays on the reverse floater:	13.50%
Issuer receives on the reverse floater:	LIBOR
Issuer pays on the plain vanilla swap:	LIBOR
Issuer receives on the plain vanilla swap:	7.50%
All-in Cost for Issuer:	6.00%

The keys to the success of these issues are as follows:

1. Investors do not believe the current Deutschemark yield curve.
2. Investors would like a security that gives a higher return as rates fall.
3. The reverse floating structure fits this view perfectly.
4. The investor market remains somewhat inefficient, allowing for advantageous cost of debt for the issuer.

The advantage in these deals for banks is obvious. They keep their investors and issuers happy, earn arrangement and underwriting fees, and can also participate in the hedging of these transactions after they are issued.

The preceding discussion focused on reverse floater transactions from a primary market issuance perspective. Reverse floaters, however, are just as applicable in the secondary market. In fact, Exhibit 4, which was used to illustrate the cash flows of a reverse floater, also shows how a company could structure a reverse floater in the secondary market. The company could achieve the same result by entering into two separate swaps, as shown in Exhibit 4, or by simply doing one swap for twice the notional amount of the underlying asset.

Conclusion

Reverse floaters illustrate how issuers can exploit a window of opportunity—in this case a yield curve that differs dramatically from the expectations of many investors. The market for reverse floaters will not, however, last forever; in fact, the recent Bundesbank cut in rates may start to bring the yield curve in line with investor expectations, or vice versa. Investors will also become more sophisticated regarding the pricing of reverse floaters, thereby diminishing their appeal to issuers.

Nonetheless, these structures provide a good example of how the creative financial engineering of basic products can yield opportunities for intermediaries. In particular, reverse floaters illustrate how bank customers can take advantage of the shape of, and expected movements in, the yield curve.

Nor are reverse floaters of interest only to bankers in Europe: Analyzing transactions in other markets can help bankers create "new" applications in their own markets. If public debt is not available, the same result can be achieved by using combining bank loans or private placements and interest-rate swaps. Bankers need not take the investor's view; for a borrower, for instance, a banker could synthetically re-create a structure that lowers interest expense as interest rates rise. By keeping up-to-date with current market deals and applying those ideas to their own customers, bank officers dramatically improve the opportunity for value-added service and profitable business.

23

Range Floaters

Structured Notes for Investors with Views on Volatility

What Are Range Floaters and Why Have They Been So Popular?

The first six months of 1994 witnessed the issuance of more than US$3 billion in the form of structured notes generically called "range floaters." They are also called corridor notes, fairway bonds, accrual notes, and digital or binary notes. Regardless of the name, the structure of all of these notes has been the same: An issuer pays a premium spread over (typically) three-month LIBOR, but only on those days when LIBOR (or, increasingly, some other indexlike foreign-exchange rates) is within a certain range. If LIBOR should move above or below the defined range on any given day, then the interest accrued for that day is zero. Investors are therefore earning a premium spread on a short-term floating-rate note in exchange for taking a view on the volatility of LIBOR (or some other index) over the life of the note, which typically is one to three years. Examples of recent range floater issues are listed in Exhibit 1.

The product behind these deals is the binary or digital option. A digital option is one in which the payout on the option is a fixed amount, regardless of how far into the money the option may move. In a range floater, the investor is selling a series of digital options to the issuer, who is paying for these options by paying a premium spread over LIBOR on the notes. The issuer can then sell these same digital options to the bank underwriting the note at a higher price, thus hedging the issue back into floating at sub-LIBOR levels.

Much like reverse floaters (see Chapter 22) and other structured deals, these notes are targeted at investors willing to take a view on changing market conditions in exchange for a pickup in yield over plain vanilla alternatives. Most early range floaters were issued in U.S. dollars, and the range used for the notes was based on three- or six-month LIBOR. When the Federal Reserve bank engaged in a series of tightenings in the first and second quarters, aggressively pushing up short-term U.S. interest rates, LIBOR approached or passed the upper boundary of many of these range floaters. As a result, these notes lost value and fell out of favor. Since then, variations of the basic range floater theme have appeared, in particular notes that accrue interest based not on interest-rate ranges but rather foreign exchange-rate

Transaction Sheet: Range Floaters

Issuers	Double-A or better European banks or government-backed borrowers
Investors	Institutional investors, mutual funds, pension funds, retail investors
Underwriters	Major investment, merchant, and commercial banks
How Bank Profits	Underwriting fees, spreads on hedging transactions
Fees	Typically 10 to 15 basis points
Deal Size	Generally US$100 to US$200 million
Major Players	Morgan Stanley, Goldman Sachs, Salomon Brothers, Merrill Lynch, Swiss Bank Corporation, Union Bank of Switzerland, JP Morgan, Chase Securities
Risk Considerations	Issuer is fully hedged; investor takes risk that volatility forecast will prove incorrect and interest will not accrue; intermediary takes on only normal underwriting risks.
Competition/ Life Cycle	Digital options are still relatively new, restraining competition, but competition will grow as understanding of digital options increases.

Exhibit 1   Selected Range Floater Issues

Issuer	Lead Bank	Amount	Coupon (basis points over 3-month LIBOR)	Maturity in Years	Ranges
Council of Europe	Salomon Brothers	US$100 million	60 basis points	1	0.0–4.00% (months 1–6) 0.0–4.25% (months 6–2)
Rabobank	Samuel Montagu	US$100 million	50 basis points	1	DM1.62 – DM1.88 (months 1–12)
Hong Kong MTRC	Morgan Stanley	HK$250 million	125 basis points*	3	3.25–4.25% (months 1–6) 3.25–4.75% (6–12) 3.25–5.25% (13–15) 3.25–5.50% (16–18) 3.25–5.75% (19–21) 3.25–6.25% (22–24)
Pemex	Chase Securities Swiss Bank Corporation	US$200 million	205 basis points	3	3-month LIBOR – 0.20% to 3-month LIBOR + 0.50%; based on 3-month LIBOR 2 days before note issuance
Oster-reichische Posparkasse	Credit-anstalt	US$100 million	4.50%** (in US$)	1	3-month Lira LIBOR: 7.50–9.00% (months 1–6) 6.50%–8.50% (months 7–12)

* Over 3-month HIBOR
** Fixed rate

ranges. Despite the rise in U.S. interest rates, yields on plain vanilla alternatives in most currencies remain relatively low. Because of this, structures like range floaters, which give investors enhanced yield in exchange for taking a market view, remain popular.

This chapter examines the rationale behind range floaters as well as the digital options that are used to create and hedge these structures. Digital options are an increasingly common product among bank product specialists, and a working knowledge of these products will prove beneficial for both relationship managers and derivatives marketers.

Who Issues Range Floaters? Who Buys Them?

So far, the issuers and general terms of most range floaters have had several common characteristics:

Issuers	AA or better (e.g., highly rated European banks and government-related borrowers)
Tenor	One to three years
Coupon	Three- or six-month U.S. dollar LIBOR + above-market spread
Ranges	Three-month LIBOR in various currencies, the spot FX rate in several currencies

Early forms of structured notes, like reverse floaters, targeted investors who did not believe the implications of the shape and direction of the yield curve or, more specifically, the forward curve. These notes were structured so that these investors could achieve enhanced yields if their view of the yield curve proved correct.

In contrast, range floaters are not structured so much to take advantage of a yield curve being *wrong* as they are structured with a specific view of the *volatility* of that yield curve. Consider the example of a range floater issued by Rabobank, the AAA/Aaa–rated government-supported Dutch bank:

Exhibit 2 Rabobank FRN Ranges and Implied Three Month Forward Rates

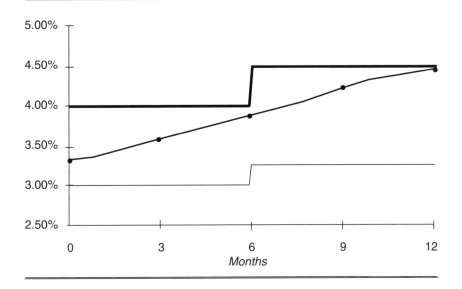

Issue Date	February 23, 1994
Amount	US$100 million
Issue Price	100.00% (par)
Coupon	Three-month U.S. dollar LIBOR + 0.60%
Tenor	1 year (February 23, 1995)
Ranges	Accrues interest on those days when three-month U.S. dollar LIBOR lies within:

                             3.00%–4.00% (first six months)
                             3.25%–4.50% (second six months)

For the coupon, LIBOR will be set at each quarterly reset date, and that rate will hold for the entire quarter. For example, if LIBOR is 3.50% on a given reset date, the investor will earn 3.50% + 0.60% = 4.10% for that quarter, paid in arrears. However, the investor will earn this 4.10% only on those days when three-month LIBOR is within the specified range for that reset period. In other words, for coupon purposes, LIBOR is reset each quarter; for interest accrual purposes, LIBOR is examined daily.

Note that the range that three-month LIBOR can float within increases in the second six months. This is in response to the upwardly sloping U.S. dollar yield curve at the time of issuance. In fact, as Exhibit 2 shows, the implied forward curve for three-month U.S. dollar LIBOR at the time of issuance falls well within the specified ranges for this issue.

An investor with a significantly different view about forward three-month U.S. dollar LIBOR would not be interested in this deal, for that view would imply that LIBOR had a good chance to fall outside the specified ranges a large percentage of time over the life of the deal. The investor who bought this deal is not disagreeing with the direction or general levels of LIBOR. Rather, the investor is earning a premium spread (Rabobank could issue a plain vanilla FRN at flat LIBOR or perhaps even sub-LIBOR) in exchange for taking the view that LIBOR will not be particularly volatile over the life of the note. If this is in fact the case, the investor will earn the full premium spread. If the investor is wrong, and LIBOR rises or falls out of the range, then the investor will not earn the full premium, and in fact could actually end up with an overall yield of less than LIBOR flat. For most range floaters, LIBOR needs to remain within the specified ranges roughly 65% to 80% of the time for the investor to break even with a plain vanilla FRN alternative.

Following the launch of this issue, the U.S. Federal Reserve tightened rates several times, and three-month U.S. dollar LIBOR stood at 5% in late July of 1994. This particular note has not turned out well for the investor.

How Are Range Floaters Structured and Hedged?

The Rabobank issue can be used to illustrate the structure and hedging techniques behind range floaters. In the simplest terms, Rabobank issued a floating-rate note to investors with a series of caps and floors embedded into the note. These caps and floors result in Rabobank having to pay no interest on any day when three-month LIBOR falls outside the specified ranges. Rabobank is paying for these caps and floors by paying a premium spread on the coupon, in this case LIBOR + 0.60%, when on a plain vanilla FRN it could probably achieve at least flat LIBOR.

As with most option-linked capital markets issues, Rabobank will not leave this range floater unhedged. Rather, it will sell to the underwriter of the note (Union Bank of Switzerland in this case) the same series of caps and floors that it purchased from the investors. The premium it will receive for these options is greater than what it paid to the investors, and Rabobank will end up with floating-rate money at sub-LIBOR levels. The target all-in funding cost for most of the existing range floaters has been estimated to be LIBOR less 20 to 30 basis points.

From one perspective, these notes do not seem much different from collared floaters, which have been seen in the market for several years and which also embed an interest-rate collar into an FRN. What makes range

---

Exhibit 3   Payout Profile of Rabobank Range Floater (First Six Months)

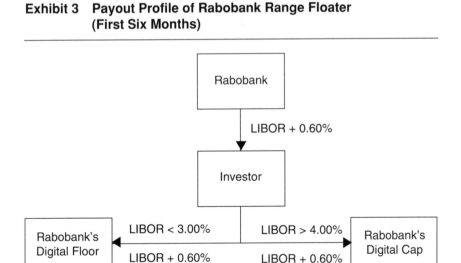

floaters unique is the nature of the caps and floors. When interest rates rise above the cap strike or fall below the floor strike on any given day, the investor earns zero for that day. With a normal cap or floor, the amount of payout depends on how far into the money rates have moved relative to the strike price of the option. With range floaters, the amount of payout on any given day is known in advance and does not depend on how far into the money the option may be. In other words, once the option goes into the money, regardless of how far, the payout is a set, fixed amount.

The caps and floors in range floaters, then, are not plain vanilla options but rather are what the market calls *binary* or *digital* options. These options are either "on" or "off" (thus the name "binary"), and if on, then the payout under that option is a fixed amount, regardless of how deep in the money it may be.

The structure behind the Rabobank issue can be re-created using these digital options. The payout profile for the first six months (when the defined interest-rate range is 3.00% to 4.00%) is shown in Exhibit 3.

Rabobank has purchased a series of *daily* binary caps and floors from the investor. In the first six months, each of these floors and caps has a strike price of 3% and 4%, respectively. In the second six months, the respective strike prices on the daily floors and caps change to 3.25% and 4.50%. The

Exhibit 4   Using Digital Caps and Floors to Cut Borrowing Costs

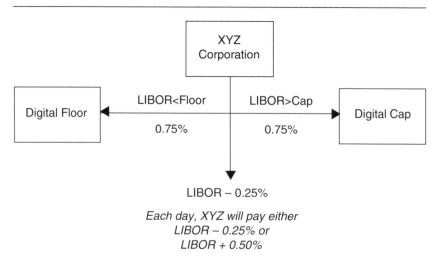

annualized cost of these caps and floors is 0.60%, the spread paid over the flat LIBOR that Rabobank could achieve on a plain vanilla FRN. (Remember that Rabobank will hedge this issue out and end up with an all-in cost of LIBOR less 20 to 30 basis points.)

The payout on the options is fixed at three-month LIBOR + 0.60%. That is, regardless of how far above 4% or below 3% rates may move on any given day, the payout under the exercised digital option is fixed at LIBOR + 0.60%. Because this is also the rate on the note itself, if one of the options is exercised on any given day, the net return to the investor is zero. There will be a new digital cap and floor each day of the note, and each will be valid only for that one day. Because LIBOR resets quarterly on the note, the hedging bank will use the implied forward three-month rates (as shown in Exhibit 2) in determining the appropriate LIBOR levels when calculating the fixed payout (LIBOR + 0.60%) under the series of daily digital caps and floors.

Can Digital Options Be Used in the Secondary Hedging Market?

Digital options may also appeal to corporate borrowers in the secondary market. Consider the example of the XYZ Corporation, which can borrow under its bank revolver at flat LIBOR. XYZ believes that interest rates will more or less follow the implied forward curve and will not be overly volatile. Such a borrower may seek to reduce its borrowing cost by selling digital options, using the premium to reduce costs.

Assume that the payout under the digital options is fixed at 0.75%, and assume that by selling a series of digital floors and caps XYZ can earn an annualized premium of 0.25%. The net result is shown in Exhibit 4.

As long as LIBOR remains within the specified range (in this case determined by the strike prices on the floors and caps), the options remain unexercised and XYZ achieves an all-in cost of LIBOR – 0.25%. If LIBOR either rises above the cap strike or falls below the floor strike (keeping in mind that it can never do both at the same time), then XYZ will pay out 0.75% under the option and will achieve a net borrowing cost for that day of LIBOR + 0.50%.

This concept can be extended to other markets besides interest rates. A company with sizable foreign-exchange flows can use digital options to either lock in rates or earn premium and reduce costs. Chapter 14, which discussed trigger swaps, showed how a company can use interest-rate swaps and digital FX options to hedge multiple exposures simultaneously.

What Are Some of the Variations of Range Floater Structures?

The Rabobank issue is typical of many of the initial range floater issues that came out in early 1994. In these issues, the ranges were linked to LIBOR and were set prior to issuance. With the pursuant tightening by the U.S. Federal Reserve bank, however, many of these deals are bumping up against their upper ranges and have lost tremendous market value.

This has not resulted in the death of range floaters, however. It has simply resulted in other types of structures. Examples of three of these variations are outlined in Exhibit 1.

In the Pemex issue, the ranges were not set at the announcement of the issue but rather were determined by looking at three-month LIBOR two days prior to the launch of the issue and setting the upper range at that LIBOR level + 0.50% and the bottom range at that LIBOR level – 0.20%. This reduced the risk to the investors that LIBOR would change significantly between the announcement and launch dates of the issue.

In the Rabobank issue, the boundary range was not tied to interest rates at all but rather to the Deutschemark/U.S. dollar exchange rate. Specifically, the investors will earn LIBOR + 0.50% on every day that the Deutschemark/U.S. dollar spot exchange rate is between DM1.62:US$1 and DM1.88:US$1. In this case, the investors are earning a premium coupon in exchange for taking a view on exchange rates, which recently have been much less volatile than interest rates (particularly U.S. interest rates).

In the Osterreichische Postparkasse issue, investors are again taking a view on interest rates, but in this case the view is on three-month Italian lira rates. With the recent upsurge in U.S. rates, the market will probably continue to see range floaters tied to other interest rates besides the U.S.. Which rate these notes will be tied to will depend on the market view of the volatility in those rates.

Another variation is exemplified by a structure offered by J.P. Morgan called a "Constant Spread Range Index Security," or CS-RIBS. In these notes, the boundary ranges are not set at the beginning of the note but rather are set as a constant spread around LIBOR, determined at each reset period. This is similar to the Pemex issue but takes it one step further. For example, the range may be set at three-month LIBOR +/– 0.25%, reset each quarter at the current three-month LIBOR level. This further reduces the volatility risk to the investor, because this risk is now limited to the next rollover date rather than predetermined for the whole note prior to issuance, as with the original range floaters.

Other variations of range floaters have also been seen in which the boundary ranges are linked to the market price of a specific stock, linked to the differential between two different interest rates, or linked to specific swap rates. In reality, the only limits to creating range structures are investor demands and liquidity in the hedging of these deals.

Summary: What Are the Key Points to Remember about Range Floaters?

Range floaters are simply a form of structured note in which the investor accepts an enhanced yield in exchange for taking a view on a particular market index. In most cases, that index has been LIBOR, but the market is increasingly seeing notes indexed to FX rates, equity prices, and other indices. In addition, recent structures have attempted to reduce the investor risk to some degree by determining the boundary ranges every reset period rather than up front.

The derivative product behind all range floaters is the binary or digital option, which is an option with a fixed payout regardless of how far in the money the option may be. As banks and corporations become more comfortable with the mechanics and pricing of digital options, they are used more in the secondary hedging market where, because of the fixed payout profile, they can often cost less than plain vanilla options. Relationship managers with a good understanding of digital options can structure cost-effective, high value-added solutions to their customer's needs.

24

Equity Derivatives
Genesis of a Market

New financial techniques and products often result from changes in regulatory, market, and economic conditions. A regulatory change in Japan, twin global equity market collapses, and a new paradigm of global economic integration have spawned the equity derivatives market.

Equity derivatives are important to bankers for three reasons. First, the use of equity derivatives is growing at a time when the use of many traditional banking products is stagnant. Margins and fees are high because most equity derivatives products are relatively new and few providers exist.

Second, the ability to create and sell equity derivatives is an important complement to equity underwriting capabilities. Any financial institution seeking to sell to equity investors—from retail investors to large institutions—can use equity derivatives to create customized equity products carrying higher margins.

Finally, equity derivatives are playing a growing role in the debt business. By combining a traditional debt issue with an equity kicker—for instance, the indexation of coupon or principal payments or an attached equity option—borrowers can often gain lower all-in funding costs than a plain vanilla debt issue would yield. Much of the sub-LIBOR funding obtained by Eurobond issuers in recent months had its origin in debt combined with some type of equity derivatives product.

Summary Sheet: Equity Derivatives

Users	Equity investors from retail level to large institutions; borrowers seeking to lower funding costs by adding an equities play
Intermediaries	Investment and merchant banks
How Bank Profits	Bid/offer spread on brokered products; fees on tailored products
Deal Size	$25 million and up for equity swaps; $100 million and up for index-linked bonds and index warrants; $1 million and up for custom-tailored options
Credit Considerations	Same as for debt derivatives (counterparty risk on swaps, purchases of options)
Major Players	Bankers Trust, Merrill Lynch, Credit Suisse Financial Products, Nomura Securities
Competition/ Product Life Cycle	Early in product life cycle; spreads are still wide
Fees/Spreads	Varies by transactions; 30 basis points through the middle on the most common equity swaps; higher for less common swaps; underwriting fees on index-linked bonds and index warrants

It's common these days to hear: "You can't be in the equity business without a strong equity derivatives capability." This sounds familiar to those who anticipated how significantly swaps would transform the debt markets several years ago. But there are differences. This chapter defines the equity derivatives business, its standards and practices and assesses its importance in the global financial marketplace.

What Are Equity Derivatives?

Equity derivatives are contracts linked to individual stocks, baskets of stocks, or market indices. Asked to define the products of the equity derivatives market, the leading marketers will usually respond that the services they provide are custom-tailored. However, the major products are covered warrants, over-the-counter options, equity swaps, and index-linked bonds and warrants. Each is defined in Exhibit 1 and is discussed in more detail later.

Exhibit 1   Equity Derivatives

Covered warrants	Equity warrants sold by a third party, which may own the underlying stock
Index warrants	A warrant linked to the value of a stock market index
Over-the-counter options	Options purchased from a dealer rather than on an exchange. To satisfy the needs of the client, they can be custom-made in terms of size, tenor, and the stock(s) or indices to which they are linked.
Index-linked bonds	Bonds with the coupons or principal repayment linked to the performance of an equity index
Equity swaps	Swaps of LIBOR plus a spread against an equity index

Equity derivatives are unique in that they are the first major investment banking innovation to emerge from Asia. The explosive Japanese stock market of the 1980s provided the impetus that led investment bankers to initiate the Japanese covered warrants market. The modern generation of equity derivatives products has developed out of the covered warrants business, and warrants remain a significant focus of many equity derivatives teams. However, the definition of equity derivatives is now broader and more general. Today, equity derivatives specialists profess the ability to do anything, on an over-the-counter basis, that an investor desires.

Japan's Covered Warrants Market

The extremely profitable Japanese equity warrants business of the late 1980s was purely a product of the wildly bullish Tokyo Stock Exchange. Covered warrants, as they have become generally known, were widely distributed to investors all over the world seeking to participate in the Japanese market. The limited downside appeal of these securities was a major attraction, given the stratospheric levels of the Nikkei index. The term "covered" in covered warrants was originally meant to signify that the warrant issuer possessed the underlying shares in its portfolio, available to the warrant holders upon exercise. In 1991 it may represent simply a promise by the issuer to pay the warrant holder on a cash settlement basis.

The early activity in the warrants market was spawned, in part, by a change in Japanese law regarding the ability of insurance companies to pay dividends. Shortly after the October 1987, stock market crash, Japanese insurance companies were restricted from paying dividends out of capital gains. Given the low dividend yields of most Japanese stocks, these investors looked to the sale of options as a way to boost income on their portfolio holdings. Another factor was that up until 1990, insurance companies were also prevented from reporting income based upon the appreciation of their stock portfolios. The revenues the insurance companies generated through option premiums could flow through to net income.

The basic supply/demand profile of the early equity derivative market— i.e., the covered warrants market—is illustrated in Exhibit 2. Japanese insurance companies sold call options on stock held in their portfolios to investment banks in exchange for option premiums. The investment banks acted like brokers, selling covered warrants to eager retail investors. Warrants were mostly denominated in yen but also were issued in other currencies, particularly Swiss francs. Demand for covered warrants came from many sources, even employees within many of the investment banks, who couldn't resist the lottery-type risks and potential rewards. Japanese securities firms' practice of actively bidding up the prices of new issues helped them to win market share and maintain the illusion of a sure thing to investors.

Beyond the strategic writing of covered call options to enhance portfolio income, Japanese insurance companies were also writing puts on Japanese stocks, as well as puts and calls on stock indexes. The put writing by these large investors wasn't hedging; rather, in most cases, it represented a leveraging-up of positions on the market. So confident were most Japanese stock market investors that they were willing to double up their bets until the start of the 1990 bear market.

Exhibit 2   Covered Warrants

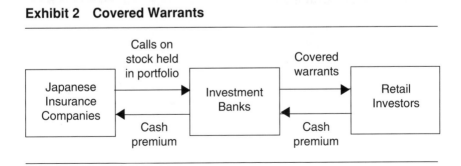

Along with the sudden supply of puts and calls on Japanese stocks and stock indices available from the Japanese insurance companies, there was an emerging demand for more tailored equity hedging products. The demand was particularly strong among the world's portfolio managers following the 1987 crash. Alan Wheat of Bankers Trust is said to have hatched the notion of a full-service equity derivatives capability at a meeting with his derivatives team shortly after the crash. Recognizing that investors would have to remain in the equity markets despite increasing volatility, Wheat believed equity derivatives would enable investors to hedge or capitalize on unfavorable market movements.

The importance of the Japanese option writers to the equity derivatives markets cannot be overstated. The liquidity that they provided to the market enabled the warrant issuers and intermediaries to earn relatively riskless profits on most of the early transactions. Exhibit 3 illustrates how intermediaries capitalized on the emerging supply of and demand for equity options.

With the 1990 decline of about 40% on most of the Japanese stock market indices, the Japanese equity warrant market has fallen on hard times. Yet, the market decline and the three-month suspension of warrant issues sponsored by the Bank of Japan during the spring of 1990 has not hurt the emerging over-the-counter equity derivatives market. Instead, the bear market in Japanese equities has created an urgency in the equity derivatives business that has caused it to be one of the few fever-pitched areas in investment banking today.

The Emergence of OTC Equity Derivatives

The most unique characteristic of the new equity derivatives market is that it remains very much a non-U.S. centered business. Credit Suisse Financial

Exhibit 3   Index Options

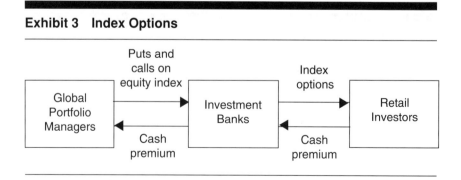

Products says that more than 90% of its global equity derivatives business in 1990 was transacted in Europe and Japan, with Japan having a slight edge. To be sure, with Merrill Lynch and the other major U.S. brokers heavily committed to the equity derivatives market, the United States will represent a center of growth in the future.

JAPAN

Ironically, the take-off point for the newly active over-the-counter equity derivatives market was the drying up of liquidity in the Japanese equity warrants market in 1990. The covered warrants market had provided Japanese investors only the ability to purchase calls on the underlying stocks. Suddenly, portfolio managers were confronted with the need for put protection and other defensive strategies. Global portfolio managers faced the necessity of hedging a variety of complex and increasingly global portfolio positions.

Japan was the fermenting ground for the new OTC equity derivatives products. As Japanese authorities groped with issues ranging from the taxation of futures transactions to the licensing of foreign futures brokers, a host of over-the-counter products were invented to meet investor needs. Nikkei swaps, Nikkei-linked bonds, and a variety of tailored options positions invented for the Tokyo market have become the typical equity derivatives products available today in other centers. The catalyst for the new activity in Japan was the sudden and dramatic fall in share values in 1990.

Just as issuers and investors in Japan were finding many new reasons to turn to the over-the-counter equity derivatives market, investors in America and Europe were also confronted with the need for better hedging tools.

UNITED STATES

The development of over-the-counter equity derivatives in the United States has been a natural evolution. Exchange-traded or listed stock options date back to the opening of the Chicago Board Options Exchange in 1973. S&P 500 futures and S&P 100 options became the standard tools for hedging and implementing synthetic portfolio strategies in the 1980s. Pure arbitrage between futures, options, and cash is a huge business, and program trading is a controversial topic among market watchers. Sophisticated new portfolio strategies, such as portfolio insurance and option replicating strategies, also rely on exchange-traded options and futures.

Yet, despite the breadth and depth of U.S. exchange-traded equity derivatives, many large portfolio managers have found the existing tools inadequate to satisfy their derivatives appetite. Limiting features of exchange-traded derivatives include lack of liquidity, inflexibility in creating structures, and little opportunity for targeted yield enhancement. Liquidity is a problem for many of the large equity portfolio managers, say $1 billion and up, who wish to actively manage their exposures.

One of the arguments for stock index futures and options is that they allow for inexpensive risk reduction (i.e., no cash market sales) and rapid risk transformation. This is true in practice only if the exchange can handle the size of the transactions and, indeed, if the exchange is open at all. Increasingly, large portfolio managers will seek the 24-hour over-the-counter derivatives market for risk-management solutions.

EUROPE

While equity departments of American investment banks focused on the exchange-traded derivatives in the 1980s, in part, due to declining profitability in all aspects of the cash business, European stock brokers continued to reap handsome profits. London's so-called "Big Bang" of 1986 killed profitability in the London cash markets, but Frankfurt, Paris, Zurich, and other centers remained lucrative. Derivatives markets in these centers lagged, in part, because the large securities firms had no real need for them to maintain profitability.

Today, change is being forced on the European centers. Equity derivatives teams have focused attention on Europe to capitalize on the need for derivatives hedging and trading. Hardly a day goes by without an issue of FAZ or DAX warrants—the two major German stock indices—and warrant issues using French and Swiss market indices are also popular. As a result, German futures authorities are under intense pressure to make the new Deutsche Terminborse (DTB) competitive while the French deregulate their markets at a dizzying pace. In 1991 the French and Swiss markets have reportedly been the most dynamic in the world for equity derivatives.

It is interesting to note that the bullishness on Europe created by the reunification of Germany combined with the actual bearishness of the moment to propel the European derivative business to near global ascendancy. Equity derivatives provided investors with a limited risk way to participate in the European stock markets.

Types of Equity Derivatives

The major types of equity derivatives are covered warrants, equity swaps, index-linked bonds and warrants, and a broad, catch-all category: custom-tailored options.

EQUITY SWAPS

Modeled on interest-rate swaps, equity swaps take the form of the payment of the growth of a share index, the Nikkei 225 for instance, versus LIBOR, which is usually denominated in the same currency as the index. There is a quoted market for S&P 500 swaps and Nikkei 225 swaps, and brokers will make prices on swaps against other major indices. In mid-February one broker quoted the Nikkei swap at "flat to plus 50" and the S&P versus US$ LIBOR at "minus 15 to plus 15." Exhibit 4 illustrates the flows involved in an equity swap, using the Nikkei 225 index.

The skewed pricing of the yen equity swap market reflects the one-sidedness of the underlying demand. While many would like to receive the Nikkei index, thereby synthetically investing in the underlying stocks, there are precious few payers of the equity index. In the absence of natural payers of the equity index, swap dealers must go to the exchange-traded markets and cash market and hedge as best they can.

Some dealers describe equity swaps as being the most commoditized of the equity derivative markets. Swaps are used by dealers to hedge various risk positions, and while some technically oriented shops are specializing in short- to medium-term equity swaps (zero to five years), many prefer to concentrate on index-linked bonds and the potentially more profitable option strategies.

INDEX-LINKED BONDS AND INDEX WARRANTS

What Bankers Trust originally called the Protected Equity Note is rapidly becoming a familiar product in the global markets. The basic structure is a zero-coupon bond, usually having a tenor of four to five years, linked to an equity index option. In February of 1991 Goldman Sachs came out with a

Exhibit 4   Nikkei Equity Swap

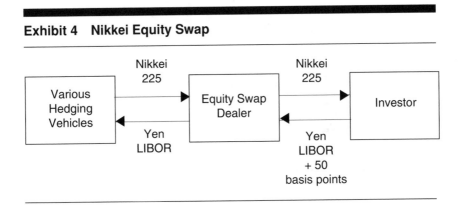

U.S. version of the hot index-linked structure, calling it Stock Index Growth Notes (SIGNS). Exhibit 5 illustrates the SIGNS structure, using the Republic of Austria as an example of an issuer. The SIGNS structure has created a problem for U.S. regulators attempting to define it as either a bond or a futures contract. In the meantime, regulators merely call it a hybrid bond. By stripping out the equity option component, the borrower likely achieved sub-LIBOR funding.

Index-linked bond transactions provide a cash market and derivatives market opportunity for the investment bank. Just as swap-driven Eurobonds provided significant juice to the fixed-income houses in the mid-1980s, equity derivative-driven issues are appearing in greater frequency today. The index-linked structure shown in Exhibit 5 has appeared in the Euromarket as a four-year zero-coupon bond denominated in ECU linked to several European equity indices. Japanese issues are, of course, also frequently linked to the Nikkei today.

Index warrants have replaced warrants on individual stocks as the most important part of the covered warrants business. The Nikkei 225 is the most well-known index and contains 22 stocks listed on the Tokyo Stock Exchange. The Nikkei 225 is a price-weighted index rather than a market

Exhibit 5   SIGNS Transaction

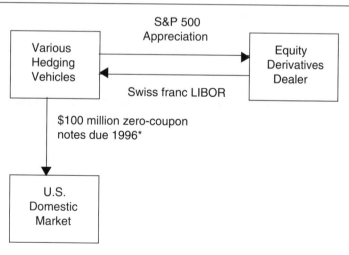

*Returns 100% of principal; pays interest based on any appreciation of the S&P 500 stock index during the life of the bonds.

capitalization index. As a result, the Nikkei 225 is affected by price changes of smaller companies with high stock prices and has been criticized as a less-than-optimum barometer of the market as a whole. The Topix index, on the other hand, is a capitalization-weighted index and is composed of all stocks on the Tokyo Stock Exchange. The Topix is available as an index on many over-the-counter equity derivatives products.

In the U.S. domestic market, where the warrants business has been relatively small, the most popular issues have been Nikkei or S&P index warrants. The worldwide change in focus from warrants on individual issues to index warrants is a manifestation of the growth in the many equity derivative products that in some way reference major equity market indices. Whether linked to bonds or sold in isolation, index warrants have become a huge business.

CUSTOM-TAILORED OPTIONS
The range of customized options provided by investment bankers on all the major stock indices, as well as on individual stocks, is very broad. Specialized index options include long-dated options, options on spreads between indices, and options on small stock market indices.

Long-dated options are usually very expensive. However, they are attractive to portfolio managers looking to protect their Japanese investments over long horizons. By adding a floor level—choosing a market level below which the put payment will no longer provide protection—the portfolio managers can reduce the price of the put insurance. Exhibit 6 illustrates the pricing for these options at various strike prices and maturities.

Individual share options are increasingly prevalent, allowing large portfolio managers to hedge huge holdings of individual shares. Basket options, covering a targeted group of stocks, have migrated from the covered warrants sector to the private hedging market. The most sophisticated providers will create almost any kind of risk return profile.

Another custom-tailored option is the over-and-out index put option. An over-and-out put option is one that automatically expires if the value of the underlying equity rises above a certain level. In exchange for foregoing protection under certain circumstances, the buyer pays a reduced premium.

The twist on the over-and-out index put is that if the index rises above a certain level, say 15% above the current level, the option will automatically expire. The buyer should not mind too much if the option expires at that point, for the put will be relatively worthless if the index rises substantially above the strike price. Exhibit 7 shows the typical terms of these options.

Exhibit 6   Long-Dated Nikkei Put Options Containing Floors

The following Nikkei 225 puts contain a floor that is one-half the current level of the index. Premium payments are made up front in yen.

European Style

	Maturity	
Strike Price	**3 Years**	**5 Years**
At the money	10.00%	11.00%
5% out-of-the-money	8.00%	9.20%
10% out-of-the-money	6.40%	7.60%

American Style

	Maturity	
Strike Price	**3 Years**	**5 Years**
At the money	11.30%	13.25%
5% out-of-the-money	9.00%	10.95%
10% out-of-the-money	7.00%	8.90%

Exhibit 7   Over-and-Out Index Put Option Features

Maturity	3 years
Strike	10% out-of-the-money (below current level)
Expiry level	15% higher than current level
Option Style	American
Price	5%
Standard Put Price	7%

Conclusion

The laissez-faire nature of global derivatives markets ensures the continued penetration of derivatives in all facets of finance. However, these innovations do not occur randomly, nor do they diffuse into new markets at the same speed or in the same form. Early activity in the derivatives market was triggered by a change in Japanese regulations. The market's growth accelerated as portfolio managers sought ways to hedge against a global bear market in equities. Because the market is still in its early stages, margins and fees are relatively high even as the amount of business grows.

It remains to be seen how the first bull run of the 1990s will affect the equity derivatives markets. The market grew up out of the boom and bust of the late 1980s and thrived in the awful markets of 1990. The next six months could well see the market peak. In the event the bull market is sustained, the old cash market may come back to rival derivatives' importance again.

25

Exotic Options
Using Embedded Options to Guarantee Returns

One of the hottest products to hit the European investment market during 1992 was "guaranteed return on investment" structures (GROIs). GROIs are money market investment vehicles with embedded options that allow retail or small institutional investors to participate in the movements of other markets. Deals have been structured using stock market indices of various stock markets (France's CAC-40, the U.K.'s FTSE-100, and Switzerland's Swiss Market Index), baskets of stocks of companies from specific countries or regions (Japan, Switzerland, Pacific Rim), and interest or foreign-exchange rates from a variety of markets. GROIs allow issuers to structure debt instruments customized to the risk/return profiles of specific investor bases and to give those investors a "one-stop" method of diversifying investment portfolios.

Though GROIs have so far been done primarily in Europe, they are of interest to relationship managers in the United States as well. Breaking down GROI structures and examining the component parts is a useful exercise in seeing how embedded options are being used by both issuers and investors to add value, and how banks are using these products to win good margin business. This chapter will discuss the probable structure behind many GROI issues, their use in the financing decisions of corporations and their applications for relationship managers.

The Generic GROI Structure

As with most so-called "exotic option" structures, GROIs are not difficult to understand, although they can be difficult to price and to hedge. Most GROI structures are variations on a common theme: a multitranche debt issue (typically short- to medium-term in maturity) in which investors can select from a variety of minimum and maximum returns depending on their expectations and risk/return preferences. The issuer uses embedded options to link the GROI returns to the performance of some underlying index, basket of stocks and/or bonds, interest rate, or exchange rate.

For example, Swiss Bank Corporation (London) issued in February of 1992 a three-tranche debt instrument in which the minimum/maximum level of return will be a combination of the return realized on the underlying

---

Summary Sheet: Guaranteed Return on Investment Contracts

Sellers	Mainly European banks and Europe-based financial subsidiaries
Buyers	European retail and small institutional investors
Intermediaries	Commercial and investment banks
How Bank Profits	Arrangement and hedging fees
Deal Size	Sold in GROI "units," with a typical deal ranging from 10,000 to 20,000 units. Each unit is worth a set amount of the underlying currency of issue, such as US$10,000, SFr5000, £1000.
Credit Considerations	None for intermediaries
Major Players	SBC-O'Connor, Union Bank of Switzerland, Credit Suisse, Société Générale, Banque Paribas
Competition/ Life Cycle	Early in product life cycle, with few banks participating. Should market expand beyond Europe or to institutional investor base, margins will diminish.

money market investment plus (or minus) a level of return determined by the
level of the FTSE-100 (London stock market) stock index in February of
1993. The minimum and maximum returns on the three tranches are shown in
Exhibit 1. Other GROI issuances by Swiss Bank or its subsidiaries have been
linked to a basket of 25 Japanese blue chip stocks, a Latin America debt
basket made up of equal portions of bonds from Argentina, Brazil, Ecuador,
and Venezuela; the SMI (Swiss Market Index), and a basket of non-Japanese
blue chip East Asian stocks.

IBM International Finance (Netherlands) has issued a GROI in which
return is linked to the ten-year Swiss Franc swap rate, and the market has
seen gold- and exchange-rate-linked GROIs as well. The only prerequisites
for constructing a GROI appear to be investor interest and a tradeable
underlying index to which returns can be linked.

Exhibit 1   Swiss Bank Corporation's FTSE-100 GROI

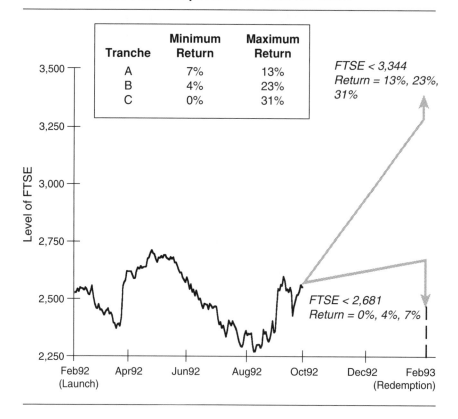

Tranche	Minimum Return	Maximum Return
A	7%	13%
B	4%	23%
C	0%	31%

FTSE < 3,344
Return = 13%, 23%, 31%

FTSE < 2,681
Return = 0%, 4%, 7%

The "Ladder" GROI Structure

One particularly interesting equity-linked GROI was issued in February of 1992 by Crédit Foncier de France via Banque Paribas and BNP. The underlying issue is an eight-year zero-coupon note, with the redemption value of the bonds linked to the CAC-40 (French stock market) index via a "ladder" structure.

In this issuance, there is a series of six thresholds, or "rungs," which represent specific levels of the CAC-40, ranging from 125% to 250% of the initial value of the CAC-40, stepping up in 25% increments. Whenever the opening level of the CAC-40 passes one of the "rung" levels, the investment yield linked to that "rung" is guaranteed to the investor regardless of future movement of the CAC-40 index. The investor also has no capped upside potential—if the CAC-40 should surpass the highest "rung" on the "ladder," the investor will realize an investment return based on the full appreciation of the index (see Exhibit 2).

The issuer of the ladder structure achieved competitively priced eight-year money with no coupon payments until maturity. The investor has tied the return of the zero-coupon issue to the performance of the French stock market.

At first glance, this transaction may seem complicated, but a look at the probable underlying structure shows otherwise. By issuing a zero-coupon

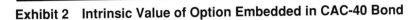

Exhibit 2   Intrinsic Value of Option Embedded in CAC-40 Bond

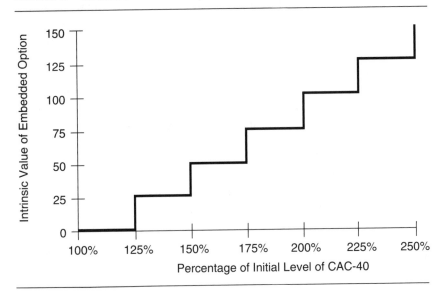

note, Crédit Foncier saves itself the annual coupon payments of a conventional debt issuance. Taking the net present value of these saved annual coupon payments gives an amount that Crédit Foncier can effectively pay to BNP and Banque Paribas to purchase the equity options required to meet the return profile of the notes. The ladder structure could be re-created by the arranging banks purchasing a simple eight-year call option on the CAC-40 struck at the money, and then locking in the "rung" levels by purchasing a series of put options on the CAC-40 struck at the laddered "threshold" levels.

Such a transaction makes all parties happy. The issuer achieves a competitive rate and makes no interest payments for eight years. The investors own a debt instrument with a guaranteed minimum return that "steps up" every time a "rung" level of the CAC-40 is reached and with uncapped equity-linked upside potential. The arranging banks have earned significant arrangement and hedging fees.

Similarities to Other Derivatives

GROIs are remarkably similar in structure to products that corporations and relationship managers have been familiar with for a long time: interest-rate collars and foreign exchange range forwards. The difference is that the investor pays for a guaranteed level of return not through an up front premium (as would be the case if a straightforward floor had been purchased), but by altering the level of minimum and maximum return.

These returns can be guaranteed by the arranging bank through the purchase and/or sale of call and put options on the appropriate underlying index or basket of stocks, bonds, or whatever underlies the GROI. The cost to the bank for buying/selling these options (plus hedging costs and arrangement fees) is passed on to the investor in the form of the various return levels. The more risk the investor is willing to take (or the more flexibility the issuer wants), the higher the maximum return—and the higher the price of the underlying options (and thus the lower the minimum return). As with all financial assets, flexibility and upside potential come at a price.

Evolution of the GROI Market

The primary issuers of GROIs have so far been European banks, their subsidiaries, and European-based finance companies. Investors have been mostly retail, viewing GROIs as an easy way to diversify their portfolios. Many retail investors have varied risk/return appetites but lack either the sophistication or time to diversify and monitor their portfolios personally. The customized nature of GROI structures allows both issuers and investors to meet their respective needs.

GROIs have been possible due to improved modeling and pricing capabilities in the options market. These structures look simple to investors and issuers but, as with diff swaps, require banks to enter into a number of underlying transactions that can be difficult to price, monitor and hedge. While banks build the cost of this into the deal, they cannot charge too much if GROI structures are to remain competitive with other debt and equity financing alternatives.

Difficulties in structuring and hedging GROIs will not limit the market's growth. Many banks have the systems and personnel required to structure these deals, and the markets to which GROI returns have been linked are deep enough and liquid enough to allow dynamic monitoring and hedging.

So far, most GROI deals have been relatively short-term in nature and tied to a standard money market index as a means of enhancing yield. The return level often takes effect one year after the original issuance of the note. While this suits the current investor's demands, it could limit the growth of the GROI market. In order to expand the issuer base of these products away from banks and finance subsidiaries, GROIs will need to lengthen in maturity so that corporate treasurers can view them as a viable alternative to, say, medium-term notes. The Crédit Foncier deal, with its eight-year zero-coupon structure, illustrates how the market will evolve should GROIs become a financing alternative for corporations.

Limits on GROI Market Growth

The growth of the GROI market will depend on investors. A large GROI market requires an investor base large enough to allow secondary trading and absorb a generous level of primary issuance. This means attracting institutional investors. But institutional investors are a double-edged sword. Their interest and investment allow for an increase in the volume of paper issued and traded. However, institutions are more sophisticated than most retail investors and are thus better able to calculate the component costs of option-linked structures. This pressures profit margins for the arranging banks and may drive the smaller arranging banks out of the market.

The other major issue facing GROIs is regulatory. In the United States, for example, many pension or mutual funds that would be the primary target of GROI issuance are prohibited either by federal regulations or internal mandate from investing in option-linked or synthetic products. A bond fund with strict investment criteria, for example, may not be able to invest in debt in which the return is based on the performance of the stock market, even if the credit of the actual issuer is acceptable. The U.S. Securities and Exchange

Commission and Internal Revenue Service have begun to look at option-linked debt in general and equity-linked debt in particular. Any unfavorable treatment by either regulatory body would devastate the development of a GROI market in the United States.

The attractiveness of GROI structures to corporate borrowers is clear. The performance of multinational companies is tied to many factors, including general economic conditions, various stock markets, bond markets, commodity prices, and exchange rates. The use of appropriate GROI structures allows companies to finance using instruments that can be structured to track and mimic changes in these various markets. From this perspective, GROIs are simply a method for corporations to fund and hedge themselves at the same time. As the ability of banks and corporations to quantify actual and economic exposure increases, the demand for competitively priced hedging methods will correspondingly increase. GROIs deals are a natural step in this process.

Conclusion

Although most GROI transactions have been done by European banks and finance subsidiaries, GROIs still have relevance to the corporate account base. As the GROI market grows and develops, corporations will see more opportunities to use these transactions as an alternative to more common financing methods. All markets have a start-up phase, and the best time to enter a market is in its development stages, when opportunistic pricing and structuring are possible.

Even if GROI structures are not directly applicable to their own accounts, relationship managers can learn a great deal about the logic and cash flows of option-linked transactions by dissecting GROI and other synthetic financing products. By breaking these deals into their component parts, relationship managers may be able to apply certain aspects of these deals to their own clients, thereby adding value. Most CFOs and treasurers look to bankers as a source of creative ideas. GROIs and other synthetic financing products provide a way to offer customers a multitude of creative financing alternatives.

26

Equity Derivatives
Linking the Equity and Debt Markets

The recent past has seen wide disparities in both the performance of global equity markets and in the views investors hold on these markets. Investors, money managers, and pension fund managers who feel that the bull run is over in the more established stock markets and are unimpressed by current fixed-income yields are increasingly looking toward more risky equity markets. Far Eastern and Latin American equity markets have benefited from investment inflows that have helped to push these local indices to record levels.

Equity derivatives have prospered in this environment, for they allow investors to act quickly and cheaply on views about the most appropriate market or sector in which to invest. These products allow investors to link the fixed-income and money markets to the different equity markets, providing a cost-effective way to change investment profiles synthetically. Equity derivatives can also be used to structure attractive financing for borrowers and to enhance the credit of certain borrowers. Finally, equity options continue to be used in structures where new equity capital is raised.

Who Uses Equity Derivatives and Why?

Investors are natural users of equity derivatives both on the supply and demand sides. Investors who think that equities will underperform other markets over a certain period and seek to protect returns make up the supply side; these investors want to pay the equity return. Investors who believe that equities offer opportunities for enhanced returns are users on the demand side; these investors want to receive the equity return.

Exchange-traded futures and options, which now exist on a variety of equity indices throughout the world, have fixed settlement dates and limited maturities. In contrast, over-the-counter equity derivatives are structured specifically to meet the settlement and maturity needs of the client. OTC equity derivatives have traditionally been driven by the interest of investors

---

Transaction Sheet: Equity Derivatives

Borrowers	Entities seeking new equity capital or institutions that can use equity as collateral for financing
Investors	Institutional investors, including mutual funds, insurance companies and other money managers
Intermediaries	Commercial and investment banks
How Bank Profits	Bid/offer spreads; fees on structured financings
Spreads/Fees	Three to five basis points on standard transactions; more for nonstandard transactions
Deal Size	$20 to $500 million for equity swaps; generally smaller for equity options
Major Players	Standard Chartered Bank, Merrill Lynch, Bankers Trust, Citibank, Banque Paribas, Société Générale, Salomon Brothers, Morgan Stanley, Goldman Sachs
Credit Considerations	Credit exposure on equity swaps, structured deals, purchases of options
Competition/ Life Cycle	Competition increasing for deals based on emerging market stocks as investors continue to seek high yields

in foreign equities: investors looking to foreign equity markets to diversify their risks and obtain otherwise unavailable investment opportunities.

Equity swaps offer investors two major advantages over holding individual equities: lower costs and the ability to track a particular index precisely.

COST ADVANTAGES
Equity swaps allow investors to earn retur:.. from equities without incurring certain costs of owning the equities. Substantial transaction costs would result from buying the equities that make up the S&P 500 index or the DAX index. Many countries also impose withholding taxes on dividends paid to foreign investors. For instance, a U.K. investor owning U.S. shares is liable for a 15% withholding tax on any dividends. The investor can avoid the withholding tax by receiving the equity index instead of owning the equities.

TRACKING ADVANTAGES
Some investors are judged on how precisely their portfolio return matches the return of a particular benchmark index. Purchasing all of the stocks in an index and continuously rebalancing individual equity positions results in transaction costs that make it difficult to match the return on an equity index. Equity swaps allow the investor to match or track the return of the index while minimizing costs.

Structuring a Plain Vanilla Swap
Equity index swaps have existed since 1991. From the investor's point of view, an equity swap allows participation in the simple price return or total return (price appreciation plus dividends) of an equity index without the need to own shares of companies that make up the index.

Exhibit 1 shows an equity swap used by an investor holding a money market instrument and seeking the total rate of return on the S&P 500 index. The return on the equity index is based on an original notional principal. The design is like that of an interest-rate swap in that the principal is not exchanged. The return on the index can be either positive or negative. If the return is negative, the investor would owe the negative return to the counterparty in addition to the LIBOR payment.

The equity swap allows the investor to switch quickly and cheaply between the money market and the equity market. The investor seeks to capitalize on the view that over the term of the swap the equity market will yield a higher return than the money market. The investor is guaranteed the

Exhibit 1   Standard Equity Swap

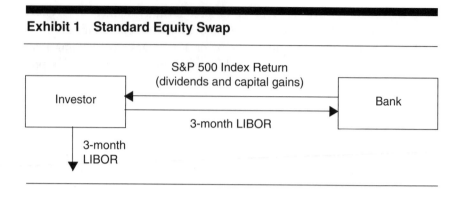

equity index return without actually having to buy the shares that make up the index.

The equity swap could also be executed with the investor paying the index and receiving LIBOR. In this case the investor is assumed to own the index and wants to swap out of the index to receive a money market rate over the life of the swap. The equity swap allows this exchange of returns without requiring the investor to actually sell the equity portfolio. In fact, short selling of stock may be difficult or even prohibited by the investor's own guidelines or by the market itself.

Equity swaps are typically structured with quarterly resets. The equity return is set in arrears at the end of each quarterly period and paid at the end of each period. The other leg of the swap can be based on a floating rate of interest over the reset period or a fixed rate of interest over the entire swap period. Equity swaps are structured on domestic and foreign indices. The equity return can be denominated in the local currency or in the currency of the client's choice.

Nonstandard Equity Swaps

In addition to swapping from LIBOR to an equity index, equity swaps allow users to switch indices, combine indices or create positions on individual stocks, baskets, or sectors.

SWAPPING INDICES

A client can enter an equity swap in which he or she pays the return in one index and receives the return in another. This may be attractive to an investor who has entered an equity swap to receive the return on the S&P 500 index quarterly for five years and now would like to receive the return on the

Exhibit 2 Swapping Equity Indices

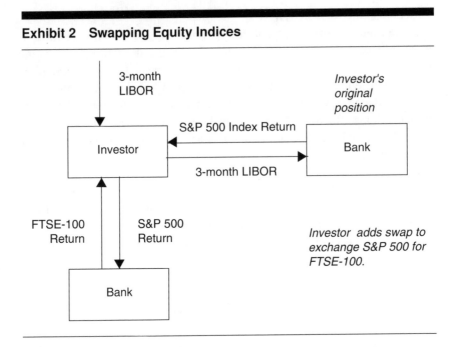

3-month
LIBOR

*Investor's
original
position*

S&P 500 Index Return

Investor

Bank

3-month LIBOR

FTSE-100
Return

S&P 500
Return

*Investor adds swap to
exchange S&P 500 for
FTSE-100.*

Bank

FTSE-100 index for a period of one year. Instead of unwinding the original swap, the client can enter the new swap in Exhibit 2. For the next year, the client will receive on a quarterly basis the FTSE 100 index. The FTSE 100 index could be denominated in dollars or sterling. After the year is up, the client will return to receiving the S&P 500 index.

BLENDED INDEX SWAPS
An equity swap can be structured in which the client can receive an equity return based on a combination of equity indices. These types of swaps have been structured for investors who want to participate in emerging markets while diversifying the risk across markets. For example, an equity index swap could be executed for $150 million notional principal in which the return is based on the following blended returns:

1. $50 million based on the DAX
2. $50 million based on the CAC
3. $50 million based on the NIKKEI 225

The blended return in this case is denominated in dollars, removing the currency risk component for a U.S. investor.

VARIABLE PRINCIPAL SWAPS

Investors may want to duplicate the return of an equity index position. If $100 million is invested in the equity market and the return for the first period is 10%, the investor has $110 million to invest in the next period. If the first-period return is negative 10%, the investor will have $90 million to invest in the next period. If the equity swap is to match the return, the swap principal must fluctuate. The principal rises or falls in the next period depending on whether the equity index return was positive or negative in the period before.

NONINDEX-BASED EQUITY SWAPS

Equity swaps are structured without an index but are customized to an investor's needs. The equity leg of the swap can be a blended position of any underlying basket of individual equities. These types of structures have been more prevalent in the equity option market.

USING EQUITY SWAPS TO "TRANSPORT ALPHAS"

Investors generally take one of two approaches to managing equity investments. A passive strategy involves trying to match the return on some index. An active strategy involves trying to manage investments to beat the return on the index consistently. The amount by which the index is bettered is known as the alpha:

$$\text{Alpha} \quad = \quad \text{Investment Return} \quad - \quad \text{Equity Index Return}$$

Equity swaps allow the investor to transport the alpha, or excess return, to whatever index is desired. For example, an investor may be able to earn consistently an excess return of 3% above the S&P 500. However, the investor may have a view that the DAX index will outperform the S&P 500 over the next two years. This investor has expertise in trading in the U.S. stock market, not the German stock market. By entering into an equity swap to pay the S&P 500 return and receive the DAX return over the next two years, the investor has achieved a return of the DAX plus 3% or the DAX return plus his or her alpha. The DAX return could be structured either in Deutschemarks or U.S. dollars. Similarly, this excess return could be transported to the fixed-income markets or money markets by having the investor pay the S&P 500 return and receive a fixed rate or a money market rate.

Using Equity Swaps to Obtain Inexpensive Financing

A few Latin American companies, particularly Mexican companies, have used equity swaps to obtain attractive financing. The structure combines a stock sale with an equity swap. The end result is cheaper U.S. dollar-based funding than could be raised in the United States.

The company sells the bank either its own equity portfolio or its own stock. The total value agreed upon for the sale is the value of the equity swap. The company pays a floating rate (LIBOR plus a spread) quarterly and receives the total return of the stock. At the end of the swap, the company may have to repurchase the equity at the current market price.

These deals pose risk for the bank in terms of both pricing and credit. The bank must take a view on the volatility of the underlying equity. The volatility plus other costs and the bank's anticipated profit factor into the spread over LIBOR that the bank receives. If the bank underestimates volatility, the spread that it has charged may be too low. Depending on the terms of the deal, the bank actually may have to sell the equity in the market at the termination of the swap. Some types of equity may be difficult to liquidate or sell.

Equity Option Structures

Most investors are probably cautiously optimistic about the U.S. and European equity markets. In the United States, inflationary concerns are causing jitters about the direction of stocks. In Europe, investors think the markets look expensive if interest rates do not come down and the economic recovery does not materialize. While investors continue to be bullish in Latin America and the Far East, the risk exists of a substantial market drop. These uncertain

Exhibit 3   Using Equity to Collateralize a Financing

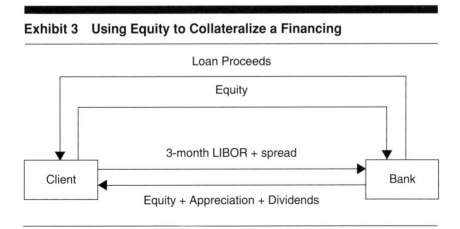

views have helped to increase the use of option structures in the equity derivatives market.

QUANTO CALLS
Most investors want to participate in the upside of equity markets, but many do not want the currency risk. The structure offered to these investors is quanto equity call options, where the exchange rate between the domestic market and the foreign-currency market is quarantined. Exhibit 4 shows a series of quanto call structures launched in early February of 1994.

LOOKBACK EQUITY OPTIONS
A lookback call option allows the buyer to exercise at the best possible price achieved during a certain period (known as the "lookback period"). Lookback options minimize market timing for the investor. Lookbacks are valuable for investors who feel the equity market has risen quickly and still feel there is more upside potential but are concerned about a slight correction. A lookback call option allows the investor to reset the strike at the best rate. If the market does pull back slightly, the strike price will be lower as well. Demand has come mostly from Europeans, especially German and Swiss investors.

The following call options were issued by KB Petercam on the Belgium-20 stock index. They were promoted as the first lookback option structured on the Belgium index. The lookback period is from February 25, 1994 to May 20, 1994. The calls are American-style and can be exercised at any time between May 23, 1994, and July 31, 1996. The level of the Belgium-20 index was 1,512 on February 2. If at any time in the lookback period the level falls below 1,512, the call strike will be reset this lower level.

The price of the option is 17.29% of par. A European call option for this period is about 14.3% of par. The lookback option is 3% more expensive than a standard call option. For a slightly higher premium the investor has eliminated the need to time the market over the three-month lookback period. If the index falls during this period, the investor will benefit from the lower price.

BARRIER OPTIONS AND COLLARS
With barrier options, the option dies or is knocked out if the stock price touches a predefined barrier. Knock-out options are cheaper than standard options because the buyer may lose the option. Investors have been buying knock-out put options where the knock-out level is above the current equity index. These options would protect the downside if equity prices fell but

Exhibit 4   Quanto Equity Call Options

Issuer	Index	Amount	Return Denominated In
SocGen	IBEX	3 tranches of 2 million calls	US$
Banque Paribas	FTSE-100	0.5 million calls	US$
Banque Paribas	CAC-40	0.7 million calls	US$
Banque Paribas	DAX	0.7 million calls	US$
Banque Paribas	Hang Seng	0.8 million calls	US$
Banque Paribas	Kuala Lumpur	0.8 million calls	US$
Citibank	Hang Seng	3 tranches of 0.1 million calls	SFr
Citibank	Hang Seng	3 tranches of 0.1 million calls	DM

would become worthless if the value of the equity index rose to touch the barrier. The view is that the knock-out strike is sufficiently above current levels so that if the option is knocked out, the investor will be in a positive position with minimal downside risk. In Switzerland, these types of knock-out options have positive tax implications. Because any profits resulting from the sale of the option or exercise of the option are not guaranteed (the knock-out feature takes care of this), any capital gains are tax-free.

Given the rise in U.S. and European equity markets during 1993, investors are looking to lock in gains. One way is to enter into a collar by buying a put on the equity index and selling a call on the equity index. If the index falls, the investor is protected below the put strike; if the index rises, the investor loses upside gains above the strike price of the call option.

Because most equity markets have experienced low volatility despite the rise in prices, option prices have decreased. Given a fixed strike for the put option, and in order to structure a zero-premium collar, the strike of the call option has to be lowered. By setting the lower strike, investors are capping their upside benefit at unattractive levels. One solution is to use a knock-in call option. This option "comes alive" only if the knock-in level is reached. By setting the knock-in level above the call strike, the investor achieves more upside potential.

BASKET OPTIONS

Basket options are structured as both call and put options (although the tendency is to sell mostly call options because it is harder to sell an option that depends on the investor thinking that the basket of equities is going to go down). These options are structured to a particular client view. Some of the more common baskets are:

NAFTA call options. These options are written on an underlying basket of Mexican company shares. The view is that the North American Free Trade Agreement (NAFTA) and Mexican financial market liberalization will improve the performance of Mexican companies.

Latin American telecommunications companies. A typical basket would contain equities from Mexican, Argentine, Chilean, and Brazilian telecommunications companies. Telecommunications companies are often among the few large-capitalization companies in certain underdeveloped equity markets. They often have good growth prospects in developing countries in need of infrastructure. Finally, they often serve as proxies for the entire stock market in a particular country. A variant includes the Philippine telecommunications company in the basket.

Using Equity Options to Raise Equity Capital

Beginning in 1991 with the first issuance of PERCS (Morgan Stanley's name for preferred equity redemption cumulative stock), corporations have used equity derivative structures to provide an incentive to investors to purchase new equity. With a PERC, investors own a hybrid type of preferred stock that converts into the company's common stock at the end of a fixed period. This hybrid earns a return higher than the dividend yield of the common shares. In return for this enhanced yield, the investor sells an equity call to the issuer. This option caps the investor's potential return from stock appreciation. Several other institutions have come up with similar products. Salomon Brothers has ELKS (Equity Linked Securities), Lehman Brothers has YEELDs (yield enhanced equity linked debt) and Bear Stearns has CHIPS (common linked higher income participation securities).

Between October of 1992 and February of 1994 (when RJR Nabisco raised $2.2 billion) there were no new major issues of PERCS. However, an option structure with similar characteristics has recently become common. Salomon Brothers calls these instruments DECS (debt exchangeable for common stock) and Merrill Lynch calls them PRIDES (preferred redeemable increased dividend securities). Similar to PERCS structures, they give the investor an enhanced fixed return over a certain period. In return, the investor does not cap the gains but only reduces potential capital gains. The structure is achieved through the purchase and sale of equity options.

In a deal launched by Salomon Brothers in February of 1994, approximately $300 million was raised for First Chicago Corporation. The underlying equity to be issued was for Nextell Communications, thereby monetizing First Chicago's investment in Nextell. The DECS are outstanding for three years with a coupon of 5.5%. The issue was priced at Nextell's then-current share price of $41. Approximately 6.5 million shares will be offered. At the end of three years the investor receives Nextell stock but loses the first 20% of the stock's appreciation.

EXAMPLE

Price of Nextell stock in February of 1997	$61.50
Percent appreciation from $41 issuance price	50%
Percent appreciation investor receives	30% (50% − 20%)
Dollar amount of investor's return	$53.30 ($41 × 1.30)
Share amount received by investor	0.87 ($53.30 × $61.50)

This payoff can be constructed by the investor through the purchase and sale of equity options on Nextell. The investor position is:

	Transaction	Purchase Option	Sell Option
1. Synthetically purchase stock 3 years from today	Buy call and sell put at the same strike ($41)	Call struck at $41	Put struck at $41
2. Swap out of first 20% appreciation	Sell call and buy call at 20% higher strike	Call struck at $49.20 ($41 × $1.20)	Call struck at $41

The two calls struck at $41 cancel out, and the investor is left with the sale of a put struck at $41 (at the money) and the purchase of a call struck at $49.20 (out of the money). The put option is worth more than the call option, and this difference is translated into an increased yield for the first three years.

The higher the strike on the out-of-the-money call option, the more price appreciation is given up in return for a higher return in the first three years. In structuring this deal, the issuer has to balance a higher yield against a lower capital return.

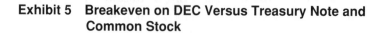

**Exhibit 5   Breakeven on DEC Versus Treasury Note and
Common Stock**

Exhibit 5 compares the all-in three-year return for the DEC structure against the return on the common stock assuming a dividend yield of 0% and the return on a three-year Treasury note yielding 4.5%. The investor buying this type of structure is looking for the stock to trade within a narrow range over the next three years. If the stock rises substantially, the common will offer the higher return. However, the DEC structure offers a higher return as long as the stock does not rise above $48.14. The three-year Treasury note offers a higher return only if the stock price does not drop below $39.70.

The issuer could either stay with the DEC structure or sell an at-the-money call ($41 strike) and buy the out-of-the-money call option ($49.20 strike). If the net proceeds are greater than the extra coupon the issuer has to pay, the issuer has a structure where a fixed amount of common stock is issued in three years, no matter where the stock price trades. In addition, the issuer has surplus funds.

Conclusion

Like currency and commodity derivatives, equity derivatives are simply another tool for linking markets. They offer investors a number of advantages —or, more accurately, the absence of disadvantages associated with owning stocks. Investors can participate in stock markets with minimal transaction costs and no custodial or tax expense, regulatory risk and (if desired) without currency risk. These derivatives also offer equity portfolio managers ways to transfer the excess return (alpha) to different markets. For borrowers, equity derivatives allow the securitization of equity holdings to achieve lower financing costs as well as the creation of various hybrid instruments that appeal to different investor audiences. Banks add value by offering products customized to client needs, whether that means setting up an equity swap based on a particular basket of stocks or marketing option structures that reduce up-front premium costs and creating new ways to raise equity capital.

27

Uncommon Equity
Using Embedded Options
to Attract Investors

New variations in capital-raising instruments continue to appear. Analyzing these new structures can help a banker to increase his or her understanding of the financial structure of the issuing firm and find variations applicable to other clients. This chapter focuses on one such structure: "uncommon equity," or equity issues containing embedded options guaranteeing some minimum level of dividends or a minimum share price.

The emphasis on equity rather than debt has become a hallmark of the early 1990s. Increased activity in both primary issuance and the equity derivatives markets attests to both the desire among investors for equity plays and the need among issuers to deleverage. Unfortunately many companies are not in a position to sell straight equity: The combination of sluggish economic activity, overleveraging or other business-specific factors deters investors from purchasing equity at a price acceptable to the issuer.

Uncommon equity presents one solution. A guaranteed level of dividends (even when combined with a mandatory conversion feature) or a floor on the share price can prove very attractive to investors while sending positive signals about the issuer. On the downside, these guarantees can cause severe cash drains or share dilution on the part of the issuer if large payouts are required.

Companies that issue uncommon equity are often in either an acquisition mode or a financial position such that issuance of straight debt or equity would be costly or impossible. Transactional opportunities that accompany the issuance of uncommon equity include funding for the future acquisition and future interest-rate management in anticipation of the issuance of new debt.

Equity, Leverage, and Earnings

Equity is the foundation of every company's capital structure. Corporate managers and their financial advisors are always pursuing the optimal balance between debt and equity. Earnings-driven companies will generally focus on the proper use of leverage to increase earnings per share. But as the 1980s proved, the use of excessive leverage can be dangerous for companies without a high degree of earnings stability across the business cycle.

Summary Sheet: Uncommon Equity

Issuers	Companies seeking equity but concerned about investor receptivity to a large common stock offering
Investors	Risk-averse investors seeking downside protection; investors willing to limit capital gains in return for higher current income
Intermediaries	Investment banks and other corporate financial advisors
How Bank Profits	Advisory and underwriting fees
Spreads/Fees	Due to complexity of uncommon equity, fee income is high; on PERCS issues, 2% to 6% is possible
Deal Size	US$200 million to US$1 billion
Credit Considerations	Guaranteed dividend payout on floor can impact cash flow of issuer, affecting creditworthiness.
Major Players	Morgan Stanley for PERCS, CVRs; ANZ McCaughan for Coles Myer noncumulative converting preference shares
Competition/ Product Life Cycle	Little competition; early in product life cycle

This trade-off is depicted in the graph in Exhibit 1, which plots earnings before interest and taxes (EBIT) against earnings per share (EPS) for two companies: one financed entirely with equity and the other with 60% debt and 40% equity. If earnings before interest and taxes has an expected value of

Exhibit 1   EPS and EBIT for Leveraged, Unleveraged Companies

Where:

Interest Rate 8% Tax Rate 50%		*Earnings Before Interest and Taxes*	*Earnings After Interest and Taxes*	*Earnings Per Share*
Leveraged Company		$0	($4,800)	($6)
Debt	$120,000	$10,000	$200	$0
Equity	$80,000	$30,000	$10,200	$13
Total	$200,000	$50,000	$20,200	$25
Unleveraged Company		$0	$0	$0
Debt	$0	$10,000	$5,000	$3
Equity	$200,000	$30,000	$15,000	$8
Total	$200,000	$50,000	$25,000	$13

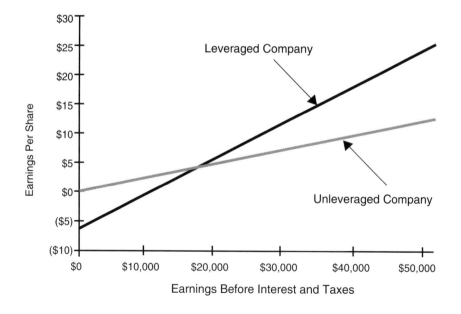

$30,000 at both companies, the one with the leveraged structure would appear to be better off (i.e., have higher earnings per share).

However, a more appropriate benchmark for capital structure is earnings volatility. A company with an expected value of EBIT of $30,000 and a standard deviation of $5,000 could easily allocate 60% of its capital structure to debt; even if EBIT was two standard deviations below the expected value, the company would still register higher earnings per share than under a less leveraged alternative. But for a company with a standard deviation of $20,000, the choice of 60% debt would be far more problematic: Although earnings per share would be higher than under an unleveraged structure during average and better-than-average years, an EBIT figure down one standard deviation would cut earnings per share to zero, and a decline of two standard deviations would generate a per-share loss of $12.25. The volatility of this company's earnings implies a less leveraged capital structure.

Many companies now find that they are more leveraged than appropriate given the volatility of their earnings or given a desire to pursue an acquisitions-oriented business strategy. For these companies seeking to reduce financial leverage at a time when management may see the common stock as undervalued, uncommon equity may offer a funding alternative.

Types of Uncommon Equity

The categories usually used when discussing capital structure are debt, equity hybrids, preferred shares and common or ordinary shares. However, uncommon equity is different: It always contains an embedded option that gives investors a guaranteed minimum dividend yield or share price. If the investor sells an embedded call, he or she gains a higher dividend yield, but potential gains from stock appreciation are capped. If the investor buys an embedded put, he or she locks in a minimum share price.

Uncommon equity has been used by a number of companies to solve specific capital-raising problems. Issuers include:

GENERAL MOTORS
When General Motors acquired Electronic Data Systems (EDS) and subsequently Hughes Aircraft, the company simultaneously created new classes of stock. In the case of EDS, it was GME shares; in the case of Hughes, it was GMH shares. Issuing these shares enabled GM to raise the necessary "flexible" capital without diluting its own shares or financing the acquisitions itself. Investors received GM shares tied to the performance of the newly acquired subsidiary.

However, in order to attract investors, GM also guaranteed that the shares would not trade below a certain level after a given period of time—that is, if the shares traded below that level, GM would effectively make up the difference. The investors get a floor, or minimum future value, on the equity they have purchased.

DOW CHEMICAL

Dow used a similar vehicle in connection with the acquisition of Marion Merrell Dow (formerly Marion Laboratories) in 1989. This time the floored equity was called contingent value rights, or CVRs. CVRs provide downside risk protection to shareholders in mergers by entitling the holders to additional payments if certain stock price performance goals are not met.

In the Dow-Marion case, the CVRs helped Dow avoid paying a large premium for goodwill (shareholders took the CVRs instead). The CVRs also reduced the cash required for the acquisition, because Marion shareholders accepted the downside price protection of the CVRs in lieu of more cash. By issuing CVRs, Dow also conveyed an important psychological message: optimism about the future stock price. As it turned out, however, Dow has made substantial payouts to holders of the CVRs; the price of Marion Merrell Dow's common stock recently traded in the US$27-27 range.

AVON

In 1988 Avon became the first company to issue the Morgan Stanley product PERCS (preferred equity redemption cumulative stock). The product is effectively a sale of common stock at today's market price in the temporary form of preferred stock. The investor receives a higher dividend than on the common but accepts a cap on common stock appreciation of about 30% over three years.

PERCS, which contain an embedded call option, clearly fall into the category of uncommon equity. In a PERCS issue the investor sells the call to the issuer, receiving a premium (in the form of higher dividends) but giving up appreciation beyond a certain level (although after conversion it would trade as the common stock it had become). After Avon's issue in 1988, no issues were done until a rash of PERCS issuances occurred in 1991, when General Motors became the second PERCS issuer and other companies followed.

The Coles Myer Case

A recent issue of preference shares provides a fresh look at the construction of uncommon equity. Coles Myer, a retailer of clothing and food, is the largest retailer in Australia, with annual revenues of A$15 billion. The company's cash flow is seasonal. Coles Myers has raised funds in all major financial markets around the world and has major U.S. and European commercial paper programs. Since the company's debt was recently downgraded

---

Exhibit 2   Coles Myer Noncumulative Converting Preference Shares

Size	Minimum of 12 million converting preference shares at A$25 each to raise a minimum of A$300 million
Entitlement	All shareholders and option holders receive one converting preference share for every 50 ordinary shares or options held on May 1, 1992
Issue Price	A$25 each (A$0.50 par and A$24.50 premium)
Base Dividend	Fully franked dividend yield of 6.8% p.a. on the issue price paid on June 11 and December 11, 1993 until conversion. Dividend is non-cumulative.
Supplementary Dividend	Paid if dividends on an equivalent number of ordinary shares (calculated at date of allotment of converting preference shares) exceed base dividends over the life of the converting preference share. Dividend is noncumulative.
Priority	Have priority to ordinary shares for payment of dividends and return of capital.
Conversion	Into a number of fully paid ordinary shares calculated by dividing the issue price by the lesser of two numbers: 1) a 10% discount to an average market price of ordinary shares at the time of conversion, and 2) A$25.
Conversion Date	June 5, 1997, unless accelerated by the company to a date no earlier than June 5, 1995
Voting	Voting rights only in certain limited circumstances
Participation	Full participation in all future issues except bonus issues

Exhibit 3   Investor Payoff Profile on Coles Myer Preference Shares

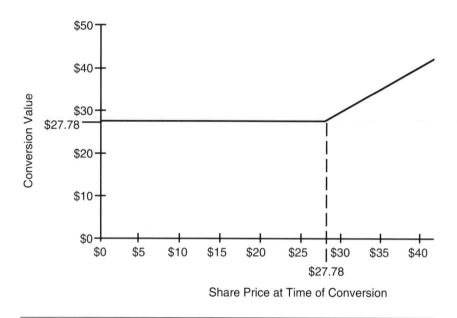

Share Price at Time of Conversion

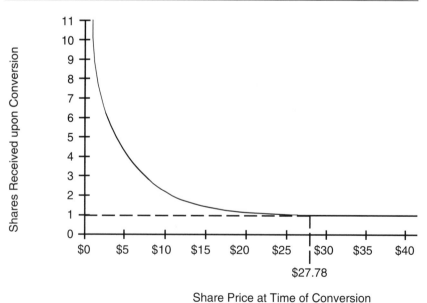

Share Price at Time of Conversion

to A-plus, Coles Myer was undoubtedly concerned about the cost of debt—especially because it has large amounts of long-term debt maturing over the next three years. In addition, the company sought capital to support ongoing business growth and to fund strategic acquisitions.

In mid-1992 Coles Myer issued a structure called converting preference shares. The terms are described in Exhibit 2. These shares contained a floor that, using the formula in Exhibit 2, worked out to a level of A$27.78 per share. At the time of issue the company's common shares were trading at a level of A$11–12 per share, while the converting preference shares sold at A$25 per share, approximately twice the price of the company's common shares.

The benefits to Coles Myer are clear. The company obtains a permanent increase in equity capital, raising the equity at twice the per-share price of the existing common. The company strengthens its balance sheet, presumably maintaining a strong credit rating and obtaining the ability to borrow more cheaply. Investors receive a high current yield as well as a minimum guaranteed price on their equity holdings (although they must wait five years to cash in this guarantee).

However, the preference shares also carry a major disadvantage for the issuer. Coles Myer has sold an option—and, as is the case in all option sales, the seller risks potentially unlimited losses.

The top graph in Exhibit 3 shows the payoff profile from the investor's viewpoint. The investor is guaranteed at least A$27.78 per share and higher prices as the common stock price increases over this level. The guarantee works by means of a share exchange: At all common share prices over A$27.78, the exchange ratio is 1:1—one share of common stock in exchange for one preference share. At common share prices below A$27.78, however, the investor receives as many shares as required to equal the payoff of the floor: two shares at a common share price of A$13.89, four shares at a common share price of A$6.95, etc. In the absence of a sustained increase in the company's share price, severe dilution is likely. However, because the company is not paying out cash (as Dow did in the case of its CVRs), the credit implications are minimal (aside from the negative implication of the company's inability to access the equity market).

Conclusion

In line with the trend toward deleveraging, bank customers will continue to look at a range of equity financing alternatives. Customers unable to sell straight equity at an acceptable price may turn to uncommon equity. Bankers need to understand uncommon equity structures for several reasons. First, the type of equity the company issues can help bankers to understand the ideal financial structure of the firm. Second, the issuance of uncommon equity has both positive and negative credit implications: positive as a result of the new equity raised, but negative as a result of the sale of a sizable option with the potential of being exercised. Finally, the issuance of equity in general, and capped or floored equity in particular, can generate a number of transaction opportunities for bankers even if they do not participate in the equity issuance itself. These include future debt issuance and forward-looking interest rate management in connection with the future debt issuance.

28

Currency Swaps
Globalization Continues

Since the now-famous deal between IBM and the World Bank in 1981, currency swaps have become the most visible symbol of the ongoing globalization of the world capital markets. The use of currency swaps is not so widespread as interest-rate swaps, but the market continues to grow and diversify (see Chapter 1). The applications of this product, and their implications, are an excellent vehicle for understanding today's markets—and the financing choices available to corporations. By examining the forces driving today's international capital and currency swap markets, bankers can better understand some of the most important factors influencing the choice of financing tools, even when currency swaps are not a viable alternative in a situation.

In many ways, currency swaps are no different than interest-rate swaps: They are an agreement to exchange payments periodically for a specific period of time. In the case of currency swaps, these payments are based on both interest rates and foreign-exchange rates. Many of the applications that apply to interest-rate swaps also apply to currency swaps, but there are additional ones as well.

Summary Sheet: Benefits of Currency Swaps

Comparative Financing Opportunities

Hedge Foreign Asset/Liability/Equity Positions

Arbitrage Differences in International Capital Markets

Exploit Investor Preference

Speculate on Interest and Exchange Rates in Different Currencies

Diversify Financing/Investment Sources

To achieve these benefits, it is necessary to alter the currency of both the principal (initial and final exchanges) and interest-rate (interim exchanges) components. This is unlike interest-rate swaps, which convert only the interim interest-rate payments.

Globalization: Real or Imagined

This buzzword is one of the most frequently used to describe today's capital markets environment. Globalization has had profound effects: enhanced ability for multinational institutions to finance globally, integration of major markets, greater choices for both investors and borrowers, more efficient use of capital, and the ability to more closely match the desires of borrowers and investors. Despite this process, however, there are still important differences between some major markets, investors, and borrowers.

It is these differences that provide the basis for currency swaps. Similarly, these differences highlight some important considerations for any potential investor or borrower. The most important forces driving currency swaps are comparative advantage financing, investor perception, structural arbitrage (tax regulations, accounting rules, regulatory requirements), and speculation.

What Drives Swaps?

In a general sense, the same factors always drive currency swaps. By exploiting investor preferences, every swap results in a comparative advantage by arbitraging among various capital markets. However, the choice of a specific swap currency, structure, and maturity depends on factors that can change quickly. The swap structure that appealed to investors and gave borrowers a comparative advantage last year may not do the same this year.

The most common swap opportunity occurs when a number of conditions come together. These factors generally fall into one of three groups: an attractive climate for issuing debt, a liquid swap market, and some artificial advantage. It is not absolutely necessary that all three conditions hold. Ideally, however, combining several of the following conditions should result in a multitude of currency swap opportunities.

Attractive Climate for Issuing Debt

Most currency swaps start when a desirable borrower goes to a stable and liquid bond market and issues debt that is denominated in a strong currency with a structure and maturity demanded by investors. Taken together, these conditions add up to comparative advantage.

The four conditions that make the issuing climate for currency swaps attractive are as follows:

CURRENCY STABILITY

An investor must be confident that, upon maturity, the investment will have sufficient value to justify the level of risk. If the currency of the investment weakens, relative to the investor's preferred currency, the value of the investment deteriorates. For instance, a Swiss investor will only invest in U.S. dollar securities if it is believed that the dollar will strengthen or at least weaken by no more than the yield advantage. In May of 1988, after the U.S. currency rebounded, Swiss demand for U.S. dollar Eurobonds surged; in October of that year, when the U.S. dollar sank, demand fell.

BOND MARKET LIQUIDITY

For many investors, the ability to alter investment strategy prior to maturity is important. This means that the bond market must be actively traded, with a reasonably narrow spread between the bid and offer prices. If the bond market is not liquid, then the bond issue must be large enough to become actively traded on its own, and must offer a yield high enough to make up for the lack of liquidity or both.

ATTRACTIVE STRUCTURE/MATURITY

Once again, not all investors react the same to the borrowing structure or maturity. Some prefer straight debt, others convertible. In some cases, borrowers are able to issue callable debt at only a slightly higher cost. Some investors aggressively seek zero-coupon investments, while others abhor them. The appetite for different structures/maturities is reflected in the yield.

DEMAND FOR ISSUER'S OBLIGATIONS
There are few issuers of debt that are perceived uniformly by all potential investors. Different groups of investors place greater emphasis on some aspects than others. Most typically, these factors include perception of credit quality, industry, market position, and name recognition.

Artificial Advantages

The combination of an attractive currency, structure, maturity, and credit may result in comparative advantage in a particular market. One additional condition that may result in a comparative advantage is a market inefficiency created by regulators.

A common regulation-driven source of comparative advantage is differences in the tax treatment of a transaction across jurisdictions. For instance, in the United States the purchaser of a zero-coupon bond must pay tax on imputed interest receipts. In Belgium, Holland, and other European countries, buyers of zero-coupon paper pay tax only on a zero-coupon bond's maturity, and then only at a capital gains rate. A number of issuers have exploited this tax advantage, floating zero-coupon paper, selling it to European investors and swapping into the desired currency.

Another regulation-based source of comparative advantage is the ability of certain highly regarded issuers to access a restricted market. Sometimes, this may be due to constraints on credit quality. Early Samurai issues, for instance, were restricted to AAA-quality borrowers. In other markets, access was controlled by central banks setting up a "borrowing queue"—a system by which issuers can only tap the market at intervals and must wait in line to do so. Borrowing queues have existed in the French franc and Dutch guilder markets, among others.

Swap Market Liquidity

In order to realize the benefits of a comparative advantage in one currency, the issuer (our client) must be able to swap the proceeds into the desired currency. This means that a counterparty must be willing to pay the currency of the debt issue in a swap at a rate attractive to both the payer and receiver. Frequently, this means that the counterparty must have a financing advantage in the currency desired by our client. Alternately, if no counterparty can be found, the intermediary must be able to create a payment stream by financing a bond denominated in the currency of the debt issue.

Exhibit 1   Is a Bond Issue/Swap Attractive?

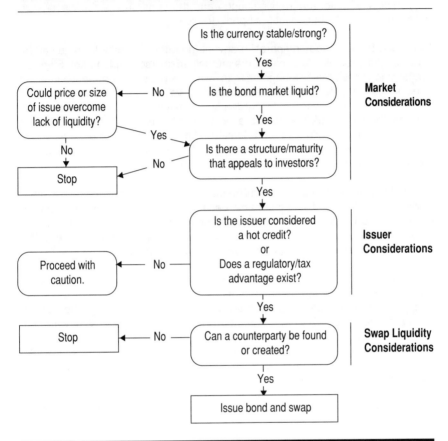

Example: The World Bank's Swedish Krona Swap

A successful swap that illustrates each of the three conditions described previously was the World Bank Swedish krona deal. In October of 1988, the World Bank issued a five-year SKr500 million Eurobond at a coupon of 10.50% and an AIBD yield of 10.07%. The bond was underwritten—and the swap reportedly arranged—by Skandinaviska Enskilda Banken (SE Banken). Although the terms of the swap were not made public, interviews with World Bank staff and independent swap dealers suggest that the swap enabled the supranational to access floating-rate dollars at about 100 basis points below LIBOR.

Investors liked the credit, currency, and coupon. The World Bank is a highly regarded AAA borrower. The Swedish krona is a strong currency, not only against the dollar but against the Deutschemark and other currencies of the European

Monetary System as well. (Since the start of 1988 the Swedish unit has appreciated almost 7% against the Deutschemark.) Although the market for Swedish bonds is not particularly liquid, the 10.5% coupon and the large size of the issue were sufficient to quell doubts about the bond's tradability.

The World Bank's huge comparative advantage derived mostly from its central bank-sanctioned ability to access an extremely restricted bond market. Swedish capital regulations prohibit foreigners from owning Swedish government bonds. As a result, few long-term krona investments are available to foreigners. This is a problem for investors, who would pay dearly to hold any currency that trades in line with the Deutschemark but carries a double-digit coupon. When the Swedish authorities agreed to allow a World Bank Eurokrona issue as part of an easing of capital barriers, investors bid up the price of the issue. The result: a yield about 100 basis points below that of a comparable Swedish government bond.

The final requirement for a successful transaction is a liquid swap market—in other words, the availability of a counterparty. Because the World Bank has no need for krona, the ability to borrow at subgovernment rates has no value unless the organization can convert the krona to dollars (or whatever currency is desired). The World Bank would like to receive five-year krona and pay U.S. dollar LIBOR.

Although the krona swap market (see Reuters page HABW) is not particularly liquid, the Swedish government bond market is. In the absence of a liquid krona swap market, SE Banken developed an alternative method to hedge the position created by the swap. SE Banken manages a large portfolio of Swedish government bonds. In structuring the swap, the bank reportedly created krona receipts by holding Swedish government bonds. This bond portfolio was presumably financed by borrowing dollar LIBOR. Because the World Bank was able to fund at subgovernment rates, there was a profit on the difference between the coupon on the governments and the coupon on the Eurokrona issue. This difference— reportedly about 100 basis points—reduced the cost of the World Bank's synthetic LIBOR obligation.

The Current Market

The trend in currency denomination of primary market swaps is linked to issuing trends in the Euromarket. Although no currency has suffered, certain currencies have found particular favor with investors. The Euromarket has seen a gain in the issuing volume of high-coupon currencies such as the Canadian and Australian dollar. This parallels a corresponding trend in currency swap transactions. Similarly, the continued growth of the ECU bond market has probably triggered an increase in the number of ECU currency swaps. Finally, the average maturity of swap transactions has shortened.

Exhibit 2 Probable Structure: The World Bank SKr Swap

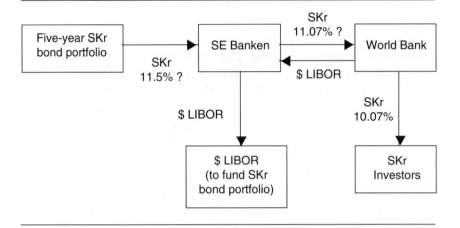

Exhibit 3 Currency Swap Volume

Currency	1987 Rank	Volume*	Probable Change in Rank—1988
US$	1	$77	unchanged
Yen	2	$27	decrease
A$	3	$14	increase
SFr	4	$13	unchanged
DM	5	$12	decrease
ECU	6	$9	increase
C$	7	$6	increase

* Volume of cash flow—U.S. dollar equivalent[new transactions in second half of 1987 (billions of U.S. dollars).

HIGH-COUPON CURRENCIES

Behind the increase in investor demand for Canadian and Australian paper—and the corresponding increase in swap opportunities—is a currency play by retail investors. The Canadian dollar in particular, and to a lesser extent the Australian dollar, tend to track the U.S. dollar more than the European currencies, sterling, or yen. Given the current uncertainty about the dollar, investors expect that these currencies will gain modestly against a weak dollar and will not weaken much against a strengthening dollar. In addition, these currencies pay extremely high coupons—on the order of 11% to 12% for the Canadian dollar and 13% to 14% for the Australian dollar.

LOW-COUPON CURRENCIES

Consisting primarily of Japanese yen, Swiss francs, and Deutschemarks, these currencies have become relatively less important in international financing. In the case of DM, one notable factor has been the threatened imposition of a withholding tax on DM bonds. While this threat recently was diluted, it has had a significant negative effect on DM financing in 1988. The globalization process in the debt and swap markets has been capitalizing on comparative advantage opportunities in these markets for several years. In some cases, these opportunities have been exhausted. While these currencies still represent significant volume (and perhaps greater *absolute* volume than in 1987), the increasing importance of other currencies has decreased their relative importance.

EXOTIC CURRENCIES

In the ongoing search for comparative advantage opportunities, less common currencies are being used as the basis for swaps. Examples include Swedish krona, Dutch guilders and Belgian francs. While the immaturity of these markets leads to an illiquid swap market, the savings generated by accessing new investors is sufficient to compensate for this problem. Essentially, this is a variation on the idea of finding a maturity or deal structure that is particularly attractive to investors—a currency that is very attractive.

MATURITIES

Another significant trend is a shorter average swap maturity. The most popular maturities in the currency swap market generally mirror those in the Eurobond market: five, seven, and ten years. In line with the shorter average maturities of issues in high-coupon, high-inflation currencies, the average maturity of swaps has probably decreased. The three-year maturity popular in Australian dollar issues and the three- and five-year maturities of Canadian issues have gained at the expense of longer maturities. Because Eurobond investors are particularly sensitive to currency risk, and because high-coupon issues carry a higher devaluation risk, investors prefer to limit their risk to these issues by purchasing shorter-maturity paper.

Conclusion

The primary force behind international bond issues and currency swaps continues to be comparative advantage financing. While the markets are becoming more global in scope, this does not mean that all investors will treat a given issuer the same. Nor does it mean that a given financing structure will be viewed the same by all investors. If all investors thought alike, comparative advantage financing would not be possible, and swaps would not make sense.

Rather, swaps (both interest and currency) serve to bridge the gap between the preference of investors and the needs of borrowers. This allows both parties to accomplish their objectives in the most attractive manner possible. Whether using swaps or not, borrowers, investors, and financial intermediaries must concentrate on several key aspects:

- In which market does a comparative advantage exist?
- What are the liquidity characteristics of the market(s)?
- Is there a financing structure or maturity that will be more attractive than others?
- Are there other factors that must be considered?
- What are the effects of the tax and accounting treatments?
- What is the impact of regulatory issues?

These issues are important whether dealing with traditional bank financing, private placements, Eurobonds, syndicated credits, or underwritten facilities. A complete solution often will involve the efforts of multiple parties within a bank: the relationship officer to identify the strengths and objectives of the borrower, the distribution side to identify the degree of receptiveness by various investor groups, and product specialists to assist in structuring the transaction—such as swaps, placements, Eurobonds, etc. As the markets become more developed and efficient, the opportunities for comparative advantage financing will become more limited. Making transactions work from this standpoint will depend on the ability to structure deals with features that are attractive to the investor: currency, maturity, and structure (i.e., embedded options). Similarly, as markets and products become more complex, the involvement of each of these parties becomes more important.

Dual-Currency Private Placements
The Rewards of Innovation

Japanese investors control a vast pool of capital, but also have unique preferences and operate under strict constraints. Any intermediary that can structure an investment acceptable to a particular group of Japanese investors, then transform it into generic U.S. dollar funding at a below-market rate, can move a virtually unlimited amount of funds from Japanese investors to Western borrowers.

This is precisely the rationale behind a growing number of dual-currency private placement transactions currently structured by Drexel Burnham Lambert, Bankers Trust, and Morgan Guaranty. For a variety of economic, institutional, regulatory, tax, accounting, and even cultural reasons, a large and profitable market has grown up around dual-currency private placements held by Japanese life insurance companies.

The market is particularly alluring to commercial banks, for private placements represent an area in which commercial banks can compete against investment banks. No underwriting is necessary, and commercial banks can originate the debt among existing customers. The main barrier to entry is the inability of most commercial banks to distribute the paper among Japanese investors.

Exhibit 1 Coupon Payments and Principal Redemption in ¥/A$ Placement

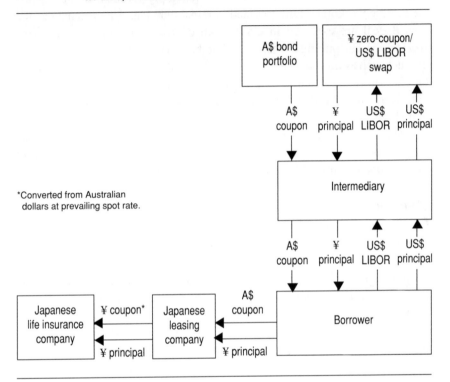

*Converted from Australian dollars at prevailing spot rate.

The dual-currency private placement is also important to banks that do not sell it. Banks that do not offer the product compete with those that do. Recent dual-currency placements allowed borrowers to access subordinated debt at 40 to 45 basis points below market. This advantage is sufficient to divert a sizable volume of financing business toward dual-currency obligations.

The market is attractive to Eurobond underwriters grappling with strong competition and stagnant volume. The dollar amount of Eurobond issues has been fairly steady over the past year. However, the dollar amount of private placements—especially those placed with non-U.S. investors—has been rising. Market participants estimate that at least $40 billion in non-U.S. private placements were done last year, and more than $3 billion were dual-currency obligations placed with the Japanese. The volume of these transactions is destined to grow as long as Japanese investors like the structure.

The spreads available to the intermediary are not public. However, the product can be very profitable. Neither the investor nor the borrower pay explicit fees. The investor and borrower are simply given all-in rates, while the precise workings of the transaction remain hidden. (The mechanics of a typical deal are explored in Chapter 40 of *The Derivatives Engineering Workbook.*) The pricing is based on what the market will bear. For a complex product such as this, at an early point in the product life cycle, sold by only a handful of vendors and exploiting a large arbitrage gap between Western borrowers and cash-rich, overregulated Japanese insurers, the profits can be quite high.

Deals generally fall between ¥5 to ¥10 billion ($40 to $80 million), with most transactions on the upper end of the range. The size and volume of transactions are limited by investor appetite rather than borrower demand.

Overview of Dual-Currency Debt

Dual-currency issues pay coupons in one currency and principal in another. The market for dual-currency securities used to exist mainly among Swiss investors, who bought Eurobonds with U.S. dollar principal and Swiss franc coupons from the early to mid-1980s. The investors liked the bonds because the Swiss franc–denominated coupon was higher than that of a similar straight Swiss franc issue. Meanwhile, the U.S. dollar principal represented a way of diversifying a Eurobond portfolio by currency, while still getting a higher than normal income stream in Swiss francs.

Issuers liked the bonds for two reasons. First, the issuer had the advantage of servicing the debt in a low-interest currency, while repaying the principal in a weaker currency. Second, assuming the borrower's base currency was the principal redemption currency (i.e., U.S. dollars for a U.S. company), the issuer had no exchange exposure on the repayment of the principal.

Dual-currency issues surfaced in a number of forms over the years. GTE kicked off the market in the early 1980s with an issue featuring U.S. dollar principal and Swiss franc coupons. In 1985, Gillette achieved a low cost of funding with a dollar/franc dual-currency convertible. Foreign interest payment securities (FIPS) were dual-currency issues with no redemption date, but with put and call options every 10 years.

All of these instruments had two things in common: Swiss investors were the main buyers and the redemption currency was U.S. dollars. In these two characteristics lay the seeds of the market's demise.

In February of 1985, the U.S. dollar plunged against all major currencies. In September of 1985, the G-5 group of central banks drove the dollar even lower. For the next year and a half the dollar continued to stumble, sometimes on its own, sometimes helped by the central banks.

Each of these declines made bonds with U.S. dollar principal less attractive to non-U.S. investors. As the Swiss franc rose against the dollar, Swiss investors saw the franc value of their dollar principal decline by almost half. As a result, Swiss investors abandoned dual-currency issues and embraced plain vanilla Swiss franc bonds.

Rise of the Yen Private Placement

The dual-currency paper placed today is different in a number of ways. The buyers are Japanese. Principal is denominated in yen, while the coupon is in a high-interest currency such as Australian, New Zealand or U.S. dollars. Most transactions take the form of subordinated private placements. Maturities range from 10 to 15 years, longer than typical Euromarket maturities. Finally, even though the investors purchase an obligation with interest in a high-yield currency and principal in yen, the borrowers (through the intermediary) can use the swap, bond, and foreign-exchange markets to transform the debt into floating-rate U.S. dollars.

Driving the unique structure of the current wave of dual-currency private placements are the needs of a specific group of investors: Japanese life insurance companies. Japanese are the world's biggest buyers of life insurance, and the Japanese insurance market is the world's most profitable. After growing at a rate of almost 15% per year throughout the postwar era, the Japanese life insurance companies have accumulated enormous reserves to invest. But because these companies provide protection to a large number of individual policyholders (more than 90% of the population, the highest proportion in the world), the Ministry of Finance (MOF) requires that the insurance companies invest more judiciously than banks.

On one hand, the insurance companies need to match the payout of dividends to policyholders. The companies cannot pay dividends out of capital gains, only current income. Current income is very low on senior yen obligations: about 4% on government bonds and 5% on high-quality corporate debt. On the other hand, the MOF prohibits the types of riskier investments that carry high yields. Subordinated debt is taboo. Foreign-currency investments are forbidden.

As a solution, the life insurers make senior yen-denominated loans to affiliated leasing companies, which invest in higher yielding paper. Most Japanese insurance companies are members of large industrial groups. Each corporate group contains a leasing company as well as a life insurance

Exhibit 2   Matching Investor and Borrower Preferences

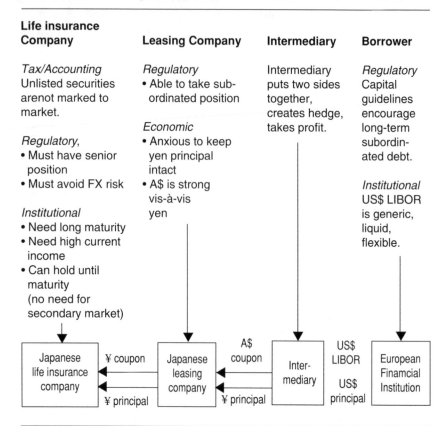

Life insurance Company	Leasing Company	Intermediary	Borrower
Tax/Accounting Unlisted securities arenot marked to market.	*Regulatory* • Able to take sub- ordinated position	Intermediary puts two sides together, creates hedge, takes profit.	*Regulatory* Capital guidelines encourage long-term subordin- ated debt.
Regulatory, • Must have senior position • Must avoid FX risk	*Economic* • Anxious to keep yen principal intact • A$ is strong vis-à-vis yen		*Institutional* US$ LIBOR is generic, liquid, flexible.
Institutional • Need long maturity • Need high current income • Can hold until maturity (no need for secondary market)			

company. The leasing companies are equipped to evaluate lower-rated credits and allowed to make subordinated and foreign-currency loans. Although the leasing company borrows senior yen-denominated debt, it can invest in subordinated foreign-currency debt.

The leasing company may be willing to invest in subordinated paper, but it will probably be unwilling to buy straight foreign-currency paper. From 1985 to 1987, the yen rose against every currency in the world. When returns were measured in yen, very few foreign currency-denominated investments were profitable. As a result, Japanese investors have made a broad statement that they wish to avoid risk indexed to items outside of Japan. However, these investors are willing to take foreign-currency risk as long as their yen principal remains intact.

Due to the recent strong performance against the yen of high coupon currencies, the logical structure—and the structure currently enjoying the most popularity—is yen principal and Australian dollar coupon payments. First, the Australian dollar was the strongest of all the major currencies in 1988, gaining about 23% on the yen and 20% on the U.S. dollar. Second, the 14%-plus coupon available on long-term Australian dollars allows the creation of a yen-denominated bond with high coupon payments.

A final twist on the structuring of the instrument is the investor's choice between public and private securities. Due to a tax and accounting quirk, Japanese investors want unlisted securities. If an unlisted security has a foreign-exchange risk, and the market value moves over the life of the security, the investor does not have to mark the value of the security to market. There is no tax event until final maturity. The result: Japanese investors generally choose unlisted securities over listed securities. Most transactions are done on an unlisted basis.

On the borrower side, the counterparty is typically a European financial institution in need of long-term subordinated U.S. dollar LIBOR debt. Behind the demand for long-term subordinated financing are the Basle Committee's risk-based capital guidelines. Financial institutions can use the debt to help achieve the mandated minimum 8% risk-based capital ratio by 1992. Borrowers seek the funds in the form of U.S. dollar LIBOR both to match floating-rate assets and because dollar LIBOR represents the most flexible currency and rate basis.

Structuring the Instrument

For a financial intermediary, the challenge is how to get from the structure desired by the investor to that preferred by the borrower. The precise mechanics of a dual-currency placement are reviewed in Chapter 40 of *The Derivatives Engineering Workbook*. What follows is a general overview of the structure used by a financial intermediary attempting to create a yen/Australian dollar private placement.

Any intermediary seeking to transform a long-term yen/Australian dollar private placement into U.S. dollar LIBOR faces several obstacles. Most important is the fact that the market for Australian dollar long-dated forward contracts is quite illiquid, and the currency swap market is only quoted out to five years.

Even if using the forward market were feasible, hedging the principal of a conventional Australian dollar fixed-income security would result in uneven cash flows. The yen trades at a steep forward premium to the Australian dollar. In the forward market, at each period in the future the Australian dollar buys fewer yen. If the principal of a conventional Australian dollar bond were hedged into yen, the yen principal returned to the investor would be less than the yen principal invested. This violates the Japanese investor's requirement that the yen principal remain intact. With its high Australian dollar coupon and low yen principal at maturity, the security would contain too much foreign-exchange risk—all of it in the coupon payments. The distorted yen cash flows resulting from this structure are shown in Exhibit 3.

Exhibit 3   ¥/A$ Bond Created Using Forward Market

Australian dollar interest rate	14%
Yen interest rate	5%
Par value of Australian dollar bond	100.00

Period	Spot and forward ¥/A$	Yen principal	Australian dollar coupon	Yen equivalent bond
0	100.0	(10,000)		(10,000)
1	92.1		14.00	1,289
2	84.8		14.00	1,188
3	78.1		14.00	1,094
4	72.0		14.00	1,008
5	66.3		14.00	928
6	61.1		14.00	855
7	56.2		14.00	787
8	51.8		14.00	725
9	47.7		14.00	668
10	43.9	4,394	14.00	5,009

Due to rounding, numbers will not add up precisely.   Internal rate of return = 5%

For the intermediary, the question is how to reduce the Australian dollar coupon and increase the yen principal. The solution lies in putting aside enough yen to pay back the face value at maturity, and using the rest to finance the purchase of a portfolio of Australian dollar bonds necessary to pay the coupon. The cash flows resulting from this arrangement—which results in less foreign-exchange risk to Japanese investors due to a lower Australian dollar coupon and the full amount of yen principal at the end—are shown in Exhibit 4.

Exhibit 4   ¥/A$ Bond Created Using Swap/Bond Markets

Australian dollar interest rate	14%
Yen interest rate	5%

Period	Spot and forward ¥/A$ rates	Yen principal	Australian dollar equivalent	Yen equivalent bond
0	100.0	(10,000)		(10,000)
1	92.1		7.40	682
2	84.8		7.40	628
3	78.1		7.40	578
4	72.0		7.40	533
5	66.3		7.40	491
6	61.1		7.40	452
7	56.2		7.40	416
8	51.8		7.40	383
9	47.7		7.40	353
10	43.9	10,000	7.40	10,325

Due to rounding, numbers will not add up precisely.   Internal rate of return = 5%

In this structure, the intermediary takes the yen principal and divides it into two portions. One portion is swapped for dollars, which are passed on to the borrower. The other portion is invested in Australian dollar bonds. At the maturity of the private placement, the swap pays back the face value of the yen placement, which goes to the Japanese investor, while the borrower repays dollars. Meanwhile, the final coupon payment depletes the portfolio of Australian dollar bonds.

The structures shown in Exhibits 3 and 4 both have the same internal rate of return when hedged into yen. But the second structure, with its lower coupon and protected yen principal, is more attractive to investors.

Conclusion

As loans become commodities and borrowers seeking generic financing increasingly bypass traditional lenders, commercial banks will be forced to develop expertise in complex structures such as dual-currency private placements. Early in the product life cycle, these transactions result in high profit margins, above-normal returns to investors, and below-market costs to borrowers. Deals such as these also displace traditional lending products, increasing competitive pressures among other financial intermediaries.

Banks that excel in these transactions possess several traits. Most important is access to investors. Once structured, the dual-currency transaction outlined previously yields funds in a generic form at below-market rates (recently 15 basis points over U.S. dollar LIBOR for customers that would normally have paid 60 basis points over). Therefore, finding borrowers is not difficult. The problem is knowing what Japanese investors want, structuring the transaction, and placing the funds.

Drexel solved this problem by setting up its own sales force and developing relationships with regional Japanese banks. These banks do not have the ability to structure dual-currency financings. However, the banks do have access to a network of Japanese investors. From this network come the buyers and market intelligence necessary to market these investor-driven deals.

Japanese life insurance companies control vast sums of capital. But their investing requirements are strict, influenced by MOF regulations, tax and accounting rules and recent negative returns on nonyen-denominated investments. Intermediaries that can create private obligations acceptable to these investors, then transform them into debt desired by Western borrowers, can profit by an arbitrage between East and West.

30

Debt Structures
Liabilities That Fill Multiple Needs

Cheap money is important, but the ideal liability addresses a customer's underlying business. The cash flows of every borrower are exposed to certain risks. Some result from the nature of the borrower's business; others result from variability in market rates such as exchange rates or commodity prices. The ideal debt structure provides liquidity while simultaneously offsetting some of this cash flow variability. Creating this ideal structure requires understanding the sources of a customer's risk: the bundle of business and financial variables that interact to create volatility in the company's cash flows.

A master at creating debt structures that serve multiple needs is The Walt Disney Company, which over the past seven years has issued a steady stream of liabilities that hedge both business and economic risk. As an A-plus-rated company with global name recognition and earnings growth exceeding 20% per annum over the last seven years, Disney has fund-raising opportunities that few other corporations can match. Nevertheless, the ideas driving Disney's structures can be adapted to many borrowers, regardless of size, industry, or nationality. Bankers able to apply these ideas can add value by devising structures that both raise cheap money and reduce the customer's risk.

Disney's MTN Shelf Offering

In August of 1992, Disney completed a shelf offering for $500 million in medium-term notes (MTNs). The MTN structures were defined broadly in order to give the company the ability to offer investors the right structure at the right time. Under the shelf registration, Disney can opportunistically respond to investor demand in a variety of markets.

MTN structures available to Disney under the shelf registration include generic fixed-rate notes; zero-coupon notes; three types of currency-indexed notes; and floating-rate notes indexed to commercial paper, LIBOR, CDs, Fed funds, Treasury bills, or the U.S. prime. In addition, the shelf registration allows Disney to devise and sell notes indexed to commodity prices, equity indices, and a catchall "other factors" category. All of the MTNs sold under the facility must have maturities of nine months or more.

The first offerings under the registration illustrated how the notes could be used to hedge the company's risks. In late August and early September of 1992, Disney issued two $18 million tranches of five-year MTNs using one of the currency-indexed structures: an MTN issue with the principal in one currency and the coupons indexed to another. This structure was similar to one used in a type of private placement marketed to yield-hungry Japanese insurers in the late 1980s: yen principal combined with coupons paid in yen but indexed to Australian dollars or Spanish pesetas.

Exhibit 1   Terms of Disney MTN Shelf Registration

Amount	$500 million
Maturity	Nine months or more
Permissible Structures	Fixed-rate; floating-rate (CP, LIBOR, CDs, Fed funds, Treasury bills, U.S. prime); zero-coupon; indexed to exchange rates, commodity prices, equity indices
Initial Issue	Two $18 million tranches of five-year currency-indexed MTNs; principal payable in U.S. dollars; coupon payable in dollars but indexed to dollar/sterling exchange rate
Dealers	Goldman Sachs, Lehman Brothers, Merrill Lynch, Morgan Stanley

The MTNs pay quarterly interest at a level based on the dollar/sterling exchange rate. As sterling strengthens over an initial exchange rate of $1.99:£1, investors receive a higher coupon; as sterling weakens, the coupon falls. The coupons have floors of 4% and ceilings of 20%. The initial MTN issuances served not only as a source of inexpensive funding, but also as a partial hedge of the U.S. company's long-term sterling receipts from licensing agreements—the company's "economic" exposure to the dollar/sterling exchange rate.

Hedging these anticipated (but not yet booked) receipts has proven difficult for many U.S. companies because of the lack of hedge accounting treatment. When options or forward contracts are used to hedge anticipated receipts or obligations, the gains or losses on the hedging instrument must be taken to income rather than netted against the gains or losses on the underlying transaction. In March of 1992, the U.S. Securities and Exchange Commission, evaluating the accounting treatment of derivatives transactions, sided with the Financial Accounting Standard No. 52, which stipulates that anticipated foreign-exchange transactions are not eligible for hedge accounting treatment.

The Disney sterling-indexed MTNs sidestep the issue of hedge accounting treatment. Because the MTNs are denominated in dollars, Disney has no foreign-currency position—only a U.S. dollar obligation indexed to a foreign currency. The company will still register accounting gains or losses on

---

Exhibit 2   Terms of Disney Participating Notes

Amount	$400 million
Maturity	Seven years
Base Interest	7.5% p.a. (payable quarterly) for first 18 months; 1.5% p.a. thereafter
Contingent Interest	50% of net revenues on portfolio of 20 to 22 Disney films. Payout starts when net revenues pass $800 million and is capped at $240 million. Net revenues defined as excess of worldwide revenues over production, marketing, and distribution costs.
Underwriters	Citicorp Investment Bank, Lehman Brothers

booked sterling receipts from its licensing agreements. But these gains or losses will be offset, in an economic if not an accounting sense, by a smaller or larger coupon payment on the sterling-indexed MTN.

Because a cap and floor limit the range of MTN coupons, the exchange rate–driven changes in the coupon payments are insufficient to hedge the full range of possible dollar/sterling exchange rates. Nevertheless, the coupons do hedge a wide range of dollar/sterling exchange rates and presumably provide cheap funds as well.

Disney has other major foreign-currency inflows as well. From the company's Tokyo Disneyland comes a stream of Japanese yen; from Euro-Disneyland, a stream of French francs. MTNs linked to these exchange rates could be forthcoming.

Disney's Participating Notes

Disney used a second innovative debt structure when it announced in October of 1992 a $400 million Euromarket issue of "senior participating notes." Underwritten by Citicorp Investment Bank and Lehman Brothers, the structure pays semiannual interest at 7.5% during the first 18 months and 1.5% per annum over the remainder of the seven-year term. In addition, investors receive a coupon contingent on the success of a portfolio of 20 to 22 Disney films, 13 of which have already been chosen.

The contingent coupon works as follows: Once the excess of worldwide revenues over production, marketing and distribution costs surpasses $800 million, investors get 50% of subsequent increases up to a ceiling of $240 million. This cash flow is expected to begin 18 to 24 months after the launch; hence the low 1.5% coupon starting in the second year. The maturity extends another five years from this point (seven years in all) because all of the revenues from a film are generally received within five years of its release.

The idea behind the participating notes is simple: Hedge business risk by allowing investors to share some upside potential while retaining control. The cash flows generated by feature films follow a highly variable life cycle: theatrical, home video, and merchandising revenues in the first year; global pay TV in the second; and network TV and syndication revenues in the final three years. The participating notes offer investors a higher upside, but also force them to take on some of this cash flow variability.

Like debt, the participating notes offer a fixed maturity and guaranteed principal; like equity, the periodic receipts (other than the fixed portion of the interest) depend on the performance over time of the underlying assets. If the film business suffers, so do the investors. The notes allow Disney to increase the flexibility and lower the risk of its financial structure—at a minimal increase in cost.

Applying Disney's Structures to Other Borrowers

Disney is a borrower apart. Its size, credit rating, earnings performance, and name recognition allow it to issue debt that other companies cannot. But while Disney is unique, the ideas behind its debt structures are universal. The functions, as opposed to the specific forms, of Disney's structures can be exploited by a wide range of borrowers.

The dual-currency MTNs partially hedge long-term sterling inflows from licensing agreements. Many companies have long-term foreign-currency inflows; many would be happy to hedge over a longer time horizon. The dual-currency structure clearly creates a partial economic hedge. And depending on the outcome of the hedge accounting debate, a debt portfolio that requires sterling payments (in Disney's case, dollar payments linked to the dollar/sterling exchange rate) could provide an accounting hedge as well. This portfolio could be created using bank loans and derivatives as well as MTNs.

The participating notes gave investors some upside potential in exchange for taking on some of Disney's business risk. Many other types of debt approach this idea. Returns on many of the junk bond structures of the late 1980s were performance-driven (albeit with far more risk). Germany's profit-participation notes offer interest at a minimum level unless the company's earnings pass a certain threshhold. Performance-driven acceleration clauses offer investors a type of upside, although this upside is measured in lower risk rather than higher returns.

However, there is one important difference between Disney's participating notes and these structures above: Returns on Disney's notes depend on an isolated portfolio of assets rather than the entire company. With the help of its bankers, the company was able to isolate a portfolio of assets and match it with investors that took on part of the risk, thus stabilizing the portfolio's cash flows. In this sense, the notes resemble a project finance structure in which investors lend to an oil drilling rig. If the rig hits oil, the investors receive high returns; otherwise (depending on the arrangement), the returns are minimal.

Conclusion

Disney's deals offer more than cheap money. Each debt issue is thoughtfully structured to reduce the risk of the company's cash flows. August's MTN issues hedged part of the company's foreign-exchange risk; October's participating notes are designed to hedge part of the company's business risk. Moreover, these structures can be duplicated using instruments available to any wholesale banker. The structure of a $400 million Eurobond can be duplicated in a $10 million private placement; the cash flows of a currency-linked medium-term note can be copied by bundling a bank loan with a range of derivatives. By studying Disney's debt and understanding what it is designed to hedge, then adapting the tools at hand, a banker can learn from Disney and apply the lessons to add value to his or her own customers.

31

Embeddos
The Rise of Embedded Derivatives

In recent years, bonds with embedded derivatives have become so prevalent that the market has invented a new term to describe them: embeddos. Derivatives embedded in bonds have included forward, swap, and option positions in interest rates, currencies, commodities, equity indices, and securities. Embeddos have in the past been primarily a Euromarket phenomenon; 1992 has seen their emergence in many domestic bond markets, especially that of the United States.

All marketers of financing products can benefit from an understanding of how the embeddo market allows issuers to save precious basis points while at the same time satisfying specific investor appetites. However, this understanding is especially important for bankers who work for institutions seeking to be significant players in derivative products. Relationship managers can originate embeddos, while syndicate and distribution specialists can identify the pockets of unique investor interest that drive the embeddo market. And derivatives traders and marketers can spot anomalies between the derivative and bond markets that create interesting embeddo opportunities.

Summary Sheet: Embeddos

Issuers	Large, creditworthy multinational corporations and supranational organizations; sovereigns; prominent issuers have included Kodak, Swedish Export Credit, the Republic of Austria.
Investors	Retail and institutional investors throughout the world
Intermediaries	Investment banks
How Bank Profits	Underwriting fees and spreads on accompanying derivatives transactions
Deal Size	$30MM and up
Fees/Spreads	Standard underwriting fees on bond portion of issue; above-normal bid/offer spreads on derivatives portion
Credit Considerations	Issuers are generally triple-A, but credits as low as single-A have issued debt with embedded derivatives.
Major Players	Goldman Sachs, Bankers Trust, Merrill Lynch
Competition/ Product Life Cycle	Competition intense, but limited to firms with excellent distribution in country of investor interest; depending on market conditions, innovation is followed by two to four months of issuance, then saturation.

Beyond providing cheap money for issuers and fancy payoff profiles for investors, embeddos drive innovation and create liquidity in the pure derivatives markets. The introduction of a new type of embeddo can have a resounding impact across many markets. This chapter starts by examining the archetypal embeddo structure, explaining what motivates each of the parties to the transaction. Trends in embeddos that emerged through the year of 1991 are then explored through exemplary deals. By examining the past and present evolution of the embeddo market, bankers should be in a better position to participate in its future.

Embeddo History

In the early 1980s there began to appear in the Euromarket structures that seemed to suggest a willingness among issuers to assume some rather bizarre risks. Bonds with attached gold warrants, debt warrants and warrants on

Exhibit 1   Kodak Gold-Linked Notes

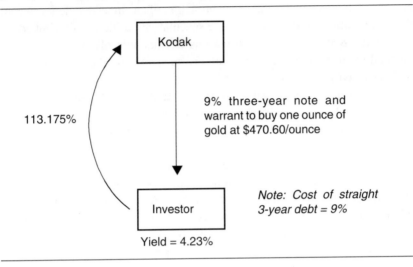

foreign currency proliferated. One classic example of such a linked bond structure is the Kodak gold-linked note illustrated in Exhibit 1.

What was Kodak's incentive for raising funds with an ultimate cost contingent on the future price of gold? Was Kodak bearish on gold, anticipating a price at the bond's maturity below the "strike" price of $470.60/ounce? If this was Kodak's view and it turned out to be right, the all-in cost of the debt would turn out to be 4.23%, almost five percentage points lower than that of a straight issue. On the other hand, if Kodak's bet turned out to be wrong—if the price at settlement turned out above $470.60/ounce—then Kodak could end up with a higher all-in cost than would have been available on a straight issue.

The first question to ask when analyzing an embeddo is: Does the issuer have any natural business that would create a desire for the embedded risk? In this example, is there any way that the sale of an option on gold can be understood to fit Kodak's book? Can it somehow be construed as a hedge of an existing business or financial risk? In this instance, and in the vast majority of these kinds of issues, the answer is no. The derivatives embedded in or linked to bonds usually have no apparent link to the issuer's business or financial condition.

The next question, then, is why an issuer of debt would add extraneous, unrelated risk positions to a debt issue. There are several possible answers:

The issuer desires a low coupon, even if there is the potential, as in the Kodak example, of a higher payout of principal at the bond's maturity; or the issuer cannot sell bonds without the added attraction of an embedded derivative; or the issuer simply wishes to assume a speculative position in the embedded derivative. While each of these reasons has undoubtedly motivated some embeddo issuers, they cannot explain the huge volume of debt with embedded derivatives that have appeared in recent years.

The reason issuers link swaps, forwards, and options to debt securities is to achieve a lower all-in cost of debt than would otherwise be available. Exhibit 2 illustrates how, in the Kodak example, the issuer can strip out the embedded risk and be left with cheap financing. By purchasing an option in the over-the-counter derivative market that is essentially identical to the one sold to investors as part of the bond issue, Kodak is effectively left with straight debt. That is because the payoff from the purchased option position will offset the higher payout of principal paid on the financing if the price of gold is above $470.60/ounce. The amount Kodak pays for buying the option ($12) is less than the cost of the gold warrants ($13.175), so the all-in financing cost is below the cost of straight debt.

The stripping out, or monetizing, of embedded derivatives enables issuers to end up with relatively cheap straight financing. But why would investors buy this sort of structure? It would seem that if the issuer is saving money by attaching the derivative, then the investor must somehow be losing money, or at least be leaving something on the table, when he or she buys an embeddo. Exhibit 3 shows how an investor might create his or her own embeddo, getting a better yield than if he or she bought the prepackaged bond with linked warrant.

Exhibit 2   Stripping Out an Embedded Option

Exhibit 3 Creating a Gold-Linked Note Structure

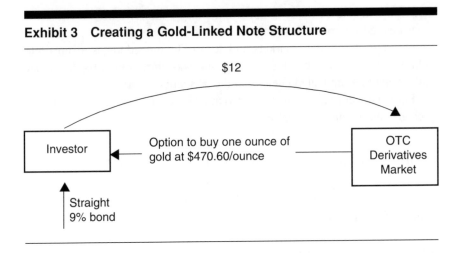

In this example, the investor buys straight Kodak debt as well as an over-the-counter gold option. This combination has exactly the same payoff profile as the Kodak embeddo. However, assuming the investor could buy the over-the-counter option at the same price as Kodak, it is clear that the investor can end up with a higher-yielding instrument than would be available through the embeddo. In essence, the cost of the option in the over-the-counter market ($12) is less than its cost when purchased through the embeddo ($13.175).

So why do investors who want the unique risks contained in embeddos embrace homemade structures instead? There are two schools of thought as to why investors buy prepackaged embeddos instead of creating their own.

THE "NAIVE INVESTORS" SCHOOL
The first school says that investors, more so than issuers, are naive regarding the workings of the derivatives market. They may not be able to price forwards and options, or they may not be able to identify the embedded position accurately. Or they may simply be uncomfortable with entering into separate over-the-counter derivative transactions. In any case, they are willing to pay a premium for the derivative that is embedded in a bond structure.

THE MARKET ACCESS SCHOOL
The second school says that the embeddo market provides investors the ability to assume risk-return profiles that would not otherwise be available. Retail investors cannot buy over-the-counter derivatives. Even if they can

participate in futures markets, there may not be liquidity in longer-term or other desired contracts. Institutional investors may be barred by regulators from certain derivatives markets and so use the embeddos as a substitute. Additionally, some embeddos may contain risk-return trade-offs that apparently cannot be replicated cheaply in the derivatives market.

For whatever reasons, investors around the world are buying embeddos in greater volume than ever before.

Prominent Embeddo Deals of the Early 1990s

This section explores some of the prominent deals of 1991, illustrating issuer and investor motivations and highlighting the role of market conditions in the timing of the transactions.

SEK's Silver-Linked Notes

In May of 1992, the Swedish Export Credit Corporation (SEK) issued $30 million in one-year debt carrying a coupon of 6.5% (see Chapter 24 of *The Derivatives Engineering Workbook*). The principal repayment is linked to the price of silver, with a spot price per ounce of $4.46 at maturity resulting in a repayment of the amount invested and an IRR of 6.5%. In contrast to the Kodak gold bond, where the embedded position is an option, the SEK structure contains an embedded forward—there are no lower or upper limits in the possible returns. As in the Kodak structure, there is every reason to believe that SEK stripped out the embedded position by entering into a side agreement to buy a forward contract on silver, leaving SEK with cheap fixed-rate financing that it could then swap into floating. SEK's savings come from the fact that the over-the-counter forward position that it purchased is cheaper than the one sold in the embeddo.

But why would investors choose to buy the embeddo rather than creating their own linked bond? By buying SEK or other triple-A debt and simultaneously buying silver futures or forwards, investors should be able to achieve a better payoff profile than was available in the embeddo. Investors have a variety of motivations for buying embeddos rather than creating their own linked structure. But clues to the timing of a bond with silver-linked risk may be found by examining market conditions prevailing at the time of the issue.

First, short-term rates were in a free fall that had begun with the onset of the U.S. recession in late 1990. Second, the silver market was beginning to show signs of life after a very long period of dormancy. The implication is that short-term bond investors seeking some kind of yield enhancement were willing to try to attain superior returns through a bet on the price of silver.

One of the most significant aspects of the SEK silver-linked deal is that it was issued as part of SEK's U.S. medium-term note program. Until very recently, embeddos were almost exclusively a Eurobond market phenomena. This has been true partly because the Eurobond market is more oriented toward retail investors, and partly because the regulation of "hybrid" bond structures in the U.S. domestic market has been unclear. However, the SEK deal showed that there is an appetite for embeddos in the U.S. market. Several other U.S. domestic embeddos have followed, including additional commodity-linked issues from SEK.

The Republic of Austria's SIGNS

This financing combined a zero-coupon bond with a call option on the S&P 500 (see Chapter 24). By purchasing in the equity derivatives market an option essentially identical to the one embedded in the bond, the issuer was left with cheap sub-LIBOR funding. The equity option sold to investors via the embeddo was more expensive than that purchased in the over-the-counter market.

This structure has appeared in virtually every major domestic bond market in 1991. The embedded option has sometimes represented a play on a different country's stock market index or a basket of stock market indexes. The small differences in the way the structure appears in each country are instructive—e.g., the Swiss version contains a very low coupon rather than a zero coupon, due to insurance company investment regulations—but the similarities are far more striking.

The obvious attraction of SIGNS and similar issues is that they allow for an upside play on various stock markets with well-defined downside protection. The most that the investor can lose is the interest that would have accrued on an interest-bearing instrument. In a world of periodic stock market crashes, and—at least in the United States—low interest rates, this seems like an attractive trade-off.

So why don't investors just buy bonds and simultaneously buy call options on the desired stock index? The reasons vary from country to country. French institutional investors are not allowed to buy listed options. Long-dated listed options are illiquid in almost every market. And all but the most sophisticated investors find it difficult to play in foreign stock or futures markets. The SIGNS-type embeddo is among the easiest ways for investors to diversify their equity portfolios globally.

Exhibit 4   Republic of Austria SIGNS Transaction

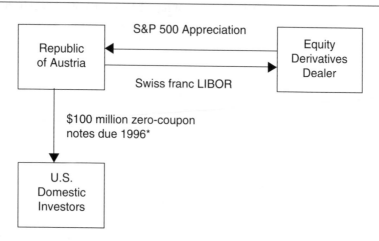

* *Returns 100% of principal; pays interest based on any appreciation of the S&P 500 stock index during the life of the notes.*

PERCS

The hottest trend in corporate financing in the United States is PERCS (preferred equity redemption cumulative stock), a new kind of preferred stock. In exchange for paying a higher dividend than would be paid on common stock, the issuer reserves the right to exchange the PERCS for common at a specified price in the future. In effect, the issuer buys an option on his or her own shares. The popularity of this structure continues to grow, as evidenced by RJR Nabisco's mammoth $2 billion PERCS offering in November of 1991.

One significant difference between PERCS and other embeddos is that for the most part, issuers have not been monetizing the embedded options. PERCS issuers could theoretically offset the option contained in the PERCS by selling options on their own shares, perhaps through a warrants issue or through a convertible bond. Even though they have not been doing so, it is a good bet that the options embedded in PERCS have been relatively inexpensive compared to their theoretical values in the over-the-counter derivatives market.

In principal, investors could replicate the PERCS payoff by buying the issuer's common stock and selling a call option on the issuer's common shares. The call would probably be priced higher than the call embedded in the PERCS, thereby providing the investor with a superior vehicle. But PERCS have been generally targeted to retail investors and equity-income mutual funds, neither of which have the ability to sell long-dated options on corporate common stock. These investors are happy to pick up yield in exchange for relinquishing some of the upside that might be available in common stock.

The popularity of PERCS can be understood in terms of the low yields available in the bond market and a relatively trendless stock market. The buyers of PERCS like the high yields and are willing to sacrifice some of the potential upside of common shares in this kind of environment.

Conclusion

Embeddos provide an easy way for investors to take views on a variety of markets. The appearance of particular types of embeddos at any given moment can often be explained by the market conditions, combined with the views of targeted investors, prevailing at the time. Banks that successfully originate embeddos are those that keep a close eye on investor trends and have a strong derivatives trading capability. In general, it is relatively easy to find issuers willing to use embeddos as a financing tool, because for them the embeddo is simply a vehicle for getting cheaper financing.

PART VI

Regulatory, Control and Policy Issues

Derivatives came under sporadic regulatory scrutiny in the late 1980s and early 1990s. This trend came to a head after the 1994 debacles associated with leveraged interest rate plays. This section discusses regulatory, policy and control issues from the viewpoint of the bank client (Chapter 32), the bank marketer (Chapter 33) and bank senior management (Chapter 34).

The first chapter in this section focuses specifically on foreign exchange risk, taking the view of the bank client. How is the client exposed to cash flow unpredictability as a result of foreign exchange fluctuations? How can the banker help to develop policies to manage this risk?

Chapter 33 focuses on the ways in which the concerns of regulators affect deal structures. Written in 1992, this chapter anticipates the derivatives debacles of 1994 and proposes a checklist of implications for marketers selling to clients exposed to regulatory scrutiny.

The final chapter takes the bank's point of view. Capital requirements help to determine the bank's cost of offering a particular product and therefore the price that must be charged and the bank's ability to compete. Low capital costs represent an advantage in any business, but this is even more true in banking, since capital adequacy rules make it difficult for banks to compensate for high capital costs by taking on additional risk.

32

Foreign-Exchange Risk
Creating Risk-Management Policies

One of the most valuable services a banker can offer to the treasurer of a company with international operations is advice in creating or evaluating foreign-exchange risk-management policies. Providing this type of advisory service can help the bank increase the profitability of foreign-exchange transactions with the customer by enhancing the relationship. Helping the treasurer to examine closely and articulate carefully the company's risk-management parameters can also make the firm a more confident user of derivatives, open to the use of specialized foreign exchange services—for instance, exotic options—that are subject to less competition.

Whether it is a growing company just turning to foreign markets or a mature multinational with a sophisticated risk management organization, three broad questions need to be addressed and written into corporate policy:

1. How will we define our foreign-exchange risks, and which will we manage?

2. How will we set risk-management objectives?

3. How will we select the appropriate tools and strategies to hedge these exposures?

Defining FX Risks

Foreign-exchange risk can be described as the way a company's cash flows, earnings, and net worth vary according to unpredictable changes in currency rates. This risk can be further defined as tactical and strategic. Tactical risks include foreign-exchange transaction exposures arising from committed cash flows, and translation exposures (exposures of the net worth of the company). Strategic exposures are often unbooked or off balance sheet and are harder to quantify. They include exposures of all foreign-currency cash flows, booked or unbooked (economic exposure), and exposures of margin and market share to foreign-exchange shifts (competitive exposure).

Summary Sheet Creating FX Risk-Management Policies

Corporate Concern	How Bankers Can Advise
Defining FX risks and deciding which to manage	Look for hidden FX risk in base currency transactions
	Consider translation hedging when debt-equity ratios are of concern, or when overseas assets may be sold
	Consider currencies in cost structure of competitors
Setting FX risk-management objectives	Don't link specific tools with specific management goals
	Avoid assuming that FX risk can be completely eliminated
	Choose a realistic benchmark for measuring performance
Selecting hedging tools and strategies	Be aware that hedging tools transform risk rather than eliminate it
	Give risk managers sufficient flexibility to select the best hedging tool in response to market conditions and expectations

TRANSACTION RISK: VISIBLE AND INVISIBLE

Transaction risks are the easiest foreign-exchange risks to identify. They also command the most attention because they impact a company's current cash flows and reported earnings. Transaction risk is the exposure of committed cash flows, including receivables, payables, loan payments, asset purchases, and sales, to foreign-exchange gains and losses as those cash flows are converted into another currency.

When a company must pay or receive foreign currency at a future date, it is exposed to the possibility that exchange rates will move. However, not all of a company's transaction exposures are booked in a foreign currency. Whenever a transaction requires currency conversion—by either the company or its customer or supplier—the company's cash flows are exposed to risk. Many such exposures are hidden in a company's base-currency transactions.

For instance, a U.S. company that asks a French customer to accept a U.S. dollar invoice may be exposed to de facto foreign-exchange risk in the form of credit risk. What if the franc declines precipitously against the dollar after the quote but before the invoice is due? If the French customer has not hedged, it may attempt to renegotiate payment terms or may simply be unable to pay in full. Currency risk has hurt the U.S. company's cash flows even though the company appeared to have insulated itself from foreign exchange risk by billing in its base currency.

Exhibit 1   Cash Flow Effects of Visible and Hidden Exposure

Amount invoiced by U.K. company:	$10,000,000 due in 90 days
Spot rate:	US$1.4350:£1
90-day forward rate:	US$1.4248:£1
Spot rate in 90 days:	US$1.4150:£1
Charge by U.S. supplier for managing customer FX risk:	2%

Action by UK Company	Sterling Outflow in 90 Days
Does not hedge	£7,067,137 ($10 million ÷ 1.4150)
Buys US$ forward	£7,018,528 ($10 million ÷ 1.4248)
Requests £-denominated invoice from U.S. supplier	£7,158,899 ($10 million + 2% ÷ 1.4248)

Exhibit 2   Deciding Whether to Hedge Translation Exposures

Hedge	Don't Hedge
Close to capital ratio covenants	No debt covenants
Concerned that lower book value of equity may increase future borrowing costs	Strong balance sheet or little foreign-asset exposure
Plans to sell foreign assets in near future or wants to maintain flexibility to redeploy assets	No plans to sell foreign assets

In the same way, a British company that will only accept sterling quotes from its U.S. supplier is likely to pay more in sterling terms than if it has accepted a dollar invoice and hedged the payment. The U.S. supplier is likely to build into its quote a safety margin that exceeds the actual forward-market hedging costs. Some companies have saved 2% to 5% per transaction—even after factoring in their own hedging costs—simply by switching to accepting quotes in the base currency of the supplier.

A company's risk-management guidelines should address the issue of whether "invisible" transaction risks should be managed. Bankers should encourage their customers to scrutinize base currency transactions carefully for such nonobvious foreign-exchange risks. A company that acknowledges these risks will probably decide to adopt a policy encouraging sales representatives to bill customers and purchasing managers to accept invoices in other currencies. Such policies make it possible to quantify more accurately and manage the company's total foreign exchange exposures of a transactional nature.

TRANSLATION RISK

Translation risk arises when a company translates its foreign-currency revenues, expenses, assets, and liabilities into the currency used to prepare its consolidated financial statements. Translation of income statement items such as sales, costs of goods sold, and depreciation affect consolidated income, but as unrealized gains or losses. A company may view translation exposures with less concern than transaction exposures because they have no impact on current income. Under generally accepted accounting practices, a company's foreign-currency assets and liabilities are translated at the current spot rate and foreign-equity accounts at the historical rate. However, any corresponding foreign-exchange gains and losses are reported in a contra-asset account in consolidated stockholder's equity, not in the parent company's income statement.

As a consequence, managing translation exposure is likely to be of less concern than managing current transaction exposures. However, in at least two cases it may be deemed prudent. If a company is considering the sale of its overseas company in the near future, FX gains and losses on the sale will have a material impact on income. Second, companies may trigger covenants on bank or private-placement debt or face downgrades by ratings agencies if they exceed certain debt-to-equity ratios. They may therefore be forced to renegotiate debt or seek new funding on less attractive terms.

Exhibit 3   Effects of a Stronger Dollar on a U.S. Exporter

U.S. Company

- Sells in Germany
- All costs are in dollars.
- Costs of local competitors are in Deutschemarks.
- German sales will respond to change in prices (demand is elastic).

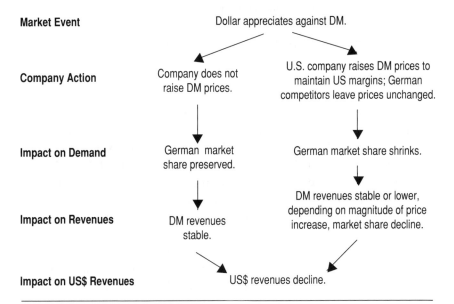

Market Event	Dollar appreciates against DM.	
Company Action	Company does not raise DM prices.	U.S. company raises DM prices to maintain US margins; German competitors leave prices unchanged.
Impact on Demand	German market share preserved.	German market share shrinks.
Impact on Revenues	DM revenues stable.	DM revenues stable or lower, depending on magnitude of price increase, market share decline.
Impact on US$ Revenues	US$ revenues decline.	

Bankers should therefore encourage companies to raise the issue of translation hedging when writing policy. Guidelines should include a directive requiring a regular review of existing translation hedging policies. Some companies may decide that because they intend to be in business in a particular foreign location for the long haul and expect foreign-exchange rates to rise and fall over time, translation hedging is unnecessary. But companies that recognize that assets may need to be redeployed due to unforeseen events may want to protect against translation losses by instituting an ongoing hedging program. Of course, companies that are operating close to their debt-to-equity covenants, who are concerned about downgradings, and/or whose foreign currency net asset positions represent a significant portion of total equity, should consider incorporating translation hedging—at least on a selective basis—into their policy directives.

STRATEGIC RISK

Strategic risk—including economic and competitive risk—is rapidly gaining recognition among large and small corporations alike. A portion of economic risk is addressed by tactical exposure management. But economic risk also includes risk to cash flows that will arise in future accounting periods. These future cash flow exposures—some more accurately measurable than others—are no less real for being unbooked.

Competitive risk, a subset of strategic risk, can affect the cash flows even of companies that sell only in the domestic market and use domestic inputs. Such companies must often compete for market share with companies with cash flows that are denominated differently or that are based in another currency.

Companies that sell at home and abroad are doubly exposed. For example, U.S. companies that manufacture in the United States saw European revenues grow sharply as the U.S. dollar fell over several years to a low in September of 1992. The domestic market share of these companies may also have expanded at the expense of their European competitors. However, these firms are now concerned about a reversal of fortunes should the dollar rise. European manufacturers with costs in European currencies will start to enjoy competitive advantages both locally and in the United States.

When an exporter faces a rising currency at home, the consequences are likely to hurt. The company may choose to maintain prices in its export markets, in which case its margins may shrink in base-currency terms without the offset of higher sales volumes. Or the company may choose to raise prices to preserve base-currency margins, accepting a lower market share and export revenues. At home the company will be similarly embattled. It may be forced to lower its prices in the domestic market to compete with foreign manufacturers. If the company maintains its prices, its market share will almost certainly shrink.

Companies that attempt to address strategic risks using derivatives face a number of obstacles. Nevertheless, the risks cannot be managed unless they are identified, and identifying the risks is a first step toward a forward-looking and proactive risk-management strategy. Therefore, companies should grapple with the nature of their strategic foreign-exchange exposures when drawing up risk-management policies before they begin to erode margins or market share. The writers of guidelines can outline broadly which cash flows are vulnerable to economic foreign-exchange risk and attempt to assess the denomination of their competitors' cash flows. Including this information in the guidelines, even in a general form, should draw senior management's attention to this category of foreign-exchange exposure.

There are two problems with managing strategic risks using derivatives. First, longer-term strategic risk is difficult to quantify and involves projections of future foreign-currency expenses and revenues that may prove inaccurate. Second, hedging unbooked cash flows can have negative accounting implications. Under many accounting regimes, a forward contract must be marked to market at the end of every accounting period. If there is no current cash flow to offset the gain or loss, marking to market can cause significant earnings volatility.

Recently the U.S. Securities and Exchange Commission (SEC) set a precedent that may further restrict the tools that companies can use to hedge strategic risks. In the past, U.S. companies could use option strategies to hedge economic exposures without marking the options to market. The SEC ruled that only simple option purchases would continue to enjoy this favored accounting status. Purchases of options to cover large, long-term exposures require a significant up-front premium expenditure.

Many companies have consequently decided to use derivative strategies to hedge economic risk as a matter of policy out to a horizon of 12 to 18 months or as far as they can quantify a foreign currency cash flow with reasonable accuracy and certainty. They may in fact be able to convince auditors that some of these cash flows—because of their predictable nature—can be used to offset the marking to market of the derivative used to hedge them.

Beyond the 18-month horizon, however, many companies have concluded that strategic risk can best be addressed through operational methods.

Policy directives might suggest changing suppliers, negotiating currency-linked contracts with vendors, switching manufacturing sites, cultivating new markets, or borrowing in depreciating currencies.

Setting Risk-Management Objectives

Companies often set unrealistic risk-management goals and impose many restrictions on how a risk-management objective should be implemented. For example, managers new to foreign-exchange markets often confuse the unexamined world of derivatives with speculation. Such a company's policy might state that it should avoid currency speculation by making all currency sales and purchases only on a spot basis to meet maturing foreign-currency commitments or receipts. The company's advisors can point out that this policy is likely to produce the same degree of earnings and cash flow volatility as one that mandates outright speculation.

Other companies issue objectives stating that margins should be preserved by covering all known future currency cash flows with forward contracts. Unfortunately, such a policy may have the opposite effect over time, exposing the company to economic and competitive risks.

These two objectives represent opposite ends of the risk-management spectrum. But both also share two misconceptions. First, they make the mistake of linking a risk-management objective to a single risk-management tool or strategy. Companies should instead be counseled by their banker to separate management objectives from specific currency instruments or strategies. Second, both objectives seem to imply that foreign-exchange risk can be avoided or eliminated. In reality, a company can trade one financial risk for another by restructuring its risk profile, but risk can never be eliminated completely.

A risk-management objective might simply state what exposures are to be managed and what benchmarks should be used to measure the manager's performance. Exposures to be managed might include committed commercial and financial transactions (or anticipated transactions out to a specified time horizon), net monetary assets, net worth, etc. A performance benchmark might be a budgeted conversion rate, the forward rate at the beginning of the period, or an average of spot rates over the term of the exposure. But the objective should avoid stating that only one management strategy be used to achieve the objective or that risk can be eliminated if the objective is carried out.

Selecting Tools and Strategies to Hedge Exposures

No strategy or tool exists that can totally eliminate foreign-exchange risk or, for that matter, any financial risk. The best a company can hope to achieve is to trade what in its own view is an unacceptable risk for an acceptable one. It can consequently be argued that no strategy aimed at a definable exposure is inherently riskier than another.

Guidelines should therefore avoid ranking particular instruments or hedging strategies according to some absolute hierarchy of risk. Instead, such directives should acknowledge that a particular hedging strategy should be evaluated in light of current market conditions and a company's expectations for future rates. Of course, a company unwilling to accept a totally unhedged position will evaluate the acceptability of strategies accordingly.

For example, a German company buys manufacturing inputs from a U.S. supplier. Because the company believes strongly that the dollar will appreciate against the Deutschemark, it may decide to cover 100% of its dollar commitment in the forward market. An unhedged position seems unacceptable in light of its market view and/or because it does not want to be unhedged as a matter of policy. Buying a U.S. dollar call option seems equally imprudent, since the company sees no point in paying a premium against the unlikely chance that the dollar will depreciate sharply. The company has therefore traded two unacceptable risks—an open short dollar position and a premium outlay for a U.S. dollar call that expects to exercise—for an acceptable one (a forward sale of Deutschemarks for dollars).

But today's acceptable risk is tomorrow's unacceptable one. And a tool that exposes a company to a particular market risk today may be rejected as too costly or imprudent under different market conditions tomorrow. If the German company were convinced that the dollar was due to fall sharply against the Deutschemark, but did not want to leave its payable totally uncovered, an option purchase might be chosen as the best strategy. Market conditions—such as the size of the forward discount or premium or the level of implied option volatility—will also affect a company's choice of instrument.

The company's risk profile could be further fine-tuned to mirror its market view more precisely using more complex option strategies, hedging only a portion of the exposure or actively trading in and out of hedges. Policies that are written with a bias toward inclusion rather than exclusion of trading instruments, styles and techniques give risk managers greater flexibility to apply different strategies and instruments to different market conditions. Caveats can be included to ensure prudence. For example, in light of turmoil in the European currency market, many companies might be tempted to issue a blanket ban on the use of proxy hedging techniques. However, a risk manager with a Dutch guilder exposure might still, for example, wish to purchase a Deutschemark option rather than pay an extra premium for a more illiquid Dutch guilder option. Such a risk may still be deemed acceptable, since the guilder/Deutschemark link has (and is highly likely to remain) unshaken despite EMS turmoil. A flexible risk policy might allow for this kind of proxy hedging scheme after senior management approval has been obtained.

Some mechanism should also exist for ongoing review of new risk-management products. For instance, companies may issue directives requiring that pricing models be well-tested, that adequate liquidity levels for trading the instrument exist and that all risk/reward tradeoffs be thoroughly analyzed before experimentation.

Conclusion

The three most important risk-management issues for any company are identifying exposures and choosing which to manage; setting risk-management objectives; and deciding on the specific tools and strategies to achieve those objectives. A company that has examined these three risk policy issues is likely to know its exposures, have a set of clear risk-management objectives, and have some flexibility in selecting the appropriate risk-management tools. For the company's bankers, this can lead to a greater volume of foreign exchange business as well as the opportunity to do a wider variety of transactions.

33

Derivatives Regulation
Implications for Structuring Transactions

With a notional outstanding amount of more than $4 trillion and compound annual growth of 30% to 50%, the derivatives market would appear to be in a position to maintain its status as the high-growth, cutting-edge financial market for many years to come. The application of derivatives to equities and commodities (as well as the more traditional foreign-exchange and interest-rate instruments) has created an environment in which the only limit to solution creation is the power of the computer and the imagination of the solution designer. Global debt, equity, and commodity markets are becoming increasingly interconnected through the use of exotic derivatives, and there is little question that derivatives have helped end-users to hedge exposures and realize attractive financing costs, and helped banks and other intermediaries increase profits.

Unfortunately, the derivatives market is in danger of becoming a victim of its own success. The high growth of the market, as well as some notable company failures, has brought the derivatives market under increasing scrutiny by regulators, all of whom appear to favor increasing formal regulation. The impact of any such regulation is unknown, but most market players agree that the existing regulatory freedom and the creative solutions such freedom allows are large contributors to the market's growth.

Exhibit 1   Checklist of Structuring Implications

For End-Users:

Does derivatives transaction replicate a cash position subject to restrictions?

Does end-user assume an off-market position in order to generate up-front income or losses?

Is deal attractive due to difference in how derivatives and cash positions are valued on end-user's balance sheet?

For Intermediaries:

What is range of ways bank could be asked to measure its exposures?

Is there agreement within bank, and between bank and regulators, on how exposure should be measured, monitored, and hedged?

Does measurement method assign sufficient weight to credit and liquidity risk?

Is bank's capital sufficient to withstand defaults based on a conservative measure of risk?

Are derivatives used to create off-balance-sheet positions that would otherwise be on the balance sheet?

Could positions create unrealized gains or losses that, if disclosed, could significantly inflate the balance sheet or shrink capital/asset ratios?

This chapter examines the concerns of regulators and the potential impact on the market as a result of increased regulation. For intermediaries, the most important current regulations are the Bank for International Settlements capital adequacy rules; for end-users, the most important regulations are the confusing mosaic of national tax and accounting rules. However, the growing concerns of regulators raise the possibility that new rules could impact current transactions. Bank relationship managers who are up to date on the changing regulatory environment are in a better position to offer appropriately structured solutions to customer financing and hedging needs.

The Concerns of Regulators

The primary concerns of regulators fall into three general categories:

1) *The sophistication of the market is increasing so fast that regulators cannot keep up.* Advanced modeling techniques and software capa-

bilities have allowed market leaders to structure amazingly sophisticated products and solutions. Products that include several options on the debt, currency and equity markets are not uncommon, and regulators fear that they, as well as the senior management at the banks trading these products, simply have no way to evaluate accurately the risk involved.

In addition, while the debt and equity markets have long-standing and well-understood regulations, derivatives are increasingly being used to create products synthetically with debt or equitylike characteristics, but which are not subject to the same regulations. Regulators fear that the market's ability to monitor and hedge the risks involved in this increasingly complex market has not kept up with new product creation.

2) *The growth in the volume and sophistication of the derivatives market has significantly increased the risk of bank's activities.* This particular concern has several aspects. First is the regulator's concerns as to whether existing capital adequacy requirements for derivatives products are sufficient to cover the risk. There is great disagreement as to how the bank's actual exposure should even be measured. Intermediaries argue that using the notional amount of transactions (more than $4 trillion) to measure exposure greatly overstates the actual exposure to the banks. In many cases (such as interest-rate swaps), only interest payments are exchanged, and there is therefore no principal risk involved. Also, if banks net offsetting transactions and calculate the replacement cost of in-the-money contracts—which banks believe is a much more accurate representation of true exposure—the result is a "market" exposure of only $150 to $250 billion as of year-end 1991.

Regulators in different countries disagree on whether netted replacement cost can be used to measure exposure, and there is no standard method to calculate exposure. The Bank for International Settlements currently does not allow netting in determining capital adequacy, and while netting has been approved in bankruptcy proceedings in the United States, its status is much less clear in Europe.

Second is concern over the nature of the products themselves. Increasing customization of OTC products has increased concern over the credit quality of counterparties. Many derivatives, such as standard swaps, caps, and floors, have large and liquid secondary markets. As products increase in maturity and customization, however, illiquidity becomes an issue, and regulators are worried that existing methods of calculating exposures and capital requirements do not adequately cover this increased risk. Also, because most derivative transactions are off balance sheet and the specific details are often highly confidential, regulators are concerned that a full picture of market risk is not available.

Finally regulators are concerned that derivatives are increasingly being used to create synthetically off-balance-sheet products that would otherwise be on the balance sheet. An example of this would be a bank entering with a counterparty into an off-market swap that resulted in a cash payment to the counterparty. This is essentially a loan from the bank to the counterparty, but because it can be classified as a swap, it would be off balance sheet. The SEC has also recently begun to investigate money market funds and their use of derivative-linked products (such as capped floaters) to bypass existing investment restrictions.

3) *The use of derivatives has increased the systemic risk of the global financial markets.* The use of derivatives has increasingly linked the global capital markets. Cross-currency transactions that tie in stock or other indices are not uncommon, and what regulators fear is that a financial shock in one market will be transmitted rapidly from market to market because of the volume of the interconnecting derivatives transactions.

Market participants argue exactly the opposite, claiming that derivatives actually reduce systemic risk because they transfer the risks more efficiently throughout the global markets. Market participants also claim that, despite the rhetoric regarding systemic risk, no one has actually identified any safeguards in the financial markets that existed prior to the advent of derivatives that have been removed by the increasing use of derivatives.

Regulators also fear that the participants do not yet fully understand how derivatives can transmit shocks from one market to another and, therefore, are undercapitalized or under-reserved for potential disasters. The concern is that the derivatives market will be the cause of the next bank credit crunch, following in the steps of Latin American debt, leveraged buyouts, and real estate. In each of these cases, it could be argued that at least part of the problem was that banks did not fully understand the risks involved in the transactions they entered.

The shocks that concern regulators are not limited to the markets themselves. The repercussions of a failure of one of the major market participants

---

Exhibit 2   Using an Off-Market Swap to Extend Credit

Notional Amount $50,000,000
Maturity   5 years

Market Swap:
Market Swap Rate: 6.50%

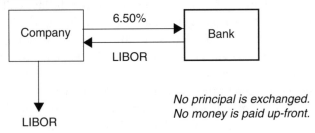

No principal is exchanged.
No money is paid up-front.

Off-Market Swap:
Off-Market Swap Rate: 8.00%

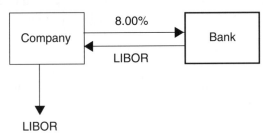

This swap is in-the-money with respect to market rates, and the bank is willing to pay a premium to enter into it. The premium will equal the PV of the difference in cash flows over the life of the swap:

n   =   10
PMT   =   (8.00% - 6.50%) ÷ 2 x $50,000,000 = $375,000
i   =   6.50% ÷ 2
FV   =   0
PV   = $3,158,398.16

This off-balance-sheet transaction can be viewed as a $3.16 million loan to the company, paid back over the life of the swap in the form of a higher fixed rate.

also cause uneasiness. So far, the market has handled very well the few well-publicized failures, but often with the help of regulators. When the Bank of New England went under in 1991, it carried on its books a notional derivatives portfolio of $7 billion. Drexel Burnham was carrying $30 billion in swaps on its books at the time of its collapse. The U.K.'s British & Commonwealth had £2 billion notional outstanding when it defaulted, and DFC, a New Zealand–based company, had to be rescued by regulators when it collapsed.

In addition, the swap market roiled but did not collapse following the Hammersmith & Fulham debacle in the U.K., in which the House of Lords declared that because British local councils were not authorized to deal in swaps, those councils were no longer obliged to honor their commitments to those swaps. Banks that were counterparties in these swaps were left with a mark-to-market exposure of almost £600 million.

Banks and other intermediaries are quick to point out that the market, through self-regulation and internal pressure, was able to absorb all of these near disasters without a general collapse of the derivatives market and with no long-term negative impact on other markets. Regulators counter that in all of these cases, the derivatives portfolios in question were relatively small and were generally well balanced. In addition, it was not the derivatives portfolio but rather other factors that caused the collapse of those institutions. Regulators fear the market impact of a sudden unwinding of a large portfolio, particularly one that resulted in large write-offs for the counterparties.

For example, Banker's Trust recently announced that it was adding $39 million to its nonperforming assets as the result of a single defaulted interest-rate swap. This type of event makes regulators ask whether derivatives are adequately regulated.

Market Impact of Increased Regulation

Market participants argue that the self-regulatory nature of the derivatives market is more than sufficient to prevent the sort of catastrophes that regulators fear, and that it is in the market's own best interest to make sure that exposure excesses or failures are absorbed in the market through a collective effort. Banks also argue that existing capital adequacy requirements are in fact more than sufficient to cover the actual mark-to-market replacement cost exposure (approximately $150 to $250 billion), and that this exposure is small relative to the size of global markets in general. (For instance, more than $600 billion is settled every day in the global currency markets.)

Many derivatives traders and marketers feel that concern on the part of regulators stems from a lack of understanding about the products and the market. Any increase in regulation, the argument goes, will limit market growth and deprive corporations' access to the increased efficiency, broader and cheaper funding, better risk management, and enhanced yields on investments that are now possible.

Nevertheless, various regulators have begun to tighten the rules. In the United States, the Financial Accounting Standards Board (FASB) recently required banks and securities firms to disclose more fully unrealized gains and losses (i.e., contingent exposures) from derivatives transactions. This requirement took effect at the end of 1993 and could result in falling capital/asset ratios or a big jump in the balance sheets of firms with sizable portfolios. Banks are concerned that this could result in additional capital requirements at a time when many firms are struggling to meet the BIS capital requirements that take effect at the end of 1992. Raising new capital at a time when bank's credit quality and shareholder appeal are low could drive up the cost of capital significantly.

Banks also fear that increased regulation will not improve the risk of the market but will simply disintermediate banks as potential dealers seek counterparties subject to less stringent regulations—for example, insurance companies or the finance subsidiaries of industrial companies. Banks also argue that increasing capital requirements will actually boost risk as the increased cost of derivatives transactions causes banks to seek higher paying (i.e., lower credit) counterparties. This would increase one of the risks that regulators fear most: the collapse of a major market player.

One of the biggest areas of controversy is the concept of netting. Netting involves reducing the exposure between two counterparties by canceling out transactions with offsetting cash flows, then calculating the mark-to-market replacement cost of the resulting exposure. Banks believe this to be a much more accurate representation of true market exposure, and they support the use of this method to calculate capital adequacy requirements.

Regulators disagree. In the United States, legislation has been passed that allows banks to net derivative exposure in bankruptcy proceedings, and reports have indicated that netting would probably be allowed in bankruptcy proceedings in 11 of the 12 European Community states. Nonetheless, existing BIS regulations require that banks calculate swap exposure on a gross basis for capital adequacy purposes. Increased capital requirements would increase the cost and reduce the profit margin of derivative products, making them less attractive to the firms that deal them.

Conclusion

Meeting customer needs through the creative use of derivatives is one of the fastest growing areas in finance today. Relationship managers who know derivatives, can identify customer applications, and can discuss these value-added solutions with clients are far ahead of traditional credit-oriented bankers in meeting customer needs. Banks with well-developed and well-integrated derivatives units almost unanimously report an increase in traditional credit business as a result of their success in the derivatives business, and for those institutions where credit is constrained, derivatives can offer a low-capital, high-return alternative to traditional financing.

While the ultimate implications of the current regulatory scrutiny for the derivatives markets are unclear, it is important that relationship managers be aware of the discussions taking place. By knowing what existing regulations allow, relationship managers can more thoroughly analyze potential solutions to customer needs. Knowledge of anticipated or expected changes in regulations can also prevent the embarrassing and damaging situation of suggesting a derivative solution that would violate the new regulations. In addition, a good relationship manager should always present all facets, both good and bad, of any potential transaction, so that the client can make an informed decision. With tax, accounting, and regulatory issues driving so many of today's financial decisions, an understanding of current rules will allow a relationship manager to gain a competitive advantage.

What some bankers view as obstacles or barriers to transactions, other bankers may view as opportunities. Increased regulation of the derivatives market may or may not be warranted and may or may not actually reduce risks. The key point for relationship managers is not whether the regulators are on the correct side of the argument. The key point is understanding changes in the regulatory environment, identifying new opportunities that arise as a result of those changes, and presenting to customers creative solutions that address that new environment. By doing so, relationship managers can play a much more consultative role with their clients and will be in a better position to win mandates.

34

Measuring Risk
An Update on Capital Allocation Requirements

Derivatives help bank customers increase their access to global capital markets and investors, manage assets and liabilities better, and widen their range of investment alternatives. All of these factors have helped to drive phenomenal growth in the derivatives industry. Further fueling this expansion have been the 1988 Basle Accords, which set lower capital requirements for derivatives than for other types of bank products. This combination of market growth and lower capital requirements has driven many of the world's major banks to reduce or eliminate capital-intensive lines of businesses (such as traditional corporate lending) and add or increase other lines of business (most notably retail operations and derivatives trading).

In light of this trend, recent developments in risk management and capital allocation are important for all bankers marketing all products with capital requirements—not only derivatives but loans, foreign-exchange services, or any products that expose the bank to credit or market risk. Capital requirements help to determine the bank's cost of offering a given product and therefore the price that must be charged and the bank's ability to compete. The release in 1993 of five major reports on risk management and capital allocation in the derivatives industry represents a tremendous quantity of seemingly dense and academic information, but the reports are likely to influence the ability of banks to market derivatives successfully. Thus relationship managers and product specialists can profit from understanding the contents and potential effects of these reports on the derivatives business.

This chapter highlights the main points of the four 1993 reports on capital allocation in the derivatives industry and discusses the potential impact of proposed regulations. It is different from the recent series on RAROC or risk-adjusted return on capital in that it focuses on regulatory oversight and derivatives rather than on internal capital allocation systems and the entire range of bank products.

Summary of the Reports

Bankers seeking to follow the progress of capital allocation rules found 1993 a difficult year. Five major reports seeking to influence the future of derivatives regulation were published: an update of the Bank of International Settlement (BIS) Basle Report, a Salomon Brothers study on capital allocation in the banking and insurance industries, the Group of Thirty (G-30) suggestions on reducing risk in the derivatives market, and the Leach Report, a blueprint for possible U.S. legislation to regulate the derivatives industry. In mid-December of 1993, the Institute of International Finance, a trade group representing 175 international banks, published a fifth report criticizing the BIS's proposals.

The Basle, G-30, and Leach Reports all pay close attention to the accurate and "prudent" measurement of the risk of derivatives transactions. Their recommendations differ, but they all agree on the need for consistent standards to measure derivatives risk. These standards would serve the dual purpose of making market participants easier to monitor and making the allocation of capital more efficient. Regulators believe that banks are underestimating (or simply do not know) the true amount of risk involved in derivatives transactions, and therefore they could be undercapitalized in the event of a market "meltdown." Risk is likely to be controlled if it is measured more consistently and accurately, allowing banks to allocate capital more effectively to derivatives businesses.

In light of this consensus on the need for improved risk measurement and capital allocation, the Salomon Brothers report is troubling. In interviewing roughly 50 international banks, Salomon Brothers found that "only a handful of banks . . . actually have installed a common, bankwide language [system] that enables estimated risk and reward to be evaluated across the product range." Furthermore, Salomon "[was] struck not only by the relative lack of

Exhibit 1   1993 Reports on Measuring Risk and Allocating Capital

Name	Author	Significance
Prudential Supervision of Netting, Market Risks, and Interest Rate Risk ("Basle Report")	Bank of International Settlements (BIS)	Updates 1988 Basle Accords; allows netting of derivatives positions; mandates the measurement of (and allocation of capital against) market risk as well as credit risk.
Capital in Banking and Insurance: Current Practice and Future Impact	Salomon Brothers	Study of how capital is being managed in banking and insurance industries. No official significance, but supports view that few banks systematically measure risk of positions.
Derivatives: Practices and Principles	Group of 30 (group of leading derivatives practitioners)	Attempts to alleviate concerns of regulators and promotes self-regulation. Makes 24 recommendations to increase efficiency and reduce risk of derivatives market.
The Leach Report	U.S. Congressman Jim Leach, Republican of Iowa	Includes 30 suggestions for U.S. legislation to be introduced early in 1994 to boost regu-lation of U.S. derivatives industry significantly.
Report of the Working Group on Capital Adequacy	Institute for International Finance (bank trade group)	Criticizes a number of points in Basle Report, including reporting requirements and method of measuring options risk.

sophisticated risk-based capital allocation procedures outside the United States but also by the lack of correlation between commitment to the capital allocation process and relative need for regulatory capital." This perceived lack of consistency and commitment to accurate risk measurement is one of the main reasons that regulators like the Basle Committee and legislators like

U.S. Congressman Jim Leach are recommending increased government supervision over the industry.

Other areas where the reports broadly agree are the issues of disclosure, accounting, management involvement, documentation, and standardization. Derivatives players report to many governing bodies with inconsistent requirements. Even the 1988 Basle Accord is interpreted by each country slightly differently, leading to unusual deal structures as banks in different countries try to gain pricing advantages by tailoring products to local interpretations of the capital rules. While avoiding specific recommendations to level the playing field, the G-30 and Leach Reports call for:

- more disclosure and more standardization of disclosure rules;
- the adoption of uniform international accounting standards;
- more understanding and involvement among senior management of institutions involved in derivatives;
- the adoption of official internal policies on capital allocation and risk measurement;
- standardization of documentation, tax treatment, and legal issues (such as bankruptcy procedures).

But while the G-30 and Leach Reports agree in concept, they differ in degree. The Leach Report recommends more conservative standards and much more government supervision and control. A Leach Report recommendation sure to generate industry opposition is the idea of making marketers responsible for determining the "suitability" of customers for derivatives transactions,

Exhibit 2   How the Basle Report Classifies Risk

Exhibit 3   Add-On Charges Based on Maturity, Notional Amount

Remaining Maturity	Interest-Rate Contracts	Exchange-RateContracts
Less than 1 year	0%	1.00%
1 year or more	0.5%	5.00%

---

including deciding whether the product is "appropriate" for the risk being managed. Market participants are sure to see this recommendation as micromanagement of their activities and as a source of risk of contingent liability and litigation.

Measuring Risk and Allocating Capital

Bank management most wants to know how much capital must be allocated against the bank's positions. The answer will help determine the bank's choice of businesses, pricing, and ability to compete. Here the implications of the 1993 update of the 1988 Basle Accord are ambiguous. Although the update permits netting (reducing the amount of capital that must be set aside), it also mandates that capital be set aside to cover both credit and market risk rather than credit risk alone. Some market participants fear that the net result—permitting netting but mandating capital to cushion against market risk—will be higher capital allocation requirements.

The following sections review two key elements of the BIS rules: the proposed rules on netting (and their impact on the measurement of credit risk) and proposed prescriptions for measuring and allocating capital against market risk.

Netting and Credit Risk

The 1988 Basle Accord dictates that banks allocate capital against gross rather than net asset positions. A bank having offsetting positions with another bank (e.g., long one swap and short another swap of the same general maturity and type) would need to allocate capital against both positions. Under April's Basle Report, these positions would be netted (as long as local law permits netting) and capital allocated only against the net position. The Basle Committee suggests that, depending on the nature of a bank's portfolio, this bilateral netting provision could reduce a bank's capital charges by 25% to 40%. Market participants believed that the original requirements vastly overstated risk and have applauded the decision to allow netting.

The decision to permit netting reduces the required capital via the rules on reserving against credit risk. Under the "current exposure method," credit exposure equals the mark-to-market replacement cost of a position (if positive) plus certain "add-on charges." When bilateral netting is factored into this measure, credit exposure equals the *net* mark-to-market replacement cost (if positive) plus the add-on charges. Because the replacement cost position can account for as much as 50% to 80% of a bank's total capital charge, the netting provision, which could reduce replacement cost by up to 50%, could reduce the overall capital charge by 25% to 40%.

The "add-on charge" component of the credit exposure measurement depends on the underlying notional amount of the transaction and its remaining maturity. The add-on charge calculation, which is summarized in Exhibit 3, has come under criticism by market participants, who believe it is far too arbitrary and inexact and who say that it overstates risk. As outlined in the G-30 report, market players would prefer to replace the add-on charges with a measure of "potential exposure" estimated more precisely using simulation (such as Monte Carlo simulation) to generate all likely outcomes for the remaining life of the transaction. This simulation would generate an expected value and standard deviation. Market participants suggest using a confidence interval of 95% (or two standard deviations) to estimate potential future exposure. The Leach Report does not disagree with this probability-based method of estimating future potential exposure but suggests that the confidence interval should be three standard deviations, which would capture 99% of all probable outcomes.

Market Risk

The 1988 Basle Accord required banks to allocate capital against risk-adjusted assets, but the risk adjustments were based mainly on the credit risk and type of asset. The accord did not recognize the *market* risk of bank transactions. Market risk can be defined as the risk to the value of assets due to movements in interest rates, equity prices, or foreign-exchange rates.

In contrast, the April Basle Report recommends that capital be allocated against both credit and market risk and states precisely how market risk is to be measured. Though market participants disagree on many of the details of how to measure market risk, the BIS's method has been applauded within the industry as a step toward more accurate risk measurement. The Basle Committee has asked market participants to comment on the measurement of market risk, and will issue final recommendations sometime this year.

When measuring market risk, the Basle Committee distinguishes between interest-rate risk, equity risk and foreign-exchange risk, and measures each of these risks separately. For debt and equity securities (or derivatives linked to these), the report further distinguishes between specific risk and general market risk:

- Specific risk is defined as "the risk of loss caused by an adverse price movement of a security (or a derivative product linked to it) due principally to factors related to the issuer of the security." In other words, it is risk that is specific to the instrument itself.

- General market risk is defined as "the risk of loss caused by an adverse market movement unrelated to any specific security."

Thus these two risks capture both the volatility of a transaction within the market and the volatility of the market itself.

INTEREST-RATE RISK

For measuring interest-rate risk, the specific risk depends on the type of debt security (or derivative linked to that security). The report proposes several categories of debt securities, as outlined in Exhibit 4.

The Basle Report recommends one of two duration-based calculations to

Exhibit 4   Specific Risk Categories for Debt Securities

Security	Definition	Residual Maturity	Charge
Government	All government paper, regardless of maturity	N.A.	0%
Qualifying	Issues (1) rated investment grade by at least two rating agencies; (2) rated investment grade by one agency and not below-investment grade by any other rating agency; and (3) unrated but deemed of investment quality by bank or securities firm, and issuer has securities listed on recognized stock exchange	up to 6 months	0.25%
		over 6 months and up to 24 months	1.00%
		over 24 months	1.60%
Other	Any issue not classified as government or qualifying	N.A.	8.00%

determine general market risk. In these calculations, the yield curve is divided into "time bands" (either 13 or 15, depending on which method is used), and the security is slotted into one of these bands depending on the residual maturity. The net position within each band is then weighted by a factor designed to reflect the price sensitivity of these positions to changes in interest rates. The factor is determined by:

a) the modified duration of a hypothetical par bond with a coupon of 8.00% and a maturity at the midpoint of its time band; and

b) an assumed yield change based on two standard deviations (a 95% confidence interval) over one month of yield changes in "most major markets." Because most yield curves are more volatile in the short maturities, the assumed yield change gradually decreases from 1.00% to 0.60% as the time band moves out the yield curve.

The modified duration for a time band is then multiplied by the assumed yield change to arrive at a "risk weighting" used to allocate capital against the net position within that band. Banks can also determine the actual duration and precise residual maturity of the security rather than using the hypothetical 8.00% bond. This will result in greater precision in measuring market risk, and the more sophisticated institutions are likely to choose this method.

A controversial point is the use of this methodology for debt derivatives (FRAs, interest-rate and currency swaps, etc.), which would therefore need to be "converted" to their underlying notional cash security positions. Market players believe this to be a relatively unsophisticated concept that does not accurately reflect the risk of the derivatives transaction, particularly for options. The Basle Report recommends that options be "converted" to the underlying notional security position on a "delta-equivalent" basis, where delta is a measure of how much the value of the option changes for a small change in the underlying position. Because option prices exhibit "curvature" (delta changes with large market movements) and "time decay" (delta changes as time changes), the Basle Report's recommendation is simplistic. An alternative is including a "gamma" (convexity) and "theta" (time) factor into the conversion calculations for options.

A final aspect of the Basle Report's recommendations on measuring interest-rate risk is the concept of offsetting positions. Few market participants run precisely matched books (where exactly matched positions are removed from any risk and capital calculations). The Basle Committee recommends allowing banks to offset positions with closely related (either by maturity or type) positions but not a 100% offset. Likewise, the time bands discussed previously are grouped into three "time zones," and positions in one time zone may be offset and netted against positions in that time zone or other time zones.

EQUITY-MARKET RISK

Equity-market risk is measured more simply than interest-rate risk. The Basle Report recommends an 8.00% capital charge for general market risk (similar to beta in Capital Asset Pricing Model theory) against the *net* value of a portfolio (long positions offset by short positions). Then a specific risk charge is added based on the *gross* value of the portfolio. The specific risk charge is 8.00% for a nondiversified portfolio, 4.00% for a diversified, liquid portfolio, 2.00% for index-related instruments, and 0% for index-arbitrage instruments.

This proposed calculation has been criticized as too liberal. Some regulators (notably the U.S. Securities and Exchange Commission) feel that using the net portfolio value in determining general market risk is unrealistic, for a long position in one stock could be netted against a short position in another stock even if the prices of the two stocks are completely uncorrelated.

FOREIGN-EXCHANGE RISK

In measuring foreign-exchange risk, the Basle Report proposes that banks follow one of two methods, one of which is significantly more sophisticated than the other.

Under the "shorthand" method, banks would calculate the net position in *each* currency and precious metal and convert them at spot rates into the reporting currency. Banks will naturally be long in some currencies and short in others, and the sum of each (all of the longs and all of the shorts) will be calculated. The larger of the two open positions (either the sum of the longs or the sum of the shorts) will be subject to an 8.00% capital charge. To this the bank would add an 8.00% capital charge to the *gross* precious-metal position.

Under the more sophisticated method, a bank would calculate a "worst-case scenario" of the currency portfolio, using a 95% (two-standard deviation) confidence interval for a two-week holding period and based on currency price movements for the previous five years. To this market risk measurement the Basle Report recommends adding a 3.00% "scaling factor" (basically an add-on "fudge factor"). Based on recent currency price movements, this scaling factor would subject a typical bank's currency portfolio to an 8.00% capital charge.

This coincidence (8.00%) draws criticism from market players who claim that the scaling factor does nothing more than bring the adjusted capital charge to the 8.00% level that the Basle Accord uses as a capital target.

Conclusion

Regulators like the Basle Committee (as well as would-be regulators like U.S. Congressman James Leach) remain concerned over the risks taken by derivatives market participants and generally favor more supervision of the industry. Market participants are lobbying against increased regulation and initiating self-policing measures both to alleviate the fears of regulators and to forestall regulatory action.

The derivatives industry is changing rapidly. Relationship managers and bankers who follow these changes closely will find themselves at an advantage in bringing value-added ideas to their customers. In addition, regulators are strongly advocating the development of more sophistication and knowledge on the part of both bankers and their customers. Staying abreast of the regulatory changes and topical market issues is one way to build that sophistication and knowledge.

About the Author

Over the past 15 years, Globecon has developed a systematic approach to implementing wholesale banking business strategies. Globecon currently works with financial institutions around the globe to assist in implementing a relationship strategy and developing superior product delivery capabilities. Globecon's consulting staff has years of hands-on banking experience. This experience, combined with a consulting practice totally focused on financial institutions, enables Globecon to bring a unique and practical approach to clients. Globecon understands the wholesale banking business and the challenges facing banks in the current marketplace.

Globecon advises financial institutions on how to implement their business strategy by focusing on human capital and the development of competitive advantage through knowledge. Globecon uses the "learning organization" concept to develop a culture of internal cooperation, free information flow, continual knowledge creation, client service based on solutions rather than products, and the building of long-term relationships.

Globecon has developed a systematic approach to learning called the *Wholesale Banker Learning System*—a comprehensive system created to enhance the competence, knowledge, and client focus of wholesale bankers—geared to the specific needs, culture, and management practices of the institution. The main components of the system are a series of classroom workshops, the *Finance Update Service,* the *Foundations of Finance Self-Instructional Guides,* which include over 30 titles. The goal of *Wholesale Banker Learning System* is to develop and sustain an organizational strategy that combines the relationship mentality with strong product delivery capability. Globecon's approach is to customize the needs of individual clients, taking into consideration the customer base and geographic location as well as the specific strategic business goals of the organization.

The Globecon Group, Ltd.
71 Murray St., 10th fl.
New York, NY 10007
Fax: (212) 227-0443